AF477736

REGIONAL INTEGRATION AND TRADE LIBERALIZATION IN SUBSAHARAN AFRICA

Volume 3: Regional Case-Studies

REGIONAL INTEGRATION AND TRADE LIBERALIZATION
IN SUBSAHARAN AFRICA

VOLUME 1:   FRAMEWORK, ISSUES AND METHODOLOGICAL
            PERSPECTIVES
Edited by Ademola Oyejide, Ibrahim Elbadawi and Paul Collier

VOLUME 2:   COUNTRY CASE-STUDIES
Edited by Ademola Oyejide, Benno Ndulu and Jan Willem Gunning

VOLUME 3:   REGIONAL CASE-STUDIES
Edited by Ademola Oyejide, Ibrahim Elbadawi and Stephen Yeo

VOLUME 4:   SYNTHESIS AND REVIEW
Edited by Ademola Oyejide, Benno Ndulu and David Greenaway

Regional Integration and Trade Liberalization in SubSaharan Africa

Volume 3: Regional Case-Studies

Edited by

Ademola Oyejide
*Professor of Economics and Director of
the Trade Policy Research and Training Programme
University of Ibadan
Nigeria*

Ibrahim Elbadawi
*Development Research Group
The World Bank
Washington, DC*

and

Stephen Yeo
*Director
Centre for Economic Policy Research
London*

First published in Great Britain 1999 by
MACMILLAN PRESS LTD

Houndmills, Basingstoke, Hampshire RG21 6XS and London
Companies and representatives throughout the world

A catalogue record for this book is available from the British Library.

ISBN 0–333–66106–0

First published in the United States of America 1999 by

ST. MARTIN'S PRESS, INC.,
Scholarly and Reference Division,
175 Fifth Avenue, New York, N.Y. 10010

ISBN 0–312–21771–4 (Vol. 3)

Library of Congress Cataloging-in-Publication Data
Regional integration and trade liberalization in subsaharan Africa.
v.<3>;cm.
Includes bibliographical references and index.
Contents: — Vol. 1. Framework, issues and methodological
Perspectives / edited by Ademola Oyejide, Ibrahim Elbadawi and Paul
Collier — Vol. 2. Country case-studies / edited by Ademola Oyejide,
Benno Ndulu and Jan Willem Gunning — Vol. 3. Regional case-studies
/ edited by Ademola Oyejide, Ibrahim Elbadawi and Stephen Yeo —
Vol. 4. Synthesis and review / edited by Ademola Oyejide, Benno
Ndulu and David Greenaway
ISBN 0–312–17321–0 (v. 1).—ISBN 0–312–21769–2 (v. 2).—ISBN
0–312–21771–4 (v. 3).—ISBN 0–312–21772–2 (v. 4)
1. Africa, Sub-Saharan—Economic integration.   2. Africa, Sub
-Saharan—Economic policy.   3. Africa, Sub-Saharan—Foreign economic
relations.   I. Oyejide, T. Ademola.   II. Elbadawi, Ibrahim.
III. Collier, Paul.
HC800.R448   1997
337.67—dc21   96–49387
                                                              CIP

This book is printed on paper suitable for recycling and made from fully managed and
sustained forest sources.

10   9   8   7   6   5   4   3   2   1
08   07   06   05   04   03   02   01   00   99

Printed and bound in Great Britain by Antony Rowe Ltd, Chippenham, Wiltshire

Contents

List of Tables

List of Figures

List of Abbreviations

ACP	Africa-Caribbean-Pacific
ADB	African Development Bank
AEC	African Economic Community
AEF	*Afrique Equatoriale Française* (French Equatorial Africa)
AERC	African Economic Research Consortium
AFTA	ASEAN Free Trade Area
AFZ	African Franc Zone
ANC	African National Congress
APEC	Asia–Pacific Economic Co-operation
ASEAN	Association of South East Asian Nations
BEAC	*Banque des Etats de l'Afrique Centrale* (Bank for Central African States)
BCEAO	*Banque Centrale des Etats de l'Afrique de l'Ouest* (central bank of the CEAO)
BLNS	Botswana, Lesotho, Namibia and Swaziland (from 1990)
BLS	Botswana, Lesotho and Swaziland (1969–89)
BOTT	Board on Tariffs and Trade (Pretoria)
CAR	Central African Republic
CBI	Cross-Border Initiative
CBLT	Lake Chad Basin Commission
CBU	completely-built-up [unit]
CCAR	*Commission de Contrôle des Assurances Régionale* (Regional Commission for Insurance Control)
CEAC	*Communauté Economique d'Afrique Centrale* (Central African Economic Community)
CEAO	*Communauté Economique de l'Afrique de l'Ouest* (Economic Community of West Africa)
CEBEVIRA	*Comité des Betail et des Industries Animales*
CEDEAO	*Communauté Economique des Etats de l'Afrique de l'Ouest* (ECOWAS)
CEPGL	*Communauté Economique des Pays des Grands Lacs* (Economic Community of the Countries of the Great Lakes)
CET	common external tariff
CFA	*Communauté Financière en Afrique*

CIC	Capital Issue Commission
CIMA	*Conférence Interafricaine des Marchés d'Assurance* (Inter-African Conference of Insurance Markets)
CKD	completely-knocked-down (unit)
CLA	Community Legislative Authority
CMA	Common Monetary Area (formerly Rand Monetary Area, now Multilateral Monetary Area)
COBAC	*Commission Bancaire d'Afrique Centrale* (Central African Bank Commission)
COMESA	Common Market for Eastern and Southern Africa
CUTT	Customs Union Task Team
DOTI	Department of Trade and Industry (Pretoria)
EAC	East African Community
EACSO	East African Common Services Organization
EADB	East African Development Bank
EAHC	East African High Commission
ECA	Economic Commission for Africa (UNECA)
ECCAS	Economic Community of Central African States
ECOMOG	Military and Security Cooperation for West African States
ECOWAS	Economic Community of West African States
EEC	European Economic Community
ESA	Eastern and Southern Africa
EU	European Union
FCD	*Fonds de Coopération et de Développement* (co-operation and development fund)
FOSIDEC	*Fonds de Solidarité et d'Intervention pour le Développement Economique de la Communauté*
GATT	General Agreement on Tariffs and Trade
GDP	Gross Domestic Product
GNP	Gross National Product
GST	General Sales Tax
HCT	High Commission Territories
IBRD	International Bank for Reconstruction and Development
IGADD	Inter-Governmental Authority on Droughts and Desertification
IGO	Inter-Governmental Organization
IMF	International Monetary Fund
IOR	Indian Ocean Rim
ISI	import-substitution industrialization

ISSEA	*Institut Sous-Régional de Statistique et Economie Appliquée*
ISTA	*Institut Sous-Régional de Technologie Appliquée*
ITT	import turnover tax
LPA	Lagos Plan of Action
MIE	multilateral industrial enterprises
NAFTA	North American Free Trade Agreement
NORSAD	Nordic funds for the promotion of private sector export in Eastern and Southern Africa
NTB	non-tariff barrier
OECD	Organization for Economic Co-operation and Development
PTA	Preferential Trade Area for Eastern and Southern African States
RI	Regional Integration
RIDP	Regional Industrial Development Programme
RSA	Republic of South Africa
SACU	Southern African Customs Union
SADC	Southern African Development Community
SADCC	Southern African Development Co-ordination Conference
SAP	Structural Adjustment Programme
SATCC	Southern African Transport and Communication
SKD	semi-knocked-down (unit)
SSA	sub-Saharan Africa
TCA	*Taxe sur le Chiffre d'Affaires* (turnover tax)
TCR	*Taxe de Coopération Régionale* (regional co-operation tax)
TCI	*Taxe à la Consommation Intérieure* (domestic consumption tax)
TIC	*Taxe Intérieure à la Consommation* (domestic consumption tax)
TINET	Trade Information Network (of the PTA)
TIP	*Taxe Intérieure à la Production* (domestic production tax)
TPG	*Tarif Préférentiel Généralisé* (generalized preferential tariff)
TU	*Taxe Unique* (single tax)
UAPTA	Unit of Account for the Preferential Trade Area
UDE	*Union Douanière Equatoriale* (Equatorial Customs Union)

UDEAC	*Union Douanière et Economique de l'Afrique Centrale* (Central African Customs and Economic Union)
UDEAO	*Union Douanière de l'Afrique de l'Ouest* (West African Customs Union)
UEMOA	*Union Economique et Monétaire Ouest Africaine* (West African Economic and Monetary Union)
UMOA	*Union Monétaire Ouest Africaine* (West African Monetary Union)
UNDP	United Nations Development Program
UNECA	United Nations Economic Commission for Africa
UTL	Unilateral Trade Liberalization
WACB	West African Consortium of Bankers
WACH	West African Clearing House
WTO	World Trade Organization

List of Contributors

Jean-Paul Azam   Centre d'Etudes et de Recherches sur le Developpement International, Clermont Ferrand; Université des Science Sociales, Toulouse

Lazare Bela   Institut Sous Regional de Statistique et d'Economie Appliquée

John Cockburn   University of Laval

Bernard Decaluwe   University of Laval

Ibrahim Elbadawi   Former Director of Research, African Economic Research Consortium; The World Bank, Washington

Charles D. Jebuni   University of Ghana

Louis A. Kasekende   Central Bank of Uganda

William Lyakurwa   Director of Training, African Economic Research Consortium

Gavin Maasdorp   University of Natal

Allechi M'Bet   University of Abidjan

Ngila Mwase   University of Dar es Salaam; UNDP

Nehemiah Ng'eno   University of Nairobi

Dominique Njinkeu   University of Laval; African Economic Research Consortium

E. Olawale Ogunkola   University of Ibadan

Ademola Oyejide   University of Ibadan

Charles C. Soludo   University of Nigeria

Stephen Yeo   Centre for Economic Policy Research, London

1 Introduction and Overview

Ademola Oyejide, Ibrahim A. Elbadawi
and Stephen Yeo

1.1 INTRODUCTION

This chapter introduces and reviews the set of seven papers contained in this volume. Six of these are devoted to the analysis of the experiences of six regional integration schemes (and their antecedents) in subSaharan Africa, while the seventh focuses on the related phenomenon of unrecorded cross-border trade flows. This volume is the third in a series of four that constitute the product of the collaborative project on Regional Integration and Trade Liberalization in subSaharan Africa sponsored by the African Economic Research Consortium (AERC) and other collaborating institutions. The other three volumes in the series address other aspects of the project. Thus, Volume I focuses on conceptual issues and methodological perspectives, Volume II is devoted to the analysis of country-specific trade liberalization experiences, and Volume IV provides a synthesis of the entire project.

Two of the seven chapters in this volume analyse the experience of regional integration schemes in West Africa – that is, the Economic Community of West African States (ECOWAS), the *Communauté Economique de l'Afrique de l'Ouest* (CEAO) and its successor, the *Union Economique et Monétaire Ouest Africaine* (UEMOA). One chapter focuses on the regional integration experience of the *Union Douanière et Economique de L'Afrique Centrale* (UDEAC) in Central Africa. Three chapters are devoted to the analysis of regional integration experiences in Eastern and Southern Africa derived from three regional arrangements: the Preferential Trade Area for Eastern and Southern Africa (PTA), including its antecedent, the East African Community (EAC) and its transformation into the Common Market of Eastern and Southern Africa (COMESA); the Southern African Development Co-ordination Conference (SADCC) and its

1

transformation into the Southern African Development Community (SADC); and the Southern African Customs Union (SACU). Finally, one chapter explores theoretical and empirical aspects of unrecorded cross-border trade in the region.

The six studies dealing with regional integration experiences used a common methodological approach and focused on the same set of issues. In particular, authors of the six regional case-studies were requested to pay specific attention to each of the following cross-cutting issues:

- assessment of regional integration experiences, as indicated, for instance, by performance in relation to objectives and targets and bearing in mind the main constraints and obstacles facing each regional integration scheme;
- implications of changing conditions for regional integration, especially in terms of consistency between country-level trade policies and regional integration trade regimes, and the linkages (if any) between political liberalization and regional integration; and
- impact of the global environment on regional integration, such as global liberalization through multilateral arrangements and bloc formation in other regions.

In addition, the authors were requested to identify and analyse special issues of specific significance for each of the six regional integration arrangements. The review that follows is organized around these cross-cutting issues.

1.2 ASSESSMENT OF REGIONAL INTEGRATION EXPERIENCE

In Chapter 3 M'Bet examines the experience of the *Communauté Economique de L'Afrique de l'Ouest* (CEAO), one of the francophone sub-regional groupings in West Africa.

CEAO grew out of UDEAO, a 1966 attempt to form a customs union by Burkina-Faso, Côte d'Ivoire, Mali, Mauritania, Niger and Senegal. UDEAO aimed to stimulate intra-regional trade through a 50 per cent tariff reduction on imports from other UDEAO members. Member states proved unwilling to implement these sweeping tariff reductions, however, as trade taxes formed a large proportion of government revenues. Without a mechanism for compensating member governments for the revenues, UDEAO foundered. CEAO, established in 1973 from the six members of UDEAO plus Togo, represented an explicit attempt to remedy the difficulties experienced by UDEAO, by establishing a mechanism – the *Taxe de Coopération Régionale* (TCR) – to compensate member governments for lost tariff revenues.

The CEAO survived for over 20 years (until 1994, when it was superseded by UEMOA). The establishment of a compensation mechanism may have ensured the political sustainability of the CEAO, but the evidence presented by M'Bet suggests that its impact on the regional economy was at best mixed and its achievements decidedly modest. This was particularly disappointing, since the initial conditions faced by the CEAO were relatively auspicious. As M'Bet notes, its member countries possessed relatively complementary production structures, with the possibility of mutually beneficial exchange between, say, the predominantly agricultural Mali and the more industrialized Côte d'Ivoire. There were relatively few physical obstacles to this trade potential: natural barriers to trade were not severe and a reasonable transportation infrastructure did exist. Moreover, the *Conseil de l'Entente*, a group comprising external donors and some of the wealthier CEAO members, provided funds earmarked to finance development projects in the less-developed areas of the CEAO, which provided additional resources to compensate the losers from regional integration.

Despite these favourable conditions, there was little evidence that CEAO played any role in stimulating regional integration. Intraregional trade grew slowly, even in comparison to the other regions of subSaharan Africa. Over the period 1975–90, for example, trade within ECOWAS grew by 11.95 per cent, while that among the CEAO members increased by only 6.95 per cent.

Why was the growth of intra-regional trade so disappointing? M'Bet identifies several explanatory factors, including the impact of external shocks and mistaken economic policies. In addition, rates of inflation were higher in the non-CEAO members of ECOWAS and as their real exchange rates appreciated, their imports from the CEAO rose – production that might otherwise have boosted intra-CEAO trade. There is no reason to mourn this growth of exports at the expense of intra-regional trade: the exports may have made the CEAO members better off and the pattern of trade welfare-enhancing.

M'Bet identifies the TCR as another important obstacle to intra-CEAO trade. This is ironic, since the TCR was designed as a mechanism to stimulate such trade. Why did the tax discourage intra-regional trade?

The TCR replaced all duties and taxes on a good imported from another CEAO member state, provided that 60 per cent of the raw materials or 40 per cent of the value added originated within the CEAO. The importing country was then eligible for 'compensation' for applying the TCR; the Community Development Fund would pay the difference between the revenue from applying the TCR and the revenue that would have been received had the ordinary import tax been levied. M'Bet argued that the TCR operated in practice to favour products from the poorer CEAO members, discriminating against those from more advanced members and from countries outside the CEAO. The results were perverse. Far from promoting efficient intra-regional specialization and strong 'regional champions', the tax maintained inefficient producers in the poorer countries and tended to erode even further the international competitiveness of these industries by sheltering them from international competition. In addition, M'Bet notes that the TCR was susceptible to fraud, given the unreliability of the data used to calculate compensation. The availability of revenue from the compensation fund also reduced the incentives for member governments to develop other sources of fiscal revenues.

Jebuni, Ogunkola and Soludo, in Chapter 2, examine the experience of the Economic Community of West African States (ECOWAS), the regional grouping established in 1975 as one of the steps towards the establishment of an African Economic Community. Some ECOWAS members also belonged to the CEAO; although the objectives of the two regional groupings were not necessarily inconsistent, the authors suggest that the loyalties (and budgets) of the member states were divided, and that this contributed to the weakness and poor performance of both sets of regional institutions.

ECOWAS aimed to achieve a number of objectives, including the abolition of all barriers to trade and factor mobility within the Community; the establishment of a common external tariff; the harmonization of agricultural, industrial and monetary policies; the joint development of infrastructure projects; the elimination of disparities within ECOWAS; and the establishment of a compensation and development fund.

The authors note that the priorities of ECOWAS clearly lay with the joint development of common resources, harmonization of sectoral policies and trade liberalization – in that order. According to the authors, the Community's major preoccupation since its inception has been the development of infrastructural facilities to create physical integration in the region, even though the trade liberalization provisions in the ECOWAS treaty were relatively elaborate, and the sections dealing with policy harmonization and resource development merely prescriptive.

The data suggest that the trade liberalization provisions of the ECOWAS treaty had little, if any, impact on intra-regional trade. In this sense, ECOWAS was a failure. The share of intra-regional in total ECOWAS trade was less than 10 per cent, and over the period since 1975 has remained stagnant or even declined. This is too simple-minded a test of the impact of ECOWAS, however, since it does not control for the other factors that might have influenced trade flows over the period. A more sophisticated approach involves the use of a gravity model to assess what trade should have taken place within ECOWAS, given levels of income and population and distances between countries. The idea here is to estimate the model using data for other regions of the world and then to use the estimated parameters to calculate potential trade between ECOWAS members, comparing these potential levels to the trade flows actually observed. Alternatively, one can estimate the gravity model for the entire (global) sample of countries and include a dummy variable representing membership in a regional integration scheme such as ECOWAS, then test for the statistical significance of the dummy variable. Research by Foroutan and Pritchett (1993) adopted the latter approach; they found that an ECOWAS dummy was not significant. Using a similar technique, Ogunkola (1994) found that the ECOWAS dummy was statistically significant, but that its impact was small. At best, then, ECOWAS has had a significant but small impact on intra-regional trade flows.

Why did ECOWAS fail in its objective of promoting intra-regional trade? The authors identify a number of factors that obstructed regional integration in ECOWAS. The existence of overlapping regional groupings, together with a large number of IGOs with conflicting mandates led, according to the authors, to unhealthy rivalries and divided loyalties among the member states. Of course, this proliferation of institutions cannot be the ultimate explanation; if the will to create effective regional institutions had existed, rationalization would have taken place. The authors attribute the continued existence of these institutions to the persistence of colonial ties, to Britain and in particular to France; many of the competing regional institutions were manifestations of one or the other colonial attachment. In this re-spect, as the authors note, recent developments give little cause for optimism. A revised ECOWAS treaty, for example, was signed on 24 July 1993; on 1 January 1994 the members of the CEAO agreed to a treaty establishing UEMOA to replace the CEAO.

More fundamentally, the authors of the ECOWAS study argue that ECOWAS failed to achieve its objective because regional issues occupied a very low place on the policy agendas of its member states or were in direct conflict with the domestic policies they pursued. This can be seen most clearly in the early stages of ECOWAS, when attempts to integrate regional markets could not possibly be reconciled with the national policies of dirigisme and strategies for industrialization based on import substitution. And even after these policies were discredited, the beneficiaries and vested interests they created continued to obstruct attempts at regional integration, since these measures threatened the rents they enjoyed.

In Chapter 4, Decaluwe, Njinkeu, Cockburn and Bela examine the experience of UDEAC. Like the CEAO, it grew out of an earlier regional grouping, the *Union Dounière Equatoriale* (UDE), an attempt to create a customs and a monetary union among the former French colonies in Central Africa.

As the authors note, trade within the region is small, 4 per cent of total trade in 1980 and only 8 per cent in 1987. The pattern of trade that emerged in UDEAC bears an interesting resemblance to the hub-and-spoke systems to which Baldwin (1995) has drawn attention. For the smaller UDEAC members, 90 per cent of their trade within Africa was within UDEAC, but for the larger members, ECOWAS (and particularly Nigeria) exerted a much stronger attraction. Gabon and Cameroon in particular traded heavily with Nigeria and Côte d'Ivoire. In terms of intra-regional trade, then, the smaller UDEAC members traded with the larger members, and the larger members with the rest of the world.

Like the CEAO, UDEAC created a number of policy instruments designed to foster regional integration, the most important of which were the common external tariff (CET), the *taxe unique* (TU) on goods traded between members, and a compensation fund.

As the authors of the UDEAC study note, the external tariff is set at a common rate across all members in order to avoid goods imported into the region being artificially routed through members with lower tariff rates. Although UDEAC did establish an external tariff regime that was in principle common to all members, it was flawed in its implementation. Since tariff revenues formed an important part of government revenues, and tariff rates varied widely across member states, government stood to lose significantly if tariffs were harmonized. In order to avoid this, members were allowed to levy a 'complementary tax' on imports from outside UDEAC. The tax was intended to be temporary, but was in fact never removed. As a result, the levels of protection varied across member states and harmonization did not take place.

The TU was designed to foster intra-regional trade, particularly in manufactured goods. It replaced all domestic and import taxes on industrial products sold within the region by registered firms, and was to be set at a rate below the common external tariff in order to encourage intra-regional trade. Firms were required to register for the TU, in order to export industrial goods within UDEAC. Registration involved an application to the national government, which in turn applied to the UDEAC Management Committee. The necessity for formal approval of the registration applications at two levels of government was costly and prone to delays, which in itself discouraged intra-regional trade. What was worse, the committee decided not only on registration, but also on the tax rate to be applied to each product produced by the firm, a rate that also varied according to the country to which the good was to be exported. The rates were set in an *ad hoc* fashion, and the political forces at work in the committee meant that widely different rates were set according to the firm, the country and the product involved. The result was an object lesson in how not to design and implement a tax. As the authors note, the implementation of the TU meant that an instrument designed to expand trade became a means of protectionism that distorted resource allocation within UDEAC, yet seemed to do little to stimulate intra-regional trade.

The authors' discussion of the *taxe unique* also offers a fascinating picture of strategic behaviour by UDEAC members. Although the UDEAC management committee was responsible for setting the rate, it operated by consensus, which meant in practice that each country determined the rate applied within its own territory. Not surprisingly, a country producing a particular good set the TU on the output of its own firms at a rate lower than that on competing products produced in other member states. The rates it applied to competing products, or products it did not produce, reflected a mixture of 'retaliation' and 'reciprocity', tempered by 'fiscal' considerations (the need to keep the tax rate high even on goods produced by domestic firms, in order to raise revenue). If countries pursue a strategy of retaliation, for example, the tax rate should be more uniform, the more countries produce the good, and the authors find that this indeed was the case.

Overall, though, strategic behaviour led to wide disparities in the tax rate, due mainly to the low rates set by countries on products produced by their own firms. These disparities appeared to widen over time, in the sense that the percentage of decisions establishing a uniform rate for the TU fell from 46 per cent to 25 per cent after 1985. As a result, exports from the region into a member country faced severe discrimination unless there were no firms in the country producing the good. And since it would appear that most firms viewed their main competitors as coming from within UDEAC, the TU tended to discourage intra-regional trade, or more precisely, offered UDEAC members a tool by which they could engage in protectionism while appearing to give allegiance to the goals of regional integration. The authors conclude that this outcome was almost inevitable, given the absence of a mechanism for compensating the losers from the integration process.

Why did UDEAC fail to establish an effective compensation mechanism? UDEAC attempted to compensate the losers through the solidarity fund and through the distribution of regional projects, but neither worked well. The UDE, UDEAC's predecessor, had established a solidarity fund financed by a portion of the revenues from the common external tariff. This functioned well, but was replaced in UDEAC by a fund financed by contributions from all member states, fixed annually by the heads of state. Not surprisingly, payments by those countries who were net contributors to the fund were subject to long delays. These delays contributed to the disintegration of the common customs service and the collection of data on intra-regional trade, and the fund had effectively collapsed by 1991. The distribution of regional projects also aimed to provide compensation by locating specific sectors of regional industry in those (predominantly poorer) countries that regarded themselves as the losers in the integration process. In practice, little or no spending seems to have been directed towards these countries, and so even this compensation instrument was ineffectual.

Mechanisms such as the UDEAC solidarity fund were the real-world analogue of the lump-sum transfers that, economic theory suggests, are an efficient means of compensating the losers from a policy change. Such transfers are efficient, in the sense that they do not distort resource allocation, because they do not affect relative prices. The failure of these 'lump-sum' transfer mechanisms left UDEAC members with only one means of protecting themselves against the changes brought about by regional integration; namely, to alter relative prices through the TU. So effective was it as a compensation mechanism that it stifled the growth of trade within the region, the primary objective of the integration process itself. The *taxe unique* thus effectively prevented regional integration from taking place at all.

The general sentiments of studies assessing the experience of regional integration in SSA is that this experience leaves a lot to be desired. These sentiments apply with equal force to the regional integration schemes in Eastern and Southern Africa. Save for the case of SACU and its monetary counterpart, the Common Monetary Area (CMA), trade expansion has been slow and intra-group trade has increased modestly, if at all. In addition, industrial, monetary, financial and fiscal policy co-ordination has been negligible outside SACU and the two monetary unions of francophone West Africa (CFA). Other shortcomings that apply to virtually all schemes are low levels of investment and growth, negligible scale economies, high administrative and operational costs, lack of political commitment, and unequal distribution of costs and benefits. Based on their review of theoretical and empirical research in the literature, Lyakurwa (Chapter 7) and especially Mwase and Maasdorp (Chapter 6) suggest that, given the initial conditions that prevailed in most African regional integration schemes, strong performance (in terms of intra-group trade) could not have been easy to achieve.

For example, Mwase and Maasdorp identify the following conditions for a regional integration scheme to be viable – hardly any of them are satisfied by any of the schemes. These conditions are that the integrating states:

(1) are at similar levels of industrial development;
(2) have competitive industrial sectors;
(3) have the potential to develop complementary industrial sectors; and,
(4) already conduct a significant portion of their foreign trade among themselves.

Also in terms of the required institutional set-up for successful integration they emphasize that governments should be prepared willingly to cede some sovereign rights to a supranational authority that has real powers to implement regional integration programmes; that members should address the problem of manufacturing concentration in a way that provides real gains to all members; and that members should harmonize their economic policies as well as contain political differences. The authors appear to subscribe to the widely accepted view that global non-discriminatory abolition of tariff and quantitative restrictions is theoretically superior to economic integration schemes. However, they argue that in an imperfect world dominated by regional groupings, regional integration in subSaharan Africa remains a viable and useful option. Furthermore, liberalizing regional integration schemes, supported by an economically strong external anchor, could be superior to a unilateral non-reciprocal trade liberalization (Collier and Gunning, 1995). This view emphasizes the role of regional integration as a lock-in mechanism to enhance national policy reform credibility and foster policy harmonization within the scheme as well as co-ordination of external economic relations with other economic blocs (Fine and Yeo, 1995).

According to Kasekende and Ng'eno (Chapter 5), implementation of PTA/COMESA objectives as stipulated in its treaties and protocol has met with mixed results. The PTA Bank has been active in infrastructure, agro-industry and tourism project lending as well as trade financing, with a cumulative approved financing reaching UAPTA65.98 million by December 1994. However, the future of the bank remains uncertain, due to the interest of SADC members of COMESA in pulling out and withdrawing their shares. After a brief surge, the activities of the clearing house and the PTA travellers' cheques virtually came to a halt as unilateral trade liberalization and exchange rate reforms took hold in the region during the second half of the 1980s. For example, the total value of intra-PTA trade transacted through the clearing house steadily increased from US\$74.6 m. in 1984 to a peak of US\$441 m. in 1989 before declining to US\$330 m. in 1991. Also, the sales of PTA cheques declined by 32 per cent, to UAPTA 8.179 m. in 1994, following a 49 per cent increase during its first two years of operation from UAPTA8.071 m. in 1989 to UAPTA12.034 m. in 1991. Perhaps the most disappointing aspects of PTA performance relate to the basic areas of macroeconomic policy harmonization and intra-PTA trade. Consistent with its share in world trade (which dropped from 0.56 per cent in 1982 to 0.4 per cent in 1993), intra-PTA exports as a share of total PTA exports declined from 7.0 per cent in 1982 to 6.6 per cent in 1992, while the share of intra-PTA imports to total PTA imports stagnated at 4.7 per cent over the period.

Except for the case of SACU, smaller schemes such as SADC did not fair any better on the above scores. Mimicking a comparable pattern to that of PTA/COMESA, intra-SADC trade, which currently accounts for less than 5 per cent of total recorded trade, rose initially but eventually levelled off following the liberalization cycle. For example, the intra-region trade increased (by 14 per cent) from US$218.5 in 1983 to US$248.8 in 1984, reached a peak of US$324.7 in 1987 before declining by 2 per cent in 1988. Lyakurwa argues that failure of member countries to achieve dynamic growth, coupled with low regional capacity to produce intermediate and capital goods (outside South Africa, Zimbabwe and Mauritius), have been the main reasons for low intra-SADC trade. Until recently, however, the lack of convertibility has also had a negative impact on intra-regional trade finance. According to Mwase and Maasdorp, based on the above criteria, SACU does not rate well despite being a very durable scheme. However, SACU meets significant requirements – requirements that remain rather elusive goals for many other African schemes. The scheme has a history of significant intra-group trade; all countries see themselves as gaining from their membership; there is broad agreement on market-based economic systems; and political differences have always been containable. The substantial dominance of the South African economies in SACU (93.4 per cent of SACU's GDP) explains the high rates of intra-group trade, but it also presents problems of appropriate compensation. For example, currently the shares of South African exports in total imports by other SACU members are 94 per cent in Lesotho, 91 per cent in Swaziland, 90 per cent in Namibia, 81 per cent in Botswana, 32 per cent in Malawi, 25 per cent in Zimbabwe and 20 per cent in Zambia. Even though the share of exports to South Africa in these countries' total exports is less (for example, 46 per cent for Swaziland, 42 per cent for Lesotho, 25 per cent for Namibia), by any standard it is not-negligible. Furthermore, out of South Africa's top 13 trading partners, four are SACU members. As a result of tariff liberalization as part of WTO agreements, the rather skewed intra-SACU trade balances (in favour of South Africa) may experience some corrections.

1.3 CHANGING ECONOMIC AND POLITICAL CONDITIONS: GLOBALIZATION AND REGIONAL INTEGRATION

Aside from administrative and institutional shortcomings and the political conflicts that characterize the operation of PTA as detailed by Kasekende and Ng'eno, the evidence clearly suggests that PTA (and other African regional schemes for that matter) were based on trade and payments regimes that are not compatible with the recent wave of unilateral trade and foreign exchange liberalizing reforms that swept African countries as part of the structural adjustment programmes. The authors argue that to the extent that PTA producers are preferred because of administrative control on foreign exchange utilization and licensing, trade liberalization is bound to constrain intra-PTA trade. Furthermore, this is also the main reason for the dramatic slowdown of the utilization of the PTA clearing house and the UAPTA travellers' cheques. By and large the response of many African countries to the oil and commodity price shocks of the 1970s and their aftermath has been expansive macroeconomic policies, over-valued exchange rates, and controlled exchange and trade regimes. As we saw from the above overview, these measures have not been conducive to overall trade or to intra-PTA trade. Now that the region is going through a transition, dominated by macroeconomic and sectoral reforms designed to correct macroeconomic imbalances and economic distortions, it is important that the tools created by the PTA secretariat in different circumstances be replaced by tools consistent with the new unilateral liberalizing reforms. Specifically, Lyakurwa suggests that long-term sustainability of SADC (and regional integration in SSA in general) hinges on creating an enabling environment for the production of goods and services, through development of physical infrastructure and co-ordination of macroeconomic policies, rather than attempting to achieve integration by drawing trade protocols that are difficult to enforce.

The authors of the ECOWAS study note that ECOWAS was very much a 'top-down' exercise in regional integration. The initial impetus for the formation of ECOWAS lay in the Economic Commission for Africa's blueprint for an African Economic Community; ECOWAS was one of the building blocks in this continental enterprise. There was little or no grassroots support for regional integration, for a variety of reasons. First, the systems of governance in place in most countries in subSaharan Africa in the 1960s and 1970s did not encourage popular participation in decision-making. Nor is it obvious that the populace would have felt moved by the prospects for a regional free trade area, even if their opinions had been solicited; intra-regional trade was very small, as were the potential benefits from its growth. In addition, as is the case outside Africa, the potential beneficiaries from freer trade did not (yet) exist (new firms that would arise in response to export opportunities) or formed only a very diffuse coalition (consumers who would benefit from more widely available and better quality imported goods). The potential losers from freer trade could identify themselves and form coalitions much more easily.

In this respect, however, recent developments give some grounds for optimism. The authors conjecture that the growth of democracy and the emphasis on more transparency and accountability in political systems might stimulate more debate on and popular support for regional integration.

The rivalry between PTA/COMESA and SADC is one of the major problems facing the two schemes. Unlike SADC, PTA is mainly a geographical grouping of a large number of African countries, reflecting the vision of UNECA, but with few shared common interests as a group. The Southern African members of SADC believe that a small grouping of countries with strong credible commitment and well-articulated policies and programmes is more effective in negotiating larger market access for its members in an increasingly competitive world economy. On the other hand, for the same reasons, the opposing view argues that larger groupings like COMESA should carry more weight and therefore should be more effective than smaller groups. The whole debate is clearly influenced by the new world trade order, associated with the creation of the World Trade Organization (WTO) and the resurgence of regionalism, exemplified by the formation of powerful regional blocks such as NAFTA, the European Union, the Pacific Rim, ASEAN and AFTA.

Kasekende and Ng'eno, and also Lyakurwa, propose a view that seems to offer an option for compatibility, based on the twin principles of 'variable geometry' and 'subsidiarity'. According to the first principle, it is possible for members to have a dual track for regional integration, where membership requirements for PTA/COMESA would emphasize broad policy co-ordination/harmonization and trade liberalization measures, while in addition to SACU and the CFA monetary unions, other smaller regional schemes like SADC and EAC could add deeper integration instruments in the areas of regional projects, labour and capital market integration, and so on. The revised COMESA Treaty appears to accommodate this 'variable geometry' view, as a logical way for a gradual move towards greater economic integration in the region. In this connection Mwase and Maasdorp emphasize the role of the Cross-Border Initiative (CBI) in reducing impediments to cross-border trade and investment. The donor-funded CBI, which covers the entire COMESA/SADC area, attempts to build on the progress towards liberalization achieved at the national and regional levels by encouraging countries to agree on harmonized reduced tariff rates. The principle of subsidiarity, on the other hand, calls for decisions to be decentralized as much as possible. This requires more involvement of civil society – especially national parliaments – in debating, conceptualizing and implementing regional integration measures. This principle is likely to be the only viable approach to achieving meaningful and durable regional integration, given the political liberalization that has swept through the continent. This dual track approach also holds promise for minimizing the conflicts of divided loyalties between larger and smaller schemes that contributed to the problems of regional integration in SSA.

Developments in the global economy, particularly in the late 1970s, had an important impact on the economic performance of UDEAC members and to some extent on the success of UDEAC itself. The member states of UDEAC vary sharply in size, income levels and economic structure. Agriculture dominates the economies of the CAR and Equatorial Guinea. Others (Congo and Chad) produce oil and consequently enjoy significantly higher incomes. Only Cameroon enjoys a diversified economic structure – industry and agriculture in addition to its oil. It also dominates the grouping, producing almost 50 per cent of its GDP. This dichotomy in economic structure had important consequences for UDEAC over the period 1970–90. The oil shocks, for example, had a sharply asymmetric effect on the oil producers and the oil consumers, making the setting of policy within UDEAC especially problematic.

The ECOWAS study finds some grounds for optimism in more recent developments, however, in particular the adoption of structural adjustment programmes in the 1980s. The implementation of these programmes, could, the authors argue, prove conducive to regional integration, and in particular intra-regional trade and factor mobility. The reduction in currency over-valuation and the creation of an environment more favourable to exports can be expected to stimulate exports, both within and outside the region. Measures to increase competitiveness and transparency within the domestic economy may also facilitate capital mobility and cross-border business dealings.

Structural adjustment programmes may, however, give rise to some developments that discourage attempts at regional integration. One possibility the authors discuss is the impact of trade liberalization on government revenues, a factor that is particularly important given the large share of trade taxes in total government revenues in subSaharan Africa. Tariff revenues may either rise or fall in response to a liberalization reduction in tariff rates; lower rates will reduce revenues, *ceteris paribus*, but a rise in the volume of imports following a cut, or the replacement of quotas by tariffs, tend to increase revenues. The net effect could in theory go either way, and since the empirical evidence gives no indication of any consistent relationship between liberalization and revenues, the authors do not believe this represents a serious obstacle to regional integration. Structural adjustment programmes might also lead to balance of payments difficulties if imports respond more promptly than exports to the liberalization measures, and regional trade liberalization might be difficult to implement during a period of balance of payments difficulties. Here again the theory gives no reason to expect that the balance of payments must necessarily worsen following a liberalization, and it may indeed improve. If so, this would create more favourable conditions for a regional trade liberalization.

1.4 SPECIAL ISSUES

Why did the CEAO survive for over 20 years, despite its apparent lack of success in fostering trade integration? Survival might be explained simply by inertia, but M'Bet argues that the explanation lies elsewhere: CEAO was kept alive by internal support for monetary union. The support for monetary union can be explained in turn by 'political' factors – namely, the desire to band together in the face of a powerful and potentially dominant neighbour, Nigeria. Aid flows also played a role; it was important to sustain the *Conseil de l'Entente*, which provided access to external donor funds.

Throughout its existence, the members of the CEAO also belonged to a monetary union, UMOA, sharing a common currency and central bank. The relationship between 'trade integration' and monetary integration is still the subject of considerable debate within the research and policy communities. Some members of the EU, for example, believe that full integration of goods and factor markets cannot be sustained without exchange rate stability, which in turn cannot be achieved without a monetary union and common currency. Without exchange rate stability, it is argued, countries will be tempted to engage in competitive devaluations, and this will undermine political support for the free movement of goods within the EU. The EU offers the example of a regional integration scheme that has integrated its goods and factor markets and now wonders whether to carry out a full monetary integration. The CEAO offers in some ways the opposite case, in which a monetary union existed before attempts were made to integrate the goods market.

What role did UMOA play in the attempts to achieve trade integration? M'Bet argues that the monetary union had a mixed impact. The poorer members could not adjust their exchange rates against fellow CEAO members in order to improve their competitiveness; in practice the TCR seems to have been used instead for this purpose. On the other hand, the monetary union may have fostered a high degree of factor mobility, and the relatively high mobility of labour may have acted as a substitute for exchange rate adjustments. In particular, the poorer members may have exported their labour forces to the more advanced coastal countries, and migrant remittances may have substituted for earnings from exports of goods.

The monetary union had other, less desirable, effects. Its members had perforce a co-ordinated and rigorous monetary policy, in which their currency was linked to a relatively strong currency, the French franc. At the same time, members were able to operate uncoordinated – and in practice very loose – fiscal policies. It is exactly this prospect that alarms the Bundesbank (the German Central Bank) as it contemplates the prospect of European Monetary Union. It has also given rise to the 'convergence criteria' in the Maastricht Treaty – criteria for public sector deficits and the level of public debt that must be satisfied before a country can join the monetary union.

As M'Bet notes, the same debate arose during 1993 within the CEAO and was partly responsible for its replacement in 1994 by UMEOA, which was intended to encompass trade integration (the role of the former CEAO) and monetary integration (the role of the former UMOA).

The members of UDEAC, like those of the CEAO, are members of a monetary union whose currency, the CFA franc is pegged to the French franc (and indirectly to the Deutschmark). The monetary union had an important impact on macroeconomic performance in both the CEAO and UDEAC, and this clearly affected the success of the regional integration efforts. But in which direction? There is a strong school of thought, in Europe at least, that a monetary union is essential if the 'deep' economic integration exemplified by the single market is to be politically and economically sustainable. Without stable exchange rates, it is argued, countries will be tempted to engage in competitive devaluations, which will tend to undermine popular acceptance of and political support for an integrated market. 'The playing field is not level' – countries that devalue are not playing by the rules and are viewed as 'cheating'. In addition, uncertainty over future levels of the exchange rate may discourage flows of long-term capital and foreign direct investment. According to this line of argument, monetary unification and trade integration go hand in hand.

Opponents of this view argue that exchange rate movements are essential in adjusting to shocks, whether these arise from outside the integrating region or are part of the process of adjustment to increased economic integration within the region. On balance, the evidence suggests that at least during later periods (the mid to late 1980s) monetary unification certainly did nothing to foster increased regional integration, and may have acted to discourage intra-regional trade.

Work by Devarajan and de Melo (1987, 1990) suggests that the monetary union did provide a nominal anchor for the CFA zone countries, allowing them to achieve significantly lower inflation rates than other countries in subSaharan Africa. But the nominal anchor had costs as well, in the form of lower growth rates of exports and income. This cost was small in the period before 1982; the 1987 study by Devarajan and de Melo notes that the CFA countries had in fact slightly higher growth rates over the period 1960–82, but their 1991 study suggests that the costs rose during the 1980s. Growth rates in the CFA were still higher (but not significantly so) and export growth and investment were significantly lower than elsewhere in SSA and there was less current account adjustment to external shocks within the CFA (after controlling for size of shocks).

In principle, then, monetary unification might act either to encourage or to discourage the growth of intra-regional trade and other forms of regional integration. There are strong reasons for believing that the monetary union acted to discourage regional integration, or at least the growth of intra-regional trade. By fixing the exchange rates of its members relative to each other, the monetary union ruled out the possibility that countries could adjust to a growth in regional trade by movements in their exchange rates. In addition, the pegging of the CFA to the French franc (and the consequent over-valuation) acted to reduce growth and exports within both UDEAC and CEAO. The over-valuation of the CFA franc clearly made imports from the rest of the world more attractive relative to domestic production. Without the monetary union, an over-valued currency in one country of the region might have led to increased imports from its regional neighbours, but since the currencies were linked in the monetary union, such an increase in intra-regional trade did not take place. Instead, the increased trade seemed to flow to ECOWAS, possibly because its members (particularly Nigeria) had even more over-valued exchange rates.

It seems unlikely, on the other hand, that the monetary union in UDEAC (and the CEAO) played any role in increasing political support for the integration of regional markets and the growth of intra-regional trade. The experience in both UDEAC and CEAO suggests that there was little or no political support for intra-regional trade; this can be seen clearly in the setting of the *taxe unique* rates in UDEAC.

It is conceivable that support would have been even lower in the absence of the monetary union, but this seems implausible. In any event, the monetary union was not a strong enough force to stimulate intra-regional trade. M'Bet argues that the monetary union did play a role in the survival of the CEAO by sustaining a spirit of regional cohesion. It might also be argued that the creation of common regional monetary institutions not only nurtured this spirit of regional co-operation, but also gave government officials in UDEAC (and CEAO) the experience of working together in formulating and implementing policies on a regional basis. Interestingly enough, something similar (but in reverse) seems to have taken place in the early stages of the European Community. Giavazzi and Giovannini (1989) have argued, for example, that the experience of co-ordinating European agricultural and industrial policies in the 1950s and 1960s made it easier for European governments to establish the institutions necessary for monetary co-operation (the European Monetary System and the Exchange Rate Mechanism).

So it is possible that the experience of operating the institutions of the monetary union played a role in fostering regional co-operation in other fields, such as the harmonization of customs procedures and accounting practices. Why was the relatively successful cooperation in the monetary field not repeated in other areas, such as the liberalization of intra-regional trade? The answer seems to lie in the role of external guarantors, a factor emphasized by Collier and Gunning (1995) and by Fine and Yeo (1995) in their analyses of the political economy of regional integration. UDEAC and CEAO members buried their differences in the monetary policy field because they had something to lose – the financial support provided to the BCAO by the French treasury. In the case of intra-regional trade, there was no external agency in a position to apply sanctions should trade liberalization not take place. Regional trade integration meant immediate short-term losses to domestic producers and the public revenues; the gains would only accrue to consumers and to firms with export potential, who were weakly represented in the political system.

The authors of Chapter 2 draw attention to two factors specific to the region that have conditioned the success (or lack thereof) of ECOWAS. The first is the overwhelming dominance of Nigeria, with two-thirds of the ECOWAS population and one half of its GDP. The other members of ECOWAS, tiny by comparison, fear that any opening of markets will flood their markets with Nigerian, goods (produced more cheaply for the large Nigerian market), while their own goods will remain uncompetitive in Nigerian markets.

A free trade area or customs union dominated by a single large nation need not necessarily be doomed to failure. The large member may find it possible to persuade its neighbours to agree to regional market integration by making side payments that in effect 'buy off' the potential losers among the smaller members. The dominant country may contain a larger number of the potential gainers from integration, who may be able to coalesce more effectively through their national government in order to pursue regional liberalization. Whether Nigeria would have been able, or willing, to play such a hegemonic role within ECOWAS remains doubtful, but the presence of a second dominant 'regional' power – France – certainly prevented it from playing that role. The authors note the widely held view that ECOWAS is governed by two powers – France and Nigeria – and that to understand whether any policy of the community would work or not, one needs just to understand what the two countries think of it.

France has continued to play an active role in the region through its influence over its former colonies, the members of the CEAO and UEMOA. It is difficult for them to implement policies (including preferential tariffs for ECOWAS members as against third countries) that would hurt French commercial interests, as the authors note. The result has been a polarization of ECOWAS into two groups, the former colonies of England and those of France, as well as the existence of rival regional groupings such as UMEOA with different and conflicting policy agendas. It is not clear whether this is the result of deliberate policy on the part of France, or whether its former colonies find it convenient to use France as a counterweight against the influence of their dominant neighbour.

Whatever the explanation, the result, as the authors observe, has been paralysis within ECOWAS. Again, as with the case of a single dominant regional power, paralysis need not have been the inevitable outcome. Members of the European Community during the 1960s, it might be argued, have faced a similar situation, with a powerful and dominant neighbour (Germany), together with a more distant but an even more powerful nation, the United States. Why did this not lead to paralysis within the European Community, as was the case with ECOWAS? One explanation might be that Germany and the USA were more evenly matched in terms of economic and political influence, but a more convincing explanation lies in the closer correspondence between the political and economic interests of the two countries, due in large part to the cold war and the perceived threat from the Soviet Union.

The framework paper by Fine and Yeo (1995) emphasizes the important role played by non-economic, and in particular political factors in providing the impetus for regional integration schemes, citing the role played by the cold war in the initial efforts to create the European Community in the 1950s. Jebuni, Ogunkola and Soludo draw attention to a number of interesting recent parallels within ECOWAS. ECOMOG, the monitoring and security cooperation mounted by ECOWAS in Liberia, has played a role in reviving enthusiasm for regional co-operation within ECOWAS, at least on matters of political security, and, according to the authors, has acted to resurrect the spirit of ECOWAS and advertised the potential political benefit of the Community. Whether the underlying rivalry between France and Nigeria and the resulting polarization of the Community will allow progress to be made towards deeper regional integration is still unclear.

Until recently, SADC has been a regional grouping with a specific political objective – to minimize economic and political dependence of the 'front-line' states on South Africa. To this effect, SADC has been successful in mobilizing substantial donor funding. However, after the democratic transformation in South Africa, the politically motivated funding will certainly be reduced. On the other hand, with South Africa now a member of SADC, it may act as a conduit through which external resources, including foreign direct investment, may be channelled to the rest of the region, especially if political stability is fully restored to Angola and Mozambique. In addition to the issues related to the relationship with COMESA, the important question that should be addressed by SADC members is, that should SADC press for extending the SACU agreement to its members now that South Africa is also a SADC member? In the view of Mwase and Maasdorp, it is doubtful whether SACU could be extended in the near future. Due to requirements such as compatibility of macroeconomic policy (interest rate, inflation and exchange rate), currency convertibility and extent of trade liberalization, only Zimbabwe would appear to have a chance from among other SADC members.

The shares of government revenues provided by SACU proceeds in Lesotho, Swaziland, Botswana and Namibia are quite substantial. For example, in 1990/91 these shares were 14.5 per cent for Botswana, 57.7 per cent for Lesotho, 32 per cent for Swaziland and 43.8 per cent for Namibia. Despite the fact that South Africa has been concerned about its declining share of customs revenue, other SACU countries are equally concerned that there will be further industrial polarization, with South Africa attracting the bulk of new industrial development. Mwase and Maasdorp argue that as in the case of the defunct EAC, it is unlikely that the redistribution of custom/excise duties revenue will adequately compensate the smaller SACU member countries. Hence, in their view, the longer-term sustainability of SACU hinges on the progress in attracting more investment and locating new industries in these smaller countries, in order to narrow the enormous gap that exists now between South Africa and its less developed partner states. However, it has been argued that it may not be politically feasible to include the smaller SACU countries in a co-ordinated industrial programme together with neighbouring South African provinces. Thus, even though compensation for industrial concentration via the revenue-sharing formula does not, in principle, solve the problem, it could be the only practical solution available (McCarthy, 1996). But recent political developments in South Africa itself (that is, emergence of majority rule) may render this political constraint less important.

The phenomenon of unrecorded cross-border trade is an important issue of specific significance for most of SSA's regional integration schemes. As Jean-Paul Azam (Chapter 8) suggests, the presence of substantial unrecorded cross-border trade can be viewed as an indication of both the failure of the relevant regional integration schemes and the potential for intra-regional trade. The ineffectiveness of existing regional integration schemes in successfully harmonizing trade, exchange rate and general macroeconomic policies provides a significant rationale for the continued vitality of this phenomenon. At the same time, the exclusion of this trade from official records leads to estimates of intra-regional trade that are substantially lower than the actual values. Thus, more effective regional integration can be expected to promote greater intra-regional trade by eliminating the obstacles whose costly avoidance currently generates unrecorded cross-border trade.

References

Baldwin, R. E. (1995) 'Review of Theoretical Developments on Regional Integration', mimeo (Nairobi: AERC).

Collier, P. and J. W. Gunning (1995) 'Trade Policy and Regional Integration: Implications for the Relations between Europe and Africa', *World Economy*, **18**: 387–410.

Devarajan, S. and J. de Melo (1987) 'Evaluating Participation in African Monetary Unions: A Statistical Analysis of the CFA Zones', *World Development*, **15**(4): 483–6.

Devarajan, S. and J. de Melo (1990) 'Membership in the CFA Zone: Odyssean Journey or Trojan Horse', PPP working paper 482 (Washington, DC: World Bank).

Fine, J. and S. Yeo (1995) 'Regional Integration in Sub-Saharan Africa: Dead End or a Fresh Start?', mimeo (Nairobi: AERC).

Foroutan, F. and L. Pritchett (1993) 'Intra-Sub-Saharan African Trade: Is it too Little', Policy Research working paper 1225 (Washington, DC: World Bank).

Giavazzi, F. and A. Giovannini (1989) 'Can the EMS be Exported? Lessons from Ten Years of Monetary Policy Coordination in Europe', CEPR Discussion paper no. 285.

McCarthy, C. (1996) 'Regional Integration in Sub-Saharan Africa: Past, Present and Future', mimeo (Nairobi: AERC).

Ogunkola, E. O. (1994) 'An Empirical Evaluation of Trade Potential in the Economic Community of West African States', final report (Nairobi: AERC).

2 A Case-Study of the Economic Community of West African States (ECOWAS)

Charles D. Jebuni, E. Olawale Ogunkola and Charles C. Soludo

2.1 INTRODUCTION

The Economic Community of West African States (ECOWAS), comprising 16 countries of the West African sub-region, was established in 1975 with the ultimate objective of forming an economic community. It was the product of the Pan-Africanism sweeping the African continent at the time, as well as the efforts of the private sector lobby and the encouragement of the Economic Commission for Africa (ECA).

Although the treaty was signed in 1975, five protocols attached to the treaty were not ratified by the required minimum number of states until November 1976. The community was therefore not operational until early 1977.

After the ratification, the Lagos-based secretariat of the community set about identifying priority areas of concern through commissioned research. Priority areas of action for 1979–81 were agreed at a summit in Dakar in 1979. Protocols and conventions were prepared and ratified by member states. Between 1979 and 1989 about 30 such protocols and conventions were ratified. The trade liberation scheme of the community, which was expected to begin two years after the ratification of the treaty, started in 1990.

Thus between 1977 and 1990, the community was preoccupied with the establishment of institutions deemed important for its success, and the ratification of protocols and conventions to clarify issues relating to the community. Not much else seems to have been achieved. Then in 1992, following a number of developments within their domestic economies and the international environment, the treaty establishing ECOWAS was revised as an attempt to re-vamp the community.

This brief story shows that the history of ECOWAS falls into two phases: the initial period up too 1990 and the period of the revised treaty starting 1992. In this chapter we shall refer to the earlier period as ECOWAS part I and the period of the revised treaty as ECOWAS part II.

In discussions of the low level of trade among ECOWAS members a number of authors have seen the problems of integration in terms of the similarity of production bases, concerns about lost revenues and balance of payments, transportation difficulties, and sometimes even linguistic barriers. These so-called constraints are symptoms of more fundamental difficulties. The largest volume of world trade takes place among countries with similar production structures and resource endowments.

It is argued in this chapter that the more fundamental problems arose from misconceptions about the basis for integration, domestic policy frameworks at variance with the ideals of integration, a non-existent or weak domestic support/political base for integration, and an approach that was both ambitious and legalistic. These factors have resulted in lack of commitment to the implementation of ECOWAS protocols.

Since the second half of the 1980s, the wave of both economic and political reforms sweeping across Africa has given rise to a need to re-examine and rededicate ourselves to the ideals of ECOWAS. These efforts are buttressed by changing world economic conditions and a changing technology in which location is increasingly unimportant in world comparative advantage.

2.2 ECOWAS PART I: 1975–91

Initial Conditions

To understand the success or failure of ECOWAS and the approach adopted, it is necessary to examine the prevailing conditions in the region prior to the establishment of the community. The interplay of these conditions with the world environment constitutes the fundamental explanation of ECOWAS difficulties.

One striking feature of the grouping is the diversity of the member states in terms of their economic size and potential. Twelve of the 16 members are classified among the least-developed countries. The majority of the member states are, individually, too small in terms of income level and market size to ensure a take-off to self-sustained economic development. In terms of population, four countries have populations of less than a million, while only four have populations of over 10 million. In many of the countries, the smallness of the domestic economy is compounded by poor endowments of natural resources, and human capital is very poorly developed.

A peculiar structure of ECOWAS, which distinguishes it from any other regional group in the world, is the immense discrepancy in market size, production and trade between the largest number, Nigeria, and the other members. Table 2.1 shows the considerable variation among member countries in terms of GDP and population. GDP ranged from about $79 m. in Guinea-Bissau to $11.6 bn for Nigeria in 1970. Only three countries, Nigeria, Ghana and Côte d'Ivoire, had GDPs of more than $1 bn each for both 1970 and 1975. Though growth rates were positive, they were generally low. Nigeria and Côte d'Ivoire dominated, with average growth rates of 8.1 per cent per annum between 1970 and 1975. Thus individual country markets were too small to support viable industries and the total market size for the 16 member countries was less than $50 bn.

Population among member countries ranged from less than 300 000 for Cape Verde to 56.6 m. for Nigeria. Population growth rates, however, were high. In terms of linguistic differences, there were only three official languages, English, French and Portuguese. This is much fewer than in the European Union, for example.

More important, however, in understanding the dilemma ECOWAS was to face, is the domestic economic policy framework adopted by member countries. At the time that West African leaders signed the ECOWAS protocols in 1975, most countries were pursuing import-substitution industrialization strategies behind high protective walls. Post-colonial political leadership was imbued with economic nationalism. Each national state was committed to its own development and the possibility of being the most developed country in Africa. This nationalism combined with a development theory of the 1950s and 1960s that preached *dirigisme* led West African states to adopt state-led, import-substitution development strategies. The

Table 2.1   Some economic indicators for ECOWAS

Country	GDP*			Population		
	1970 (m.)	*Average annual growth (1970–5)*	*1975 (m.)*	*1970 (m.)*	*Average (m.)*	*1975 (m.)*
French-speaking						
Benin	332	1.5	353	2.7	2.38	3.00
Burkina Faso	335	2.6	390	5.6	2.22	6.20
Côte d'Ivoire	1 147	8.1	1 662	5.5	4.15	6.80
Mali	338	3.9	397	5.5	2.35	6.20
Niger	647	–1.2	569	4.2	2.72	4.80
Senegal	865	3.5	972	4.2	2.89	4.10
Guinea	n.a.	n.a.	n.a.	3.9	1.23	2.30
Togo	253	3.4	306	2.0	2.47	1.40
Mauritania	197	1.7	195	1.2	2.32	1.60
English-speaking						
Liberia	n.a.	n.a.	n.a.	1.4	3.00	2.90
Sierra Leone	383	3.9	435	2.7	1.97	0.55
Gambia	n.a.	n.a.	n.a.	0.46	3.32	9.80
Ghana	2 214	1.5	2 166	8.6	2.65	66.60
Nigeria	11 594	8.1	15 207	56.6	3.18	
Portuguese-speaking						
Guinea Bissau	79	4.1	97	0.53	3.58	0.63
Cape Verde	n.a.	n.a.	n.a.	0.267	0.80	0.278

Notes:
* Calculated from average annual growth (per cent) given in World Tables (from the data files of the World Bank).

resulting import-substitution syndrome, with accompanying over-valued currencies and controlled regimes, generated rents that developed powerful supportive vested interests. The beneficiaries from this system were usually the politicians, the bureaucrats and the military corps. They also included the workers and managers of the dependent industries that relied on the largess of the state and import licences. These groups also constituted the ruling coalition and therefore could not be expected to implement policies that would erode their rents.

In West Africa the fact that almost every country was pursuing these types of domestic economic policies reinforced every other country's beliefs in the policies, in spite of the apparent adverse

Table 2.2   The structure of trade of the West African countries,
1971–95

SITC section	% share of section in:	
	Average	*Total*
0 Food and live animals	17.4	13.4
1 Beverages and tobacco	0.1	1.7
2 Crude materials, excluding fuels	16.4	2.5
3 Minerals fuels, and so on	59.2	6.3
4 Animal and vegetable oils, fat	2.3	0.5
5 Chemicals	0.3	9.5
6 Basic manufactures	3.1	24.1
7 Machines and transport equipment	0.5	33.0
8 Miscellaneous manufacturing	0.2	6.6
9 Goods not classified by kind	0.4	1.6

Source: Calculated from Table 6 of ECA (various issues), *Foreign Trade Statistics for Africa*, Summary Tables C (New York).

economic consequences. Thus this negative neighbourhood effect reinforced and deepened the policies, with no group of countries emerging to champion the cause of ECOWAS.

Table 2.2 presents the structure of trade of member countries prior to ECOWAS. Though exports of these of countries consisted largely of agricultural and mineral products, imports were mainly manufactured products. Table 2.2 shows that over 95 per cent of exports consisted of agricultural and mineral products, with mineral fuels dominating. These products were exported largely to the industrialized countries along colonial lines. Only 4.2 per cent of exports went to destinations within the region in 1975. On the import side, over 75 per cent consisted of manufactured products. If one adds processed food from SITC 'O', the proportion exceeds 90 per cent.

This pattern of exports and imports suggests two ways to increase intra-ECOWAS trade. For one, considerable industrial development was required to provide competition with the imports from the industrialized countries. For another, substantial increases in growth and per capita incomes was necessary in order to increase demand and intra-ECOWAS exports without displacing imports from industrialized countries.

The Treaty Establishing ECOWAS

In summary, the goals and aspirations as set forth in the treaty showed that the community aimed to raise the standard of living of its peoples; increase and maintain economic stability; foster closer relations among its members; and contribute to the progress and development of the African continent.

The specific objectives based on the aims and purposes stated above are that the community shall, by stages, ensure:

- elimination of customs duties and other charges with respect to trade flows among member countries;
- abolition of quantitative and administrative restrictions on trade flows among member states;
- establishment of a common customs tariff and a common commercial policy towards third countries;
- abolition of the obstacles to the movement of persons, services and capital within the community;
- harmonization of agricultural policies and the promotion of common projects in the field of marketing, research and agro-industrial enterprises;
- joint development and evolution of common policy in infrastructural facilities such as transport, communications, energy and other;
- harmonization of economic and industrial policies and elimination of disparities in the level of development;
- harmonization of monetary policies; and
- establishment of a fund for co-operation, compensation and development (FCCD).

The first three objectives listed above relate to customs and trade matters. These matters were elaborated upon in Chapter III of the treaty. The matters were to be implemented in stages. The first stage was to last the first two years of the community, during which period member states were neither to impose new import duties and taxes, nor to increase the existing ones. In the second stage, the succeeding eight years, member states were to reduce progressively and then eliminate import duties. The third stage was the following five years, when members were expected gradually to abolish existing differences in their external customs tariffs.

Chapter IV (Article 27) enjoins the member states to abolish all obstacles to free movement of the community's citizens and their residence within the community. The citizens were to be allowed to work and undertake commercial and industrial activities within the community unhindered.

Harmonization of policies was also directed at agricultural sectors. The treaty viewed co-operation in agriculture and natural resources as consisting of two stages. The first involved harmonization of agricultural policies. At this stage, member states were enjoined to exchange information on experiment and research results and rural development programmes. It also envisaged joint development of programmes for basic and in-service training in existing institutions. The second stage involved evolution of a common agricultural policy.

The treaty identifies the following infrastructure development: roads, railways, shipping and waterways, air transport, telecommunication, and postal services. Co-operation and joint development of infrastructure facilities is very important, given that reliable communication services and a good network of transportation system (road, water and air) are prerequisites for increasing intraregional trade flows. Indeed, a situation where traders are sure of uninterrupted provision of these services helps in reducing cost of transactions (time and money).

Industrial development and harmonization also received the attention of the treaty. As with the harmonization of agricultural policies, member states are enjoined in the first stage to exchange information on major industrial projects. The treaty also says that member states should commission, finance and develop industrial projects jointly. The second stage, which involves the harmonization of industrial incentives and industrial development plans, aims to ensure similar industrial climates in order to avoid disruption of industrial activities that might result from dissimilar industrial incentives. The member states are enjoined to exchange their industrial plans so as to avoid unhealthy rivalry and waste of resources. The third and final stage entails exchange and training of skilled professional and managerial personnel of the community. In this stage also, member states are encouraged to engage in joint ventures.

Co-operation in monetary and financial matters entails establishment of bilateral (in the treaty) and multilateral (in the long run) systems for the settlement of accounts as well as of a committee of West African banks. This committee, made up of the governors of the Central Issue Committee, was set up to take care of issues relating to shares and stocks and mobility of capital, and to seek to harmonize rates of interest on loans prevailing in member states.

The treaty made provisions for other issues such as energy and mineral resources, social and cultural affairs, and settlement of disputes.

From these objectives and provisions of the treaty, it is clear that co-operation and joint development of common resources, harmonization of sectoral policies, and trade liberalization are the key components of the community's agreement. Co-operation and joint development of basic common resources is aimed at creating physical integration of the region. This aspect of the community's agreement is directed mainly towards two issues. First, it intends to take advantage of economies of scale embedded in the provision of such facilities as roads, railways, shipping and international waterways, air transport, and telecommunications, and so on. Related to this is that these infrastructural facilities usually involve huge sunk cost. Thus, the community rather than the individual country is in the best position to mobilize the required funds or arrange for finance. Second, co-operation and joint development of common resources are critical as long as the community intends to carry the least-developed members along with its programmes and projects. This aspect may prove indispensable for the survival of the community.

Harmonization and joint development of the community are necessary for effective trade liberalization. It is envisaged that well-coordinated industrial plans can deliberately influence the range of goods produced in the community in such a way that complementarity of goods and services is ensured. In other words, some provisions are required for effective take-off of co-operation, and joint development helps ensure even and accelerated development of the region.

Initial Delays in Getting the Agreement off the Ground

The provisions of the treaty are meant to be implemented through protocols and conventions. Indeed, five initial protocols annexed to the treaty provide details of the agreement on the following issues: definition of the concept of products originating from the member states; re-exportation within the region of goods imported from third countries; assessment of loss of revenue by member states as a result of implementing the provisions of the treaty; the Fund for Co-operation, Compensation and Development; and contributions by member states to the budget of the community.

The treaty has been criticized as being too ambitious, too general and lacking in effective strategies (Ebifie, 1984; and Tokuta, 1984). The conceptual problem of the community was also noted by ECOWAS (1985) when it observed that apart from matters relating to customs and trade, which were relatively elaborate, other provisions of the treaty were better passed as mere prescriptions of harmonization and co-ordination of policies. Thus, the implementation[1] of the provisions of the treaty started with clarification of issues and development of strategies. Much of the burden of designing clear documents was shifted to the design of protocols. These protocols were neither readily available nor promptly adopted by the member states. Some issues of common interest that the treaty did not include initially were deemed acceptable by the council. Protocols and conventions were used to annex such issues to the treaty; mutual assistance in defence is one example.

Indeed, when the community became operational in 1977, the secretariat began to identify priority areas for action. As part of the effort, some ten research projects were undertaken. Issues such as economic conditions of the region, recorded and unrecorded intra-regional trade flows, import and export regimes, profiles and potentials, and joint promotion were studied. Others included co-operation and trade in food products, livestock products, and forestry and forest products. Studies were also carried out on fiscal co-operation and harmonization, on monetary and financial obstacles to trade expansion in the region, and on currency convertibility in the region.

As a result of the commissioned studies, priority areas were set at the 1979 summit at Dakar for the period from 1979 to 1981. The areas identified were: trade and customs, fiscal and monetary matters, immigration, industrial co-operation, and agricultural co-operation.

Protocols and conventions were prepared and ratified by member states; some 30 of these[2] had been ratified by 1989. They clarified and improved the provisions of the treaty, and were intended to serve as the mechanism for implementation. The protocols covered almost all the areas of the regional integration efforts, except for issues relating to the harmonization of agricultural and industrial co-ordination. Trade and customs matters and issues relating to free movement of factor inputs, especially labour, dominated these instruments. (See Appendix Table 2 A.1 for the summary of distribution of protocols and conventions by main issues.)

Institutions of the Community

The community established institutions where necessary for effective management of day-to-day activities, as well as some specialized and technical commissions. The executive secretariat in consultation with the council of ministers and the authority of the heads of states is responsible for the overall implementation of the provisions of the treaty. The technical and specialized commissions were established to make recommendations with respect to issues relating to their specific areas. The areas identified are:

- trade, customs, immigration, and monetary/payment matters;
- industry, agriculture, natural resources;
- transport, communications, energy; and
- social/cultural affairs.

Other institutions necessary for promoting intra-regional trade flows were established. The West African Monetary Agency (WAMA), an autonomous body that grew out of the West African Clearing House (WACH), was set up to facilitate multilateral payments in the sub-region and to provide means of overcoming the multiplicity of currencies in the region. As noted earlier, the Capital Issue Commission (CIC) and the West Africa Committee of Bankers (WACB) were also established.

The Fund for Co-operation, Compensation and Development, the financial arm of the community, has several functions. The most important of these are to mobilize financial resources for the implementation of community projects and to supervise payment of compensation to member states that have incurred losses in revenue as a result of the implementation of the provisions of the treaty. The latter especially covers implementation of the trade liberalization scheme and the effect of the location of community projects in different member states.

The reasons for establishing the fund are not far-fetched: an integration programme such as that of ECOWAS usually favours one set of countries more than others. Thus it is necessary to design a compensatory scheme in such a way that net gainer pays net loser.

Infrastructural Development

The community's projects are mainly in the area of infrastructure. The two major road projects are at various stages of completion: the 4767 km. trans-coastal highway linking seven countries and the 4633 km. trans-Sahelian highway. These road projects are designed to open up some member states. Telecommunications is another project area of the Community designed to facilitate growth of intra-ECOWAS trade.

Trade Liberalization Scheme

In addition to all these supportive measures, a multi-phase trade liberalization scheme has just taken off. The scheme, which was meant to begin two years after the treaty became operational, finally got off the ground on 1 January 1990. At the moment, it is in its second phase, which entails total liberalization of trade. The scheme comprises two phases, consolidation of customs duties and non-tariff barriers and the total liberalization of trade. The consolidation, which was designed for the first two years, was conceived as the basis for the gradual removal of tariffs. Under this procedure, member states are not bound to reduce or remove import duties. Rather, they are expected not to fix new duties, or to charge or increase existing ones.

The total liberalization second phase is based on three product types and three groups of countries for its implementation. The first product types include unprocessed goods, which comprise animal, mineral and plant products. These products are not eligible for compensation for loss of revenue suffered as a result of their importation from member states. The second group of products is referred to as traditional handicraft products, and the third group is classified as industrial products produced within the community.

The first two groups of commodities have been enjoying free movement within the community (that is, without duties and entry charges). The scheme's timetable for the elimination of duties and taxes for the third product group is based on the following criteria: level of development, importance of custom receipts in member states' revenue, and problems deriving from difficulty of access (landlocked members). Thus, the implementation period ranges between six and ten years, with a corresponding annual rate of reduction in duties and taxes of between 16.6 per cent and 10 per cent (see Table 2.3).

Table 2.3   The ECOWAS tariff reduction schedule

Group of countries	Implementation period of duties and taxes (years)	Annual reduction rate (%)
A. Cape Verde Burkina-Faso, Gambia, Guinea–Bissau, Mali, Mauritania and Niger	10	10
B. Benin, Guinea, Liberia, Sierra Leone and Togo	8	12.5
C. Côte d'Ivoire Ghana, Nigeria and Senegal	6	16.6

Source: ECOWAS Secretariat, Lagos.

Assessment of Implementation of Agreements

In assessing the performance of ECOWAS, a number of mechanisms may be used. One could assess it in terms of the extent to
which it was able to achieve its stated objectives. This approach is
not favoured in the literature because of difficulties in the measurement of some of the objectives. A more common approach is to
judge the extent to which the efforts of the community succeeded
in increasing intra-group trade. This is the more common method.
In this section we first assess the extent to which agreements were
implemented, and follow with the impact of the implementation
on intra-ECOWAS trade.

As the review of the treaty in the previous section has shown,
we based our assessment on the following areas: trade liberalization; free movement of factor inputs, especially labour and capital;
harmonization of agricultural, economic, monetary and industrial
policies; and joint infrastructural facilities development. The trade
liberalization scheme was to have started in 1979 (that is, two years
after the treaty became definite, given the delays in ratifying the
protocols). The take-off of the scheme was postponed until 1989,
and despite over eight protocols and conventions, the implementation of the scheme was later shifted to January 1990.

The revised timetable indicates that non-tariff barriers (NTBs)
were to be removed gradually over a four-year period (1990 through

1993) in such a way that by 1 January 1994, all such barriers would have been removed. The commencement of the second stage (immediate liberalization of unprocessed goods and traditional handicrafts) was also billed for January 1990. The implementation of the third stage, gradual liberalization of industrial products originating from member states, took off in 1992.

The implementation of the current timetable is hindered by rules of origin, lists of agreed enterprises and products, and classification of member states into three groups – among other things. The implementation of free movement of persons was met with various obstacles at the final stage. Indeed, the protocol on free movement of persons has not been implemented. The expulsion of community citizens from Nigeria in 1983 and 1985 is another experience that is being taking care of..

Harmonization of fiscal and monetary policies seems to be relegated to the background as member countries are still holding tightly to their sovereignties notwithstanding the community's agreement. The adoption of structural adjustment programmes by individual countries without reference to each other is an example of lack of co-ordination, co-operation and harmonization of policies.

The development of infrastructural facilities for the physical integration of the region has been the major preoccupation of the community since its inception. The community viewed the low level of intra-regional trade as due not only tariffs and NTBs, but mainly to formidable production and infrastructural problems. Efforts, therefore, have been directed towards creation of links among the countries through transportation and communication development.

Impact Assessment of Implementation of Agreements

Two groups of studies that attempt to measure the impact of ECOWAS on intra-regional trade can be identified. First are those that are based on trade ratios (share of intra-regional trade in total trade flows). The second group includes those based on theoretical models. The two groups of studies conclude that intra-regional trade flow remains insignificant and that it has not shown appreciable change over the years. In this section, we shall examine these groups of studies.

The trade ratios method was applied by Ariyo and Raheem (1991), De la Torre and Kelly (1992), Langhammer and Hiemenz (1991), de Melo, Montenegro and Panagariya (1992), and Foroutan (1992), among others. They generally agree that the regional efforts have not significantly affected the share of intra-regional trade in total trade flows. The measurement of trade flows has been variously defined to include exports, imports and/or the summation of exports and imports. Notwithstanding the definition adopted by various researchers, the main finding is that the share of intra-regional trade flows of the member states of ECOWAS in total trade is small (in all cases below 10 per cent) and at best stagnant. It is even declining is some cases. A typical trade ratio analysis is shown in Table 2.2.

The use of the share of intra-regional trade in total trade as a measure of the impact of regional integration has been criticized, however. The following excerpt summarizes objections to the method:

> Trade ratios are useful in providing *broad indicators* of the actual level of economic interdependence among the member countries of a grouping, but as an indicator of the degree or progress of integration they are of limited value. In the first place, the degree of integration is a relative concept that refers implicitly to the extent to which the potential for profitable integration is actually exploited. Furthermore, trade ratios throw little light on the progress of integration, because they do not reveal the degree to which the trade flows have been affected by the integration arrangements rather reflect an interdependence that would exist anyway. (Robson, 1982, pp. 161–2)

Because of the inadequacy of trade ratios for the measurement of progress of regional integration efforts, and based on the custom union theory, we turn to measurements of the trade-creation and trade-diversion effects of regional efforts. Unfortunately with respect to ECOWAS, few researchers have utilized this approach. Two studies, Foroutan and Prichett (1993) and Ogunkola (1994), are briefly examined.

Foroutan and Prichett (1993) focus primarily on the intra-subSaharan trade. The study shows that trade ratios (measured as share of intra-subSaharan exports of SSA to total exports of the SSA) indicate that intra-subSaharan trade flow is small. A gravity model was used to compare actual trade with what such a model would predict. The result of the analysis shows that the gravity model predicts very well the low level of intra-SSA trade. In other words, given the determinants of trade flows, intra-SSA trade is not low because of factors that work differentially against such trade, rather it is naturally low. The study concludes that 'increasing intra-SSA trade is not just a matter of removing discriminatory distortions or biases in infrastructure. It requires positive action such as providing differential incentives to intra-regional trade'.

The estimate of the dummy variable for ECOWAS that was included in the gravity model was neither significant nor consistently defined, as it was positive and negative in import and export equations, respectively. This implies that ECOWAS has not significantly affected intra-ECOWAS trade.

Ogunkola (1994), unlike Foroutan and Prichett (1993), focused on the regional integration efforts in West Africa with emphasis on ECOWAS. But he also utilized a gravity model to explain the impact of ECOWAS and to measure trade potential in the sub-region. Two periods were used: average trade flows for 1970–2 as the pre-integration period and average trade flows for 1978–80 as the post-integration period. Comparing the estimates of the dummy of ECOWAS in the two periods, the study concludes that – though marginally – integration efforts by the community have affected intra-regional trade flows in the sub-region. This conclusion is based on the changes in the estimated dummy variable from negative 0.1614 (pre-integration efforts by ECOWAS, intra-regional trade flow would, perhaps, have been lower than it was during the post-integration period.

These studies (Foroutan and Prichett, 1993; Ogunkola, 1994) corroborate others that base their analysis on the ratios. In other words, they confirm that intra-regional trade flows in the sub-region are small.

Assessment of Potentials for Integration

In assessing the potential for integration of the sub-region, short-run analysis seems to dominate discussions on the potentials for integration of the sub-region. This type of analysis is based on the fact that for meaningful trade to take place between partners, there must be coincidence of wants. Therefore, the structure of demand for and supply of foreign goods in the sub-region is usually employed to support the argument. For example, Agu (1992), among others, has argued that West African economies produce similar products, primary products, hence there is no basis for their coming together.

The historical structure of demand for and supply of foreign goods over the 18 years (1970–87) is used to explain complementarity in

Table 2.4 Share of intra-ECOWAS exports for selected years (%)

Year	%
1970	3.0
1975	4.2
1980	3.5
1985	5.3
1986	6.7
1987	6.4
1988	7.8
1990	6.0

Source: De la Torre and Kelly (1992).

Table 2.5 The structure of exports of West African countries, 1970–87

SITC classification	Average share of the section (%)				
	1971–75	*1976–80*	*1981–85*	*1976–87*	*1970–87*
0 Food and live animals	17.4	15.2	13.8	16.0	16.5
1 Beverages and tobacco	0.1	0.1	0.1	0.1	0.1
2 Crude material, excluding fuels	16.4	0.2	10.4	10.9	12.0
3 Mineral fuel, and so on	59.2	68.8	69.1	66.5	65.6
4 Animal and vegetable oils, fats	0.3				
5 Chemicals					

Source: Calculated from Table 6 of ECA (various issues), *Foreign Trade Statistics for Africa*, Summary Table C (New York).

the exports and imports of the sub-region. If the structure is maintained, then the demand for different categories of foreign goods gives an indication of what the present trade liberalization scheme aims to appropriate.

The value of exports and imports, which are shown in Appendix Tables 2A.2 and 2A.3, respectively, indicates that on average West Africa exports less than it imports. Tables 2.5 and 2.6, on the other hand, show the structure of exports and imports, respectively, using five periods. Although there are some minor fluctuations, we chose to analyse the structure of exports and imports using the 1970–87 period, which encompasses all other periods. More importantly, the structure of exports is significantly different from that of imports. Mineral fuels (SITC 3) averaged about 65.6 per cent of total exports for the period. Other major exports include food and live animals, which constitute about 16.5 per cent of total exports, and crude material excluding fuels (SITC 2) amounting to about 12 per cent of total exports. Basic manufactured goods averaged about 2.1 per cent and animal and vegetable oils, fats, and so on, accounted for about 1.5 per cent of total exports for the period under consideration. Other categories of export were beverages and tobacco, chemicals, machines and transport equipment, miscellaneous manufacturing, and others; these accounted for 0.1 per cent, 0.4 per cent, 0.5 per cent, 0.3 per cent and 1.1 per cent, respectively.

The structure of imports on the other hand, as revealed in Table 2.6, reflects more diversification than exports. Each of the import sectors recorded above 1 per cent of total imports for the period. The major importing sectors are machinery and transport equipment (SITC 7), 35.4 per cent of the total imports; and manufactured goods (SITC 6), 21 per cent of total imports. Food and beverages (SITC 0 and 1), chemical and related products (SITC 5), mineral fuels (SITC 3), and miscellaneous manufactured articles (SITC 8) accounted for 14.9 per cent, 9.1 per cent, 7.7 per cent and 6.1 per cent of the total imports, respectively.

The community is, therefore, a net exporter – mainly in mineral fuels (SITC 3) and crude material (SITC 2). On the other hand, the community is a net importer of machinery and equipment (SITC 7), manufactured goods (SITC 6), chemical and related products (SITC 5), and miscellaneous manufactured articles (SITC 8). However, two countries could have identical factor endowments and yet trade with each other at intra-industrial levels if there were a possibility of product differentiation.

What the above analysis illustrates is that failure to implement the ECOWAS protocols left the structure, destination and composition of exports and imports unchanged from the initial conditions. The region is still a net exporter of mineral fuels and crude materials and a net importer of machinery and equipment, manufacturing goods, chemicals, and related products.

Theoretically, a group of economies will benefit from a regional integration arrangement if certain conditions are fulfilled. The theory

Table 2.6   The structure of imports of West African countries,
1970–1987

SITC section	Share of the section in average total (%)				
	1971–75	*1976–80*	*1981–85*	*1976–87*	*1970–87*
0 Food and live animals	13.4	13.0	16.8	15.1	14.9
1 Beverages and tobacco	1.7	1.3	1.2	1.3	1.3
2 Crude materials excluding fuels	2.5	1.7	2.2	2.0	2.1
3 Mineral fuels and so on	6.3	6.9	8.1	8.0	7.7
4 Animal and vegetable oils, fats	0.5	0.9	1.3	1.1	1.1
5 Chemicals	9.5	7.1	10.2	9.0	9.1
6 Basic manufactures	24.9	22.1	19.1	20.3	21.0
7 Machines, transport equipment	33.0	39.2	34.0	35.7	35.4
8 Miscellaneous	6.6	6.8	5.6	6.1	6.1
9 Goods not classified by kind	1.6	1.0	1.5	1.3	1.4

Source: Calculated from Table 6 of ECA (various issues), *Foreign Trade Statistics for Africa*, Summary Tables C (New York).

of the customs union postulates such conditions, as comparative advance and a non-homogenous production structure, just to mention two, are necessary factors for successful regional integration. However, in the long run, further analysis of regional integration efforts suggests that success may not be based on these conditions. Rather, it may be premised on economies of scale in production and consumption and investment structure. Thus there is a distinction between short-run and long-run analyses of regional integration efforts. Indeed, regional integration efforts in the short run may be directed at creating conditions for the long-run viability of such organizations.

The economies of a sub-region will in the long run benefit from regional integration efforts in terms of economies of scale and efficiency from competitive production and consumption. However, such benefits depend on the success of the short-run relationship, especially efforts at creating physical integration and establishing regional policy for the sub-region. In the short run, complementarity and comparative advantage in production of merchandise, among other issues, are the main focus.

For ECOWAS, the need to alter production structure is an integral part of the community's treaty. Provisions relating to harmonization of polices were designed to ensure that projects and plans are not unnecessarily duplicated in the sub-region. The community prefers laying a sure basis for future meaningful integration and co-operation. At the initial stage, therefore, the community kept away from project orientation; rather, it focused on developing regional policies and programmes to ensure the long-term survival of the body (ECOWAS, 1985).

The potential for integration for the region should thus be cast in the long-run perspective, as short-run analysis will offer little insight into the aspirations of the regional efforts.

Some Issues and Constraints

In the preceding section, we demonstrated first that most ECOWAS protocols were not implemented; and secondly that, in spite of the long-run potential for increased intra-regional trade, the existence of ECOWAS does not seem to have made any difference. This failure could be attributed to a number of factors. In this section we examine some of these constraints.

Domestic Economic Policies

One of the major factors responsible for both the non-implementation of the treaty and protocols and the ineffectiveness of ECOWAS in increasing intra-regional trade was the continuation of the initial domestic policy framework in the member countries.

As indicated earlier, all the makers of ECOWAS at the time of signing the treaty were pursuing state-led, import-substitution industrialization strategies. These policies continued even after the signing of the treaty. Promoting the ideals of ECOWAS required increasing exports, especially of the non-traditional type, and lowering tariffs. The domestic policy strategy adopted required higher tariffs and discouraged exports. Thus the domestic policy stance of most governments was at variance with the conditions required for the success of ECOWAS.

The initial structure of exports and imports dictated that to increase intra-regional trade, manufactured exports had to increase. It is possible that the initial experience with import-substitution industrialization could have provided a basis for the take-off into exporting through learning-by-doing effects or exports of Linder-type products. This, however, required a change in strategy and domestic policy framework. Such change did not occur, for reasons discussed earlier. This hampered the realization of the intent of the ECOWAS treaty and protocols in several ways.

First, the institution of general controls on international trade in terms of tariffs and non-tariff barriers tends to affect adversely overall exports and intra-regional trade. The incidence of these taxes is borne to a large extent by the export sector. Estimates of the incidence of these taxes on exports are not available for all ECOWAS countries, but two examples will illustrate the point. For Ghana it is estimated that approximately 74–85 per cent of the import tax is shifted to the export sector, and an estimate of 55–90 per cent for Nigeria. These negative effects on exporting were reinforced by an inappropriate combination of macroeconomic and exchange rate policies. The results were economies bound to their traditional exports whose direction, flow and composition were determined largely by their colonial heritage.

Second, as we saw earlier, the resulting import-substitution mode, with its over-valued currencies, controlled regimes and opportunities to skim off state largesse, had the support of powerful vested interests which would not be likely to support policies that would effectively erode their power base.

Nonetheless, the private sector, represented by the various national chambers of commerce, was one of the key advocates for the formation of ECOWAS. The Federation of West African Chambers of Commerce, which had been started by the Sierra Leone National Chamber of Commerce and the Lagos Chamber of Commerce and Industry in 1963, and covered most of West Africa by 1972, had among its objectives the promotion of regional integration. Pursuant to this goal, it set out on a number of campaigns and tours of the countries of the sub-region between 1972 and 1974, lobbying heads of state and other government officials on the urgent necessity to formalize the ECOWAS arrangement. The state-led development strategy had almost totally killed the private sector. What was left became dependent on the state and the rents from the import-licensing system. Furthermore, the policy and economic environment tended to narrow the horizons of firms to the domestic market.

Multiple Inter-Governmental Organization (IGOs)

The existence of numerous IGOs in the sub-region seems to be unique. These organizations overlap in different areas, especially in their objectives, aims and membership. Some, such as the Lake Chad Authority, extend beyond the regional boundary. Even within the regional confines, this multiple existence (overlap and duplication in most cases) impinges on the effectiveness of the organizations. Members are often confronted with congruent issues or at best different levels of loyalty, that may determine fulfillment and discharge of their obligations (especially financial obligations) to different bodies. More damaging are the divergent issues and the unhealthy rivalry among some of the IGOs in the sub-region.

An important common ground for all of these bodies (different IGOs) is their relationship with developed countries (mainly their former colonial masters). To some extent the relationship is part of the fall-out from the history of the administration of these countries prior to their independence. It was noted that France administered francophone West African countries centrally, while the British administration was decentralized. The French system of governance not only brought these countries closer to each other in terms of cultural, political and economic institutions, to mention a few factors, but also brought them into closer ties with France.

Thus, the dichotomy between anglophone and francophone West African countries, which is still manifest today, can be linked to the relationship between France and Britain. For example, the francophone African countries still have their currency tied to the French franc.[3] The relatively close tie among the francophone countries in the sub-region *vis-à-vis* their anglophone counterparts cannot be easily isolated from their relationship with France.

France brought the francophone West African countries to the EEC long before the Lomé convention, which formally defined the relationship between 46 developing countries in Africa, the Caribbean, the Pacific (ACP) and the EEC. The relationship between

Table 2.7   Taxation on international trade and transactions as % of total central government current revenue

Country	1992	1989	1987
Sierra Leone	34.9	44.6	24.7
Nigeria	n.a.	16.4	6.6
Mali	n.a.	12.0	28.1
Burkina-Faso	n.a.	38.9	39.4
Ghana	n.a.	35.2	42.5
Togo	n.a.	32.3	32.3
Guinea	74.4	n.a.	n.a.
Côte d'Ivoire	29.1	n.a.	n.a.
Liberia	n.a.	34.6	26.9

Source: The International Bank for Reconstruction and Development, *World Development Reports* (1989 and 1991).

these countries and the EEC on the one hand, and the ECOWAS on the other, may not be complementary (Olofin, 1977). The Lomé Convention is more on the exchange of raw materials originating from these countries and manufactured goods originating from the EEC. On the other hand, ECOWAS is expected to promote industrialization of the member states. In fact, if the countries in the region were able to turn their raw materials into manufactured goods, then the demand for manufactured goods from the EEC and the other developed countries would be adversely affected. So also the supply of raw materials to the EEC would decline.

Dependence on Taxes on International Trade

The heavy dependence of various governments on taxes on international transactions is another factor that is hindering the progress of integration in the sub-region. In fact, this was the focus of Ariyo (1992), who suggested that the possible contradiction of policies geared towards enhancing intra-regional trade but which may negatively affect the realization of some macroeconomic objectives of individual member states should be thoroughly reviewed. Some of the countries still depend on taxes on international transactions to the tune of 35 per cent of government revenue. Table 2.7 presents the ratio of taxes on international trade and transactions to total government revenue.

Financial Constraints

Contributions by member states to the community's budget are not promptly honoured. In some cases, contributions by some member states for some years were not honoured at all. This has resulted in huge outstanding balances. As at January 1991, the total outstanding contribution was UA (West Africa Unit of Account) 29.633 m., which was about 30.4 per cent of the total amount due. The effect of this financial position on the operation of the community is that some programmes and/or projects are either cancelled or delayed. Delay and/or non-payment of assessed dues, delay in the ratification of protocols and conventions, and delay in the implementation of agreed programmes and projects are manifestations of the degree of member states' non-commitment to the community.

2.3 ECOWAS PART II: 1992 TO THE PRESENT

In the previous section we argued that both the economic policy framework and the nature of governance in most member countries did not augur well for ECOWAS. These circumstances began to change in the late 1980s, providing an opportunity to revamp the ailing community. Combined with world developments and the poor performance of ECOWAS, they led to a revision of the treaty. In this sector we examine the new circumstances, the revised treaty, and the extent to which the revised treaty took advantage of the new circumstances and provided a basis for better performance.

The Revised Treaty: A Panacea for the Myriad Problems of the Community?

There are some changes within and outside the region that necessitate renewed commitment to economic integration by the member states of the community. The revised treaty identified some of the issues as:

- the achievement of the community since it was established (which are not encouraging);
- the African Charter on Human and People's Rights and the Declaration of Political Principles of ECOWAS adopted in Abuja on 6 July 1991;

- the realization that a viable regional community may demand partial and gradual pooling of national sovereignties to the community within the context of collective political will;
- the Lagos Plan of Action and the Final Act of Lagos of April 1980, stipulating the establishment, by the year 2000, of an African Economic Community based on existing and future regional economic communities;
- the treaty establishing the African Economic Community signed in Abuja on 3 June 1991;
- changes in the international scene and the need to derive greater benefits from those changes; and
- the need to modify strategies in order to accelerate the economic integration process in the region.

The establishment, composition, aims, objectives and fundamental principles of the community are restated in Chapter II of the revised treaty. The aims of the community were not changed drastically from those stipulated in the old treaty, but the revised treaty spells out the aims in 15 objectives compared with 10 objectives in the old agreement. Apart from the inclusion of some issues of common concern in the list of objectives (such as harmonization and co-ordination of policies for the protection of the environment[4]), the revised treaty to some extent also incorporates the strategies to be involved. The revision, then, moved from a mere statement of intentions and general prescriptions about integration into defining strategies and even introducing sanctions where appropriate. Apart from being explicit on the stages involved, such as harmonization and co-ordination (stated as objectives (a) and (b), joint production (objective (c), a common market (objective (d), economic union (objective (e)), community (objective (i)), and so on, the revised treaty also assigns roles to the private sector (objectives (f) and (g)). The enabling legal environment and a population policy among others are listed as well.

Chapter III of the revised treaty identifies the institutions of the community, with their composition and functions well defined. The major departure from the old agreement is the establishment of the following institutions:

- a community parliament;
- an economic and social council; and
- a community court of justice.

Apart from the expansion of the community's secretariat to include the parliament and court of justice, the treaty establishes a number of technical commissions, to take care of the harmonization and co-ordination of national policies and the promotion of integration programms, projects and activities in their respective areas. The commissions are to take charge of the following areas:

(1) food and agriculture
(2) industry, science and technology, and energy
(3) environment and natural resources
(4) transport, communication and tourism
(5) trade, customs, taxation, statistics, money, and payments
(6) political, judicial and legal affairs, regional security, and immigration
(7) human resources, information, social and cultural affairs
(8) administration and finance.

The treaty gives a detailed account of the functions of each of the institutions in Chapter IV through XII. Each technical commission within its area of competence is in the main responsible for:

- preparing the community's projects and programmes;
- ensuring harmonization and co-ordination of projects and programmes; and
- monitoring and facilitating the application of the provisions of the treaty.

The revised treaty of the community thus has a broader perspective on the task ahead. The strategy of working through representative technical commissions is commendable.[5] Some issues arising from the implementation of the old treaty have not been fully taken on board in the revised treaty, however. For instance, Article 2 of Chapter II of the revised treaty, states that ECOWAS 'shall ultimately be the sole economic community in the region for the purpose of economic integration and the realization of the objectives of the African Economic Community (AEC)'.

However, though the revised treaty was signed on 24 July 1993, a sub-group surprisingly appended their signatures to a treaty establishing the Economic and Monetary Union of West Africa (UEMOA) in January 1994 at the demise of the former UMOA and CEAO. The revised ECOWAS treaty (Article 84) recognized that member states may conclude agreements among themselves and with non-member states, regional organizations or any other international organization, provided that such economic agreements are not incompatible with the provisions of the treaty. Thus, the establishment of UEMOA presumably is complementary to the provisions of the revised treaty.

Apart from UEMOA, which was established barely six months after the revised treaty of ECOWAS was signed, there are over 40 inter-governmental organizations in the region. The revised treaty is not specific about their relationships with the community, other than co-operating with them with a view to mobilizing resources in the region for its development.

As mentioned in the previous section, there are different reasons why countries come together (such as ECOWAS) and we tend to believe that where there are sub-groups within a larger group such as ECOWAS, then there are specialized benefits, and of course, costs which cannot be generalized. It may also be due to the fact that the larger group is neither efficient nor comprehensive enough in its tasks to take care of the issues being addressed by the sub-groups. Even if the sub-groups are not incompatible with the provisions of the regional treaty, the efficiency of the groups will definitely be affected, given the limited resources. Rationalization of the various groups in the region is inevitable. If this is done, attention and energy will be directed towards ECOWAS – or the emerging body.

The current stand of the community on this issue still borders on compromise, given the fact that rationalization of IGOs in the sub-region was recognized earlier and various initial steps have been taken. However, there seems to be no consensus among the various groups, especially the old CEAO and (Manu River Union) (see Ezenwe, 1992).

Closely related to the issue of multiple IGOs in the region is that actions and deeds of the individual countries are not related. The lacklustre response that greeted the implementation stage of the old treaty of the community testifies to this. The trade liberalization scheme was delayed for some years due to complaints by some member countries, even though they were actively involved in the design of the scheme. Perhaps that is why sanctions are incorporated into the revised treaty.

The timetable of the community has been revised, with stages of implementation clearly defined. The new timetable shows that within

Table 2.8 Overall position of contributions to the ECOWAS fund as at 22 October 1991 (UAm.)

Contributions	Amount due	Payment made	Outstanding	Outstanding as % of amount due
(1) Capital	72.11	48.49	3.62	32.8
1st tranche	42.68	40.98	1.70	4.0
2nd tranche	29.43	7.51	21.92	74.5
(2) S.F. Telecom	2.93	2.61	0.32	11.0
(3) Headquarters	21.18	15.80	5.38	25.4
Lomé	6.31	4.19	2.12	33.6
Abuja	14.86	11.61	3.25	21.9
(4) Compensation on budget	1.30	1.00	0.30	23.2
Total	*97.51*	*67.90*	*29.61*	*30.4*

Source: Ezenwe (1992).

a period of ten years, effective from 1 January 1990, a custom union among the member states would be established. In other words, by 1 January 2000, there would be a custom union in the region. Within the five years following the establishment of a custom union, an economic and monetary union would be established. Thus, by the year 2005, an economic and monetary union should be in place in the region.

The new circumstances

Structural Adjustment

Since the second half of the 1980s, most ECOWAS countries have embarked on some form of structural adjustment. Given the similarity of the initial economic conditions inducing them to undertake structural adjustment policies, the set of policies pursued has also been remarkably similar.

Critical to the issue of trade integration is the pursuit of national trade liberalization, reduction in the extent of over-valuation of currencies and a greater disposition toward export promotion. Table 2.9 shows that since 1985, exchange rates of most English-speaking ECOWAS members have depreciated considerably in real terms. Countries with substantial changes include The Gambia, Ghana,

Nigeria and Sierra Leone. The situation in the French-speaking countries has changed significantly since the devaluation of the CFA. These changes have tended to create a more conducive atmosphere for exports development.

At the same time, as a result of trade liberalization, the levels of both tariff and non-tariff barriers to international trade have been reduced. These policies have had a greater impact in reducing the levels of trade barriers among ECOWAS members than the ECOWAS protocols. It might be argued that this global trade liberalization could reduce the margin of advantages that may accrue from preferential trade liberalization. 'However, this very constraint may encourage speedy action by regional groups to remove other impediments to intra-regional trade . . .' (ADB, 1993).

Apart from the trade and macroeconomic component, SAPs have also aimed at generating competition within the domestic economy, increasing productivity, and simplifying and reducing the administrative, regulatory and legal impediments to efficient economic activity. If successful, these measures would make transparent the environment for business activity from one ECOWAS member country to the other. The development of transportation and communication networks should have a complementary impact on regional integration.

Furthermore, intra-regional trade is much more acceptable and the costs are lower among countries with growing economies in the context of expanding exports. This is the medium-term to long-term objective of structural adjustment programmes. Successful expansion in exports in combination with global trade liberalization could increase intra-ECOWAS trade without substantial trade diversion. The resulting economic growth and improvements in fiscal and external balances should reduce the incentive to restrict trade and lead to a further reduction in the trade and payments regimes among ECOWAS member.

A major consideration in discussions of regional integration in Africa is the role of government tax revenues. A large number of African governments depend heavily on taxes on international trade. In some cases revenue considerations have led countries to prefer to trade with the outside world rather than with each other. Countries take advantage of policy disparities within the region: trade policy, price policy, monetary policy. Some traders also benefit from the complicity of politicians and civil servants. In many countries it has proved easier to cream off rents from relations with the outside world, causing some observers to speak of *rentier* states.

These considerations have also led governments to revenue-sharing arrangements, which have tended to restrict trade among ECOWAS countries. Given the low levels of inter-regional trade, revenue losses to governments under preferential trade liberalization should be low, depending on the extent to which member countries can be induced to take advantage of the preferences and the size of the preferences.

At the theoretical level, the effect of SAP-induced trade liberalization on tax revenues depends on its direct impact on trade tax revenues and the economy's response to the changes in relative prices. Liberalization may have a positive effect on tax revenue through:

- the replacement of quotas and other quantitative restrictions by tariffs;
- reduction of duties from the prohibitive to a more normal range;
- putting low tariffs on previously exempted goods (in a situation where exempted goods form a large share of imports, perhaps due to an import-substitution industrialization policy, this change is potentially very important in terms of revenue yield);
- the likely reduction in smuggling;
- some positive effects associated with a possible change in the composition of imports in favour of the decreased incentive to a bias towards raw materials and intermediate products;
- some positive effects on tradeable output, especially over the medium term, associated with the liberalization policy.

At the practical level, 'a serious trade liberalization is as likely to increase revenues as it is to reduce them: the elimination of tariff exemption and quantitative restrictions, and the ensuing import boom, may more than outweigh the reduction in (statutory) tariffs in practice'.

Even though Greenaway and Milner (1993) find no evident relationship between trade reform and the amount of revenue collected from trade taxes, for a number of ECOWAS countries that are pursuing liberalization programmes dependence on trade taxes has decreased. In Côte d'Ivoire, the share declined from 42.8 per cent in 1980 to 27.8 per cent in 1991. The experience of Ghana suggests that liberalization may increase total tax revenues from international trade and transactions, but their share in total tax revenues may decline. This has to be set against the extra efforts made by the government to increase tax revenue collection.

An issue of considerable concern in trade liberalization among ECOWAS countries is the balance of payments effects of the liberalization. It has been argued that because trade liberalization may be expected to worsen the trade balance, in the short run at least, it may not be a viable policy option for countries with foreign exchange or borrowing constraints. These considerations may lead individual countries to begin to roll back the liberalization effort.

But both the theoretical and empirical literature indicates that the effect of trade liberalization on the external balance is ambiguous. The current account is identically equal to the difference between national savings and investment. Liberalization can therefore be expected to affect the current account if it induces a differential response in savings and investment flows.

Using this savings–investment approach and considering a model that involves reduction of restrictions on imported intermediate inputs, for example, concludes, that: 'if tradeables use both capital and intermediate imports intensively relative to the rest of the economy, liberalization leads to an increase in the level of saving and a decline in the level of investment and, hence, unambiguously to an improvement in the external current balance'. Of course, the reverse could occur under alternative assumptions.

The use of balance of payments considerations to deny access to products from other ECOWAS countries may be based on short-term trade balance and revenue considerations. Typical of this attitude are the trade relations among Ghana and Nigeria and Côte d'Ivoire. All three belong to the same customs union, ECOWAS, and all three have embarked on trade liberalization. The manufactured goods to be exported amongst them and other ECOWAS members are approved and certified by the ECOWAS secretariat. Yet customs officials deny duty free access of these goods to each others' markets.

If the macroeconomic and other policy measures under structural adjustment prove successful, they should reduce the dependence of governments on taxation of international trade and make them more willing to grant concessions to other ECOWAS countries. Similarly, the effects of these policies on the external balance of individual countries could reduce the importance of balance of payments considerations in denying market access to ECOWAS members.

In view of this potential interrelationship between SAPs and regional integration, the issue that arises is whether structural adjustment should not be co-ordinated among member countries. One of the critical elements of the economic reforms taking place within members' domestic economies is the reduction in the role of government in directly productive activities and the increased importance of the private sector. Under structural adjustment both private capital and the private sector are expected to play a leading role in development of the economy. And as indicated earlier, the private sector was one of the key players in the formation of ECOWAS. However, as the development strategy adopted by these economies reduced the role of the private sector, its involvement and role in ECOWAS diminished. Furthermore, the small private sector left in most of these economies was absorbed into the *rentier* state system and lost its ambitions beyond national boundaries.

There are no data to indicate the extent to which the new circumstances have led to intra-ECOWAS movement of capital. However, the formation of the West African Enterprise Network (WAEN), which held a conference in Accra in November 1995, is an encouraging sign of the positive role the private sector can play. The network is already leading to joint ventures among private sector individuals and enterprises with some external support.

At the same time that domestic economic policy reforms seem to be moving in the right direction in terms of ECOWAS objectives, world developments are also important. In particular these include changing world technology and the conclusion of the Uruguay Round of the GATT.

There have been dramatic changes in world technology for both production and information technology but much more so in information technology. These developments are reducing the transaction costs of international trade and changing the nature of the basis of comparative advantage. Increasingly with improvements in information technology, comparative advantage will no longer be location specific. It is becoming possible for firms to source products and services world-wide in a matter of minutes. These developments imply that unless ECOWAS is able to adapt to the new technology, there will be a tendency for firms within the region to transact business outside the region as the transaction costs will be lower.

The conclusion of the Uruguay Round GATT negotiations offers an opportunity for multilateral trade liberalization. Even though African countries' participation in the Round was minimal, the Round has implications for these economies. Its impact on Africa is expected to be felt through its effect on the world economy, reduction

Table 2.9 Index of real exchange rates of ECOWAS countries
(national currency per US $)

	1985	1986	1987	1988	1989	1990	1991	1992
Benin	–	–	–	–	–	–	–	–
Burkina-Faso	100	85	74	84	85	78	–	–
Cape Verde	100	78	67	–	–	–	–	–
Côte d'Ivoire	100	77	65	71	–	–	–	–
Gambia	100	133	96	92	112	93	103	92
Ghana	100	117	168	174	192	165	–	–
Liberia	100	93	91	87	83	–	–	–
Mali	100	–	–	76	77	70	70	–
Niger	100	86	78	63	96	89	98	–
Nigeria	100	305	351	305	304	345	335	–
Senegal	100	78	69	83	83	76	78	–
Sierra Leone	100	367	87	116	125	178	20	140
Togo	100	80	68	80	81	73		

Source: Calculated from IMF, *International Financial Statistics* (October 1992).

in tariff escalation and non-tariff barriers, loss of preferential market access, and Africa's obligations from World Trade Organization (WTO) membership.

Quantitative estimates of the impact range from a 2 per cent gain in exports to a 0.55 per cent gain. For West African countries, the significant reduction in tariff escalation for wood and paper products, leather products, and tobacco products should be encouraging. This has to be set against the increasing escalation for cocoa.

What is more important is the extent to which the Uruguay Round will encourage or discourage intra-ECOWAS trade. Global trade liberalization that is not matched by similar liberalization among ECOWAS members will tend to increase ECOWAS trade with the rest of the world and probably have adverse effects on intra-regional trade. On the other hand, the Uruguay Round offered an opportunity for African countries to 'bind their domestic reforms to an international anchor to improve their credibility'. The failure of ECOWAS countries to take the opportunity to make a credible commitment to trade liberalization might signal their continuing reluctance to liberalization trade among themselves in spite of the revised treaty.

Some Concluding Remarks

ECOWAS was established two decades ago. Its efforts at promoting regional integration have failed to reflect intra-regional trade flows. To a large extent this failure has been due to a domestic policy stance at variance with its ultimate objectives. It also stems from misconceptions about the effects of intra-ECOWAS trade liberalization on individual member countries' balance of payments and government revenues. Furthermore, the search for a credible external anchor by the French-speaking members of the community and the reversal of policies by the largest member, Nigeria, renders it a non credible anchor to ECOWAS efforts.

Changing domestic economic policies as is occurring under structural adjustment programmes in member countries appears to afford better prospects for intra-regional trade than effects at the multilateral level. It must be realized that multilateral arrangements that are not buttressed by credible commitment to domestic policy reform involving trade liberalization and the development of the private sector are unlikely to succeed. ECOWAS must therefore examine and redefine its role in the new circumstances. In this respect it must be observed that the revised treaty adopted the same ambitious approach as the original agreement. While not abandoning its overall objectives, a phased programme with a modest objective at a time is perhaps a better procedure.

APPENDIX

Table 2A.1   Summary of the protocols annexed to the ECOWAS Treaty.

		A	B	C	D
I	Protocols relating to the definition of products originating from member states of ECOWAS (5 November 1976)	X			
II	Protocols relating to the re-exportation within ECOWAS of goods imported from 3rd countries (5 November 1976)	X			

		A	B	C	D
III	Protocols on the assessment of loss of revenue by member states (5 November 1976)			X	
IV	Protocols relating to the fund for co-operation and development of ECOWAS (5 November 1976)			X	
V	Protocols relating to the contributions by member states to the budget of ECOWAS (5 November 1976)			X	
VI	Protocols relating to the general convention on privileges and immunities of ECOWAS (22 April 1978)				X
VII	Protocols on non-agression (22 April 1978)				X
VIII	Protocols relating to free-movement of persons, residence and establishment (29 May 1979)	X			
IX	Supplementary protocol of rectification of the French text of the protocol relating to the definition of the concept of products originating from member states of ECOWAS (29 May 1979)				
X	Supplementary protocol amending protocol relating to the definition of the concept of products originating from member states (28 May 1980)	X			
XI	Supplementary protocol amending Article VIII of the French text of the protocols relating to the definition of the concept of products originating from member states of ECOWAS (Treatment of Mixtures) (28 May 1980)	X			
XII	Supplementary protocols amending Article 2 of the protocol relating to the definition of the concept of originating products of member states of ECOWAS (29 May 1981)	X			

		A	B	C	D
XIII	Additional protocols amending Article 4 of the treaty of ECOWAS relating to the institutions of ECOWAS (29 May 1981)				X
XIV	Protocols relating to mutual assistance on defence (29 May 1981)				X
XV	Protocol on the establishment of an ECOWAS brown card relating to motor vehicle party liability insurance (agreement for the implementation of ECOWAS brown card scheme) (29 May 1982)		X		
XVI	Conventions regulating inter-state road transportation between ECOWAS member states (29 May 1982)		X		
XVII	Protocol relating to the definition of the community's citizen (29 May 1982)		X		
XVIII	Convention relating to inter-state transit of goods (29 May 1982)		X		
XIX	Convention for mutual administrative assistance in custom matters (29 May 1982)	X			
XX	Protocol relating to community enterprises (1984)	X			
XXI	Supplementary protocol amending Article 9, Para. 1 (c) of the ECOWAS Treaty (23 November 1984)				X
XXII	Convention on the temporary importation of passenger vehicles into member states (6 July 1985)		X		
XXIII	Supplementary protocol on the code of conduct for the implementation of the protocol on free movement of persons, the right of residence and establishment (6 July 1985)		X		
XXIV	Supplementary protocol on the second phase (right of residence)		X		

	of the protocol on free movement of persons, the right of residence and establishment (1 July 1986)				
XXV	Cultural framework agreement for ECOWAS (9 July 1987)		X		
XXVI	Protocol on the establishment of West African Health Organization (9 July 1987)		X		
XXVII	Supplementary protocol amending Articles 14 and 9 of the treaty establishing ECOWAS relating to the institutions of the community and its technical and specialized commissions respectively (25 June 1988)		X		
XXVIII	Supplementary protocol amending Article 53 of the Treaty of ECOWAS on the budget of the community (25 June 1988)	X			
XXIX	Supplementary protocol amending and completing the provisions of Article 7 of the protocol on free movement, right of residence and establishment (30 June 1989)	X			
		8	9	4	8

Table 2A.2   SITC classification of total imports of West Africa ($m.)

SITC category	1970	1971	1972	1973	1974	1975	1976	1977	1978	1979	1980	1981	1982	1983	1984	1985	1986	1987
0	376	425	485	758	1014	1091	1561	1849	2503	2622	3195	4293	3863	2897	2152	2141	1726	2039
1	51	56	58	78	99	178	260	341	235	184	242	288	240	194	147	184	207	218
2	63	77	80	110	186	239	238	248	266	380	436	494	383	385	352	439	241	272
3	121	122	153	190	603	699	847	928	1067	1368	2066	1968	1723	1174	1229	1276	1254	1414
4	19	23	17	21	38	47	69	101	182	213	251	303	247	219	250	157	172	155
5	281	346	322	433	639	935	1038	1258	1564	171	2386	2637	2218	1506	1356	1613	1400	1319
6	762	884	851	1064	1645	2549	2805	3624	4353	3837	5338	5587	4156	3088	2117	2457	2028	2163
7	853	1105	1135	1460	1901	3673	5296	7053	7867	6455	8734	1098	7944	4912	3541	3677	3262	3254
8	163	219	256	310	384	676	818	1081	1272	992	1975	1975	1346	801	433	585	554	585
9	79	94	101	83	90	94	104	221	160	205	211	224	569	179	155	246	244	217
Total	2768	3351	3458	4507	6599	1018	1299	1670	1946	1797	2483	2875	2268	1535	1173	1277	1108	1163
						1	2	3	9	5	4	0	9	5	3	5	8	6

Table 2A.3   SITC classification of total exports of West Africa ($m.)

SITC category	1970	1971	1972	1973	1974	1975	1976	1977	1978	1979	1980	1981	1982	1983	1984	1985	1986	1987
0	1028	900	834	1212	1674	1830	2268	3336	3509	3378	3520	2832	2466	2305	2934	2924	3603	3652
1	5	4	6	9	10	10	12	12	11	8	17	28	25	9	8	10	12	13
2	811	795	874	1374	1677	1462	1724	1848	1764	2362	2807	2364	2022	1895	1912	1945	1950	2234
3	725	1351	1819	2926	8623	7578	1006	1116	9205	1579	2471	1803	1375	1056	1182	1315	5967	7349
							2	6		0	8	7	3	0	2	7		
4	114	90	135	135	262	258	182	290	186	251	214	110	176	919	209	157	182	199
5	10	12	15	20	35	40	34	43	44	47	78	75	50	68	91	135	122	117
6	193	177	217	236	281	258	319	368	335	366	403	557	447	271	236	222	284	308
7	17	24	29	35	44	71	59	75	60	85	116	146	98	111	94	78	125	135
8	10	11	15	18	22	27	31	33	31	55	84	63	54	67	46	42	74	80
9	15	27	32	41	27	37	67	69	22	88	176	141	209	337	394	297	405	447
Total	2928	3391	4076	6006	1264	1157	1475	1694	1516	2243	3213	2435	1930	1581	1774	1896	1272	1453
					6	1	8	0	7	0	3	4	0	4	6	7	7	4

Table 2A.4 Performance evaluation of ECOWAS

Objectives	Instruments/Targets	Achievement/Implementation
(A) Customs and trade matters		
• Elimination of custom duties • Abolition of quantitative and administrative restriction • Establishments of a common external tariff and a commercial policy	• First two years (1977–8) for consolidation of customs duties • Third to tenth years were for liberalization of unprocessed goods and traditional handicrafts and gradual liberalization of industrial products • Eleventh fifteenth years (1987–91) for gradual establishment of common market	• Take-off has been postponed several times and new timetable puts the take-off at 1 January 1990. • Stage II is being implementated but constrained by rules of origin and list of agreed enterprises and industrial products. • Common external tariff does not exist.
(B) Free movement of factor services		
• Abolition of obstacles to movement of persons, services and capital	• Free movement of factors of production	• Protocols on free movement of persons, residence, and establishment have not been implemented. • Workers of the Community's origin were expelled from Nigeria in 1983 and 1985. • Labour movement is restricted.

(C) Development and policy harmonization

- Agricultural policies
- Common projects in marketing, research and agro-industrial enterprises
- Economic policies
- Industrial policies
- Monetary policies

- Harmonized agricultural policies
- Exchange of information on industrial projects
- Harmonized industrial incentives and industrial development plans
- Personnel exchange, training and joint ventures
- Establishment of committee of West African Central Banks (WACB), Capital Issues Committee (CIC), and Fund for Co-operation, Compensation and Development (FCCD)

- Little progress has been made in fiscal and monetary harmonizations.
- WACB, CIC and FCCD were established.

(D) Infrastructural development

- Joint development of transport facilities, communications, energy and others

- Physical integration of the region

- Two road network projects are near completion.
- Communication projects have commenced.

(E) Others

- Co-operation in sociocultural matters
- Mutual assistance in defence and non-aggression

- West African Football Union (WAFU)
- ECOMAG

Notes

1. Various studies have examined the efforts at implementing the regional agreement. Recent studies include Diouf (1990), Ezenwe (1990), Ariyo (1992) and ECOWAS (1985).
2. See ECOWAS (not dated), *Protocols annexed to the Treaty of ECOWAS*.
3. However, the recent devaluation of CFA against the French Franc may signal the beginning of gradual disengagement of France from the economic management of these countries.
4. Although the old treaty mentions issues relating to the protection of the environment, they are not explicitly stated in the objectives.
5. Although technical commissions were established in the old treaty, they were hamstrung by political factors.

References

African Development Bank (AfDB) (1993) Economic Integration in Southern Africa, vols. I, II, III. Abidjan

Agu, C. C. (1992) 'Problems and Prospects of Monetary Integration in Africa' in Nigerian Economic Society, *The Challenges of African Economic Integration*.

Ariyo A. (1992) 'Tariff Harmonization, Government Revenue and Economic Integration within ECOWAS: Some Reflections', *Development Policy Review*, **10**: 155–74.

Ariyo, A. and M. I. Raheem (1991) 'Enhancing Trade Flows Within the ECOWAS Sub-Region: An Appraisal and some Recommendations in A. Chibber and S. Fischer (eds) *Economic Reform in Sub-Saharan Africa, a World Bank Symposium*.

De la Torre, A. and M. Kelly, (1992) 'Regional Trade Arrangements', International Monetary Fund Occasional Paper no. 93 (Washington, DC).

de Melo, C. Montenegro, and A. Panagariya (1992) 'Regional Integration, Old and New' Policy Research Working Papers, no. 985 (The World Bank).

Diouf, M. (1990) 'Evaluation of West Africa experiments in Economic Integration, in *Background Papers, The Long-Term Perspective Study of Sub-Saharan Africa, Vol. 4, Proceedings of a Workshop on Regional Integration and Cooperation* (Washington, DC: The World Bank).

Ebifie, E. O. (1984) 'Central Provisions of the Treaty of ECOWAS' in A. B. Akinyemi, S. B. Falegan and I. A. Aluko (eds), *Readings and Documents on ECOWAS* (Lagos: Nigerian Institute of International Affairs).

Economic Community of West African States, The (1975) *Treaty of ECOWAS* (Lagos).

Economic Community of West African States, The (1985) *Ten Years of ECOWAS, 1975–1985* (Lagos).

Economic Community of West African States, The (1993) *Revised Treaty of ECOWAS* (Lagos).

Economic Community of West African States, The (not dated), *Protocols Annexed to the ECOWAS Treaty* (Lagos).

Ezenwe, U. (1984) *ECOWAS and the Economic Integration of West Africa* (Ibadan: C. Hurst).

Ezenwe, U. (1990) 'Evaluating the performance of West African Integration Movements', in *Background Papers, The Long-Term Perspective Study of Sub-Saharan Africa, vol. 4, Proceedings of a Workshop on Regional Integration and Cooperation* (Washington, DC: The World Bank).

Ezenwe, U. (1992) 'Rationalizing West African Groupings for African Economic Integration', *The Challenges of African Economic Integration*, Selected Papers for the 1992 Annual Conference of the Nigerian Economic Society.

Foroutan, F. (1992) 'Regional Integration in Sub-Saharan Africa: Past Experience and Future Prospects', paper presented at the World Bank and CEPR Conference on *New Dimension in Regional Integration*, 2–3 April 1992.

Foroutan, F. and L. Pritchett (1993) 'Intra-Sub-Saharan African Trade: Is it Too Little?' *Journal of African Economies*, **2**(1).

Greenaway, D., and C. Milner (1993) 'The Fiscal Implications of Trade Policy Reform: Theory and Evidence', Occasional Paper No. 9 (Washington, DC: UNDP and World Bank).

International Bank for Reconstruction and Development, The (1989) *World Development Report* (Oxford University Press/The World Bank).

International Bank for Reconstruction and Development, The (1991) *World Development Report* (Oxford University Press/The World Bank).

Langhammer, R. J. and U. Hiemenz (1991) *Regional Integration among Developing Countries: Survey of Past Performance and agenda for future policy action* (Washington DC: Trade Policy Division of the World Bank).

Ogunkola, E. O. (1994) 'An Empirical Evaluation of Trade Potential in the Economic Community of West African States, A Final Report', Submitted to the African Economic Research Consortium (AERC), Nairobi, September.

Olofin, S. O. (1977) 'ECOWAS and the Lomé Convention: An Experiment in Complimentary or Conflicting Customs Union Arrangements', *Journal of Common Market Studies*, **16** (Sep.).

Robson, P. (1982) *The Economics of International Integration* (London: Allen & Unwin).

Tokuta, R. A. (1984) 'ECOWAS Treaty and the East African Common Market Compared', in A. B. Akinyemi, S. B. Falegan and I. A. Aluko (eds) *Readings and Documents on ECOWAS* (Lagos: Nigerian Institute of International Affairs).

3 The CEAO and UEMOA within ECOWAS: The Road Ahead towards West African Economic Integration

Allechi M'Bet

3.1 CEAO REGIONAL INTEGRATION EXPERIENCE

This study examines the *Communauté Economique de l'Afrique de l'Ouest* (CEAO) integration experience. More specifically, we examine the transition from the CEAO to the *Union Economique et Monétaire Ouest Africaine* (UEMOA). We also touch on developments in UMOA, the *Union Monétaire Ouest Africaine*, which was established in 1962, and relationships with ECOWAS, the Economic Community of West African states.

The study is organized as follows: Section 3.1 reviews the origin, objectives and performance of the CEAO. Section 3.2 analyses how the changing economic environment led to the 'death' of CEAO and concomitant 'birth' of UEMOA. Section 3.3 looks at the impact of the European monetary integration on UEMOA, specifically the changing role of France within the European Union and France's new role in the franc zone after the historic devaluation of the CFA franc. Section 3.4 makes some concluding remarks on the sequential approach to regional integration in Africa.

Historical Background and Objectives

At its establishment, the CEAO comprised six countries: Burkina-Faso (formerly Upper Volta), Côte d'Ivoire, Mali, Mauritania, Niger, and Senegal. (Benin and Togo have been observers.) The CEAO was founded in 1973 in response to a major drawback of its predecessor, the *Union Douanière de l'Afrique de l'Ouest* (UDEAO) or the West African Customs Union, which had grouped the same countries.

The UDEAO was established on 3 June 1966. Its particularity as a classical customs union was to forgo the principle of free movement among member countries and to implement a preferential regime and the absence of a common tariff. This preferential structure was characterized by a 50 per cent reduction on customs duties on imported goods from UDEAO countries. However, when a country felt the need to provide adequate protection to its industries, the customs duties could be increased to a level as high as 70 per cent instead the 50 per cent.

This constituted the major drawback of the UDEAO, which was associated with the inequities inherent in the compensation of lost customs duties. For importing UDEAO countries whose fiscal revenues depended largely on custom duties, and who could not be compensated by other forms of tax revenues, to give up customs duties meant to substantially reduce fiscal revenue that might affect economic development. This led to active resistance by quantitative restrictions and by tariff manipulation or by passive resistance in the form of complicated administrative machinery. The result was that UDEAO failed to compensate member governments adequately for trade diversion and hence could not achieve its objectives. Induced losses in revenues emerged over time.

The CEAO emerged from the ashes of the UDEAO. Like the UDEAO, CEAO members were all former French colonies. Unlike the UDEAO, it comprised seven member states, the six UDEAO members plus Togo, the all of which are French-speaking. Moreover, even as the CEAO was established, the same countries were already members of UMOA, the West African Monetary Union, which had been in operation since 1962. In addition to having French as a common language, UMOA members used a common monetary unit, the CFA franc, that is pegged to the French Franc at a fixed parity. The CEAO thus already showed some harmony as in integration scheme at the monetary level.

In order to avoid the shortcomings UDEAO, the CEAO founders aimed to design more adequate instruments of compensation and a better system of sharing the benefits derived from the scheme. Accordingly, the CEAO was set up to compensate the losses of revenues from customs duties of importing countries. The instrument designed was the *Taxe de Coopération Régionale* (TCR) or regional co-operation tax. In addition, the CEAO was to promote actions in favour of the least-developed members, as will be discussed later on.

The treaty establishing the CEAO was signed in 1973 in Abidjan, Côte d'Ivoire. The original objective was 'to favour the harmonious and balanced development of economic activities of member states in a view to improving as quickly as possible the standards of living of the populations'. The specific objectives were:

- to implement at regional level an active co-operation and economic integration policy, particularly the development of agricultural activities, livestock, fishery, industry, transportation, communication and tourism; and
- to increase the trading of industrial and agricultural products of member states by establishing among themselves an organized trading area.

In order to achieve the stated goals, the treaty designed instruments to foster economic development. These were the *taxe de coopération régionale* (TCR) mentioned earlier, the *fonds de coopération et de dévelopment* (FCD), and the *fonds de solidarité et d'intervention pour le développement économique de la communauté* (FOSIDEC) or the community funds for solidarity and economic development. We will come back to these policy instruments when assessing the performance of the CEAO.

Although the CEAO grouping was theoretically well suited and favourable to intra-regional trade, there were four main characteristics that were perceived as particularly conducive for higher trade flows. First, the countries showed some complementary structures. For example, intersectoral divisions of labour are important in trade between Burkina-Faso and Mali, as potential agricultural product exporters, and Côte d'Ivoire and Senegal, two relatively industrialized members. An indication of the complementarity is the relatively high level, by African standards, of intra-regional trade (7 per cent of total exports in 1985).

Second, contrary to the situation in many African countries, natural barriers to trade, such as prohibitive transportation costs, are lower than elsewhere in subSaharan Africa. Railway links set up during colonial times exist between Mali and Senegal and between Burkina-Faso and Côte d'Ivoire.

Third, a high degree of factor mobility prevailed within CEAO countries. The monetary union, with its common central bank, allows for free mobility of capital, and labour mobility is high as well. However, empirical investigation reveals that the net effects of factor mobility on trade are at best mixed. On the one hand, countries are unable to use exchange rate adjustments such as devaluation as an instrument of economic policy because of the rules of the franc zone to which UMOA belongs. This has dire consequences for landlocked Sahelian countries, which are unable to depreciate their currency as members of UMOA, in order to improve their competitive edge *vis-à-vis* the more advanced coastal countries like Côte d'Ivoire. On the other hand, the factor mobility that always existed within the region, tends generally to lower information and transaction costs in intra-regional trade, which has a stimulating effect on trade. In addition, under conditions of full labour and capital mobility, workers from less-developed areas can work in the coastal countries and send income remittances to their home countries, thus contributing to the sustained import demand necessary for industrial development.

Fourth, another integrating organization, a more political one, co-existed with the CEAO. Called the *Conseil de l'Entente*, it included almost the same countries as the CEAO. That council made funds available outside the UMOA framework to 'finance development projects in the less-developed areas', hence acting as a compensating system among member countries. Contributions to the entente fund came from external donors and, among CEAO members, predominantly from the wealthier countries such as Côte d'Ivoire and Senegal. This expression of solidarity is well-appreciated by smaller landlocked Sahelian countries.

Despite these favourable conditions, efficient intra-regional specialization never emerged in the CEAO. One reason was the several successive external shocks and, in the larger countries, overall economic policy failures (for example, government over-spending in Côte d'Ivoire following the commodity price boom of the late 1970s). Another impediment was the TCR, the functioning and the impact of which we will assess. The TCR was the CEAO's primary policy instrument, but proved to be a rather complicated and sometimes conflicting mixture of allocation and distribution objectives.

Despite these shortcomings, the CEAO was kept alive by internal support for the monetary union. The officially unstated objective was the desire to maintain an economic coalition against the political and economic potential of Nigeria within the Economic

Community of West African States (ECOWAS), and – most important – the need to retain access to external funds allocated for regional co-operation projects.

The Comparative Performance of the CEAO: the TCR Impact

While CEAO institutions have come to perform quite satisfactorily, progress in implementing the ECOWAS treaty has been mainly limited to a set of decisions reached in political enthusiasm, the application of which remains hypothetical. In both the CEAO and ECOWAS treaties, raw products and products of traditional handicrafts originating from member states are free of all duties and taxes normally levied at entry, but not from international taxes equally levied on domestic goods. Industrial products originating from member states are subject to the regional co-operation tax (TCR) in CEAO countries and admitted to a general preferential tax regime in ECOWAS.

Table 3.1 shows the geographical characteristics of CEAO and ECOWAS countries, while Tables 3.2 and 3.3 present the average annual growth rate within ECOWAS and the CEAO.

Tables 3.1 to 3.3 indicate that overall for the period 1975–90, the growth rate of intra-community trade flows within ECOWAS was faster than that of the CEAO, contrary to the tendancies observed by studies done a decade ago. Indeed, the intra-ECOWAS annual trade-flow growth rate was 11.95 per cent against 6.95 per cent for CEAO.

Mali, Niger and Burkina-Faso have trade-flow growth rates considerably above average (see Table 3.2). This is due to the fact that the growth of their share is directed more towards ECOWAS countries than other CEAO numbers. This stems from the difficulties of promoting exports among CEAO countries that confronted the TCR for more than a decade, essentially relating to the overall hike of the TCR rates in all CEAO countries in order to increase foreign trade revenues.

However, the high growth rate of intra-ECOWAS trade flows in some countries could be partially explained by high inflation rates experienced by non-CFA ECOWAS countries.

Nevertheless, it should be mentioned that the CEAO is the only integration scheme that has achieved the highest degree of 'institutional integration' among several such schemes in Africa and even among all developing countries. Indeed, in the CEAO Regional

Table 3.1   Geographical characteristics of the CEAO and ECOWAS countries

| | | | GNP per capita | |
| | | | --- | --- |
Country	*Population (000s)*	*Area (1000 km²)*	*US$*	*The annual average growth (1965–89)*
Benin	4 600	113	380	–0.1
Burkina-Faso	8 800	274	320	1.4
Côte d'Ivoire	11 700	322	790	0.8
Mauritania	1 900	1 026	500	–0.5
Mali	8 200	1 240	270	1.7
Niger	7 400	1 267	290	2.4
Senegal	7 200	197	650	–0.7
Togo	3 500	57	390	0.0
CEΛO				
Guinea	600	246	430	n.d.
Guinea–Bissau	960	36	180	n.d.
Liberia	2 500	111	n.d.	n.d.
Cape Verde	361	4	780	n.d.
Sierra Leone	4 000	72	220	0.2
Ghana	14 400	239	–1.5	390
Nigeria	113 800	924	250	0.2
Gambia	849	11	240	0.7
ECOWAS average			407	–0.1

Table 3.2   Annual average growth rate of intra-community trade level out of total trade level, the CEAO and ECOWAS, 1975–90 (%)

| | *Level growth rate* | | *Share growth rate* | |
| | --- | --- | --- | --- |
	CEAO	*ECOWAS*	*CEAO*	*ECOWAS*
Burkina-Faso	9.60	13.26	–1.26	–0.26
Côte d'Ivoire	9.40	10.00	2.73	3.80
Mali	0.00	18.00	8.20	10.40
Mauritania	7.46	8.93	4.20	–0.60
Niger	8.13	19.86	10.20	13.53
Senegal	7.13	8.60	4.40	3.46
Average	6.95	13.11	4.75	5.06

Source: M'Bet and Camara (1993).

Table 3.3   Annual average growth rate of intra-ECOWAS trade, 1975–90

	Level	*Share*
Benin	10.80	7.40
Burkina-Faso	10.89	0.24
Côte D'Ivoire	10.40	4.24
Mali	17.81	5.31
Mauritania	8.75	−0.69
Niger	19.86	13.50
Togo	27.27	12.37
CEAO average	*15.11*	*6.05*
Cape Verde	–	5.85
Gambia	12.45	5.45
Ghana	52.58	42.43
Guinea	9.44	−0.32
Guinea-Bissau	40.90	25.24
Liberia	23.06	12.48
Nigeria	10.18	6.76
Senegal	8.64	3.63
Sierra Leone	30.21	56.50
CEDEAO average	*19.53*	*12.52*

Source: M'Bet and Camara (1993).

Integration scheme, apart from Mauritania, all countries use the same monetary unit – the CFA franc – a common central bank, and a fairly sophisticated system of credit and investment.

A traditional explanation of the low level of intra-community trade flows is based upon the high degree of production specialization in the respective economies. This argument does not hold in West Africa, where an assessment of agricultural production reveals that the West African countries have different specialities. For instance, most trade analysis in the CEAO and ECOWAS emphasized industrial development against agricultural produce that is heavily traded within the sub-region.

What is the essence of the regional co-operation tax (TCR)? This tax is a special preferential regime aimed at limiting intra-regional competition through tax rates that favour products from poorer member countries over those from more advanced countries. The tax raises effective rates of protection through tax escalation and promotes regional import substitution through explicit discrimination against third-country sources. The costs of this policy have affected both groups of countries in the CEAO. By maintaining through artificial fiscal measures inefficient industries in the poorer countries and protecting industries in the more advanced countries against outside competition, the TCR contributed to the further erosion of the international competitiveness of these industries.

The regional co-operation tax has been substituted for all duties and taxes levied on imports from member states. An industrial good is admitted to the TCR regime when at least 60 per cent of the raw materials used in the processing originates from member countries, or the value added exceeds 40 per cent of the final value of production. Industrial products originating from member states and not admitted to the TCR regime are subject to the import tax that would be applicable to them if they originated from a third country.

The difference between the import proceeds accruing to a member country, the TCR and the amount that would result if the same products were taxed if they originated in a third country, is the capital loss incurred by member countries and gives rise to the payment of compensation from the community development fund.

The amount of the community development fund is determined by the annual conference of heads of state in terms of total amount of capital losses that are likely to be incurred by member states as a result of the application of the TCR. Member states' contributions to the fund are proportional to their share of intra-community trade in industrial products. Two-thirds of the fund are allocated to importing countries in compensation for their capital losses, the remainder is shared among the least-developed countries in the CEAO and is intended to finance development projects.

From 1974 to 1981, member states' contributions to the fund amounted to CFAF20 320 m., of which Côte d'Ivoire contribution represented CFAF11 333 m. and Senegal's share was CFAF8212 m. In terms of compensatory disbursement, Upper Volta (now Burkina-Faso) and Senegal received 56.5 per cent, while 14.4 per cent went to Mali and 13.8 per cent to Niger. Mauritania, the last in intra-community trade, received 9.9 per cent while Côte d'Ivoire, the major trading partner, received only 11.2 per cent. As to community development from 1974 to 1979, priority was given to national projects in the least-developed countries in CEAO: Burkina-Faso, Mali, Mauritania, and Niger. Community development projects have taken the lead since 1979.

The third institution established by the CEAO is the solidarity intervention fund for community development. The main objectives are to provide guarantees and counter-guarantees to loans contracted by member countries under specific rules; to grant loans to member countries under certain conditions; and to provide subsidies for feasibility studies when countries are applying for loans in international financial markets. The resources of the fund include ordinary and special contributions by member countries. The capital of the fund is fixed at CFAF5 m. and annual contributions are set at CFAF1.5 m., of which the Côte d'Ivoire accounts for half and Senegal for CFAF250 m. In May 1980, the fund guarantee potential was put at CFAF30 m.

The CEAO countries, in search of a better economic community, have established institutions that operate quite efficiently despite their shortcomings. It is clear that Côte d'Ivoire, as the major trading partner and the most advanced country in the area, provides more than half the financial contributions to the fund. Therefore, accomplishment of CEAO objectives in terms of community agriculture, industry, trade, transport and communication, cattle breeding and fishery development will be largely influenced by Ivorian economic conditions. This was particularly felt at the sixth conference of heads of state in October 1981 in Niamey (Niger) at which Côte d'Ivoire and Senegal came under attack from other members. The two countries were reluctant to pay their contribution to the community development fund, arguing that the data on which the calculations were based have never been accurate. The main reason was that the two major CEAO exporters have recorded declines in budget revenues against increasing expenditures. The situation was more alarming in that the countries' past dues amounted to CFAF5 bn, or 1.33 times the total received by all the sectors in terms of national and community development programmes over the 1974–9 period. It should be noted that the CEAO also provides a secured outlet to the Ivorian manufacturing industry. For instance, in 1975 Côte d'Ivoire accounted for 75 per cent of the manufactured products exchanged in the CEAO, against 54.4 per cent in 1978. However, the gains for Côte d'Ivoire from intra-community trade must be compared with its contribution in order to find out whether the CEAO represents a net loss to the country.

The establishment of the preferential tax regime is seen to be a positive step on the path towards a full customs union, a CEAO objective for 1990.

The UDEAO did not survive because the founders failed to resolve properly the problem of compensation as a result of elimination of tariff barriers within the former Federation of Francophone West Africa. We shall derive some lessons from that compensation scheme when discussing UEMOA later on. At its establishment, UDEAO trade revenues represented more than 50 per cent of the budget revenues of member countries. Given the internal tax structure and tax base, no significant revenues could be derived from the domestic market. This is still true today and no economic integration scheme would survive if the treaties did not provide for compensation for member countries' losses.

Shortcomings of the TCR

The TCR can be criticized on the grounds that it provides opportunities only to the firms operating in the formal sector. Even in this sector, firms may not qualify to benefit from the special tax regime. In the mid-1980s, 212 enterprises within the CEAO were admitted to the TCR regime compared to 91 in 1975. Côte d'Ivoire had 115 enterprises, compared to 1 for Mauritania, 64 for Senegal, 14 for Burkina-Faso, 13 for Mali, and 5 for Niger. In 1980, 450 enterprises operated in the Ivorian manufacturing sector. If one excludes bakeries, repair shops and other activities that are not export-orientated, an estimated 350 entreprises manufacture exportable goods. Still, only 115 firms (about one-third) were admitted to the TCR. It is not certain how many firms will engage in intra-community trade, but it can be argued that TCR requirements exclude a number of them from regional trade.

Three additional problems may be identified with the TCR system:

(1) The system may lead to fraud due the unreliable nature of the statistical data on which compensations are computed. If this occurred, importing countries would be penalized because of the loss of revenues that would be derived if the goods imported were not admitted under the TCR system.
(2) The system may be criticized in that it amounts to a subsidy on manufactured exports. In fact, the system protects industries within the CEAO against outside competition. In the long run, however, firms under the TCR regime may find it difficult to adjust to new combinations of factors and lose substantial shares of their markets.

(3) The TCR system may tend to prevent the institution of effective domestic fiscal policies to generate budget revenues in importing countries. Since contributions to the community development fund are proportional to the volume of regional trade, it can be argued that more effective trade policies will increase fund resources for compensation. These resources constitute real budget revenues to the least developed countries and may actually work against internal fiscal policy reform.

Consequently, the TCR practice would be counter-productive in the long run if CEAO countries did not undertake steps to eliminate gradually the TCR system before 1990, when a full customs union is expected. More concerted regional development combined with national developments strategies geared to growth will increase the opportunities to generate more initial fiscal revenues in the long run. Until recently, most CEAO countries had little hope of generating budget revenues except through trade taxes and foreign aid.

This assessment indicates that a degree of integration has been achieved within francophone West Africa. The institutions established, despite some inherent difficulties, operate quite efficiently. The countries have harmonized their customs laws and regulations and adopted common customs nomenclature. Thus, despite its short-comings, the TCR constitutes a major innovation in the preintegration era.

In the area of rural development the countries have set regional development programmes according to factor endowments of member countries. More co-operation is expected in agriculture and cattle breeding. The objective of CEAO countries is to achieve self-sufficiency in food production. In the field of industrialization, more co-operation is needed in order to avoid duplication that distorts resource allocation for a very narrow market. Some rationalization is needed.

3.2 THE EFFECT OF A CHANGING ECONOMIC ENVIRONMENT ON WEST AFRICAN REGIONAL INTEGRATION: THE DISAPPEARANCE OF CEAO AND THE EMERGENCE OF UEMOA

As stated earlier, the CEAO countries were all members of the UMOA. But the UMOA has experienced two major reforms since its establishment in 1962.

First, in 1973, it undertook a reform of its institutions so as to reinforce the cohesion of member countries through a better-managed monetary policy. At the same time, Mauritania withdrew from the UMOA and created her own currency called the *ouguiya*. Second, on 2 October 1989, the rules of intervention of the central bank, the BCEAO, were revised, granting a more dominant role to a market-determined system.

All CEAO members except Mauritania use the CFA franc as common currency. Therefore the withdrawal of Mauritania from UMOA made trade settlements more difficult among members due to the presence of a non-convertible currency alongside the CFA franc.

Another crucial element that began to emerge in the UMOA in the early 1980s, when the first structural adjustment programmes were implemented, is associated with the duality of economic policy in UMOA countries. On the one hand, these countries have a co-ordinated monetary policy and on the other hand they have different non-harmonized fiscal policies. Hence BCEAO officials emphasized at a conference in Dakar in January 1993 the need to match monetary integration and economic integration. It recognized that up till then the UMOA had been characterized by two centres of decision-making:

(1) a monetary policy falling within the competence of community institutions and
(2) an economic and budgetary policy falling under the authority of member states according to their own needs.

The need for more co-ordinated overall economic policy emerged. This led to the reshaping of the regional integration schemes, sparked partly by the European single market, which called among other things for standardization of norms and procedures; environmental regulations; and the harmonization of macroeconomic policies, monetary and fiscal.

To this end it was important to resolve the duality problem by harmonizing the management of public finance, debt, external payments and pricing policies in member states. Indeed, a viable integration scheme requires compliance with the fundamental criteria of the convergence of national economic and budgetary policies.

The question arises as to the degree of convergence of economic policies in UMOA countries with respect to the potential interactions between monetary and macroeconomic policies, especially fiscal policies. In fact, based on key macroeconomic indicators such as public finances, external debt, current account and price levels, UMOA countries showed some notable discrepancies. In order to correct these distortions in national budgetary policies, UMOA authorities proposed the creation of the Economic and Monetary Union of West African States – UEMOA. The move excluded the superposition or juxtaposition within the UMAO geographical area of several integrating schemes. This has motivated the dissolution of the CEAO, a decision that effectively integrated its trading aspect into the monetary harmonization of the UMOA to create UEMOA, which is externally anchored by France. That decision took place on 15 March 1994 at the special summit in Ouagadougou, Burkina-Faso. Essentially this decision allows UMOA countries to remove Mauritania, which is no longer part of the monetary union, from the CFA countries integration scheme.

In what follows we present first the need for harmonization policies in UMOA, followed by UEMOA integration strategies.

The Need for Macroeconomic Policy Harmonization

It has been argued by economists that a regional integration scheme can be viable in the long run only if the macroeconomic policies of the different member countries have sound monetary and budgetary components policy that are convergent.

The degree of economic convergence is usually measured by key indicators associated with public finances, external indebtedness, current account and tendency of price level. For instance, in the Maastricht treaty of the European union, certain criteria must be met such as the convergence of macroeconomic policies before the emergence of a unique currency. These criteria concern mainly (1) public indebtedness of less than 60 per cent of GDP; (2) a budgetary deficit of less than 3 per cent of GDP; (3) a maximum inflation rate that cannot exceed by 1.5 per cent the inflation rate of the three countries with the lowest inflation rate in the union. What is the situation regarding UMOA economies?

Divergence at the Public Finance Level

The slowdown of economic activity in recent years, stemming to a large extent from the sluggish international markets of export commodities, is reflected through the public finance stance. During the 1980–90 period, large and persistant budgetary deficits emerged, despite unsuccessful structural adjustment programmes implemented by all UMOA member states. Overall, the budget deficit amounted to about 9.1 per cent of GDP across the UMOA. However, notable divergences exist around that average deficit–GDP ratio across countries. During the period the deficit–GDP ratios vary from a low 5.6 per cent to 14.7 per cent of GDP.

Divergences at the External Indebtedness Level

The comparative analysis of indebtedness ratios indicates some notable dispersion at the national levels. Around the average ratio of 59.0 per cent, some real discrepancies appear in debt service ratios to public receipts. Indeed, a wide range of divergence exists, from 16.4 per cent to 77.5 per cent.

Divergences at the Current Accounts Level

Like the budget deficit, the current accounts also show contrasted ratios of deficit to GDP. The spread is from 2.9 per cent to 9.5 per cent around an average of 7.2 per cent observed between 1980 and 1990.

Divergences at the Price Level

The institutionally restrictive monetary policy and the favourable export crop prices in recent years helped slow the inflationary pressures in UMOA countries. The average inflation rate using the GDP deflator was –2.0 per cent in 1990. It slightly increased to 1.0 per cent between 1991 and 1992. The spread was relatively narrow across countries, moving from –1.0 per cent to 3.0 per cent at the end of 1992. It appears that UMOA's rigorous monetary policy for over three decades helped achieve notable results, namely at the price level.

These results, however, are overshadowed by the persistent divergences in public finances (budget deficits) and in external payments. The co-existence of a stable monetary policy and an uncoordinated fiscal policy can in the long run undermine the very existence of the union if corrective measures are not taken to harmonize both monetary and fiscal policy.

The 1994 change in CFA parity makes such policy convergence even more compelling so as to secure a more competitive position for UMOA products. The double constraints of consolidating the union as well as achieving more competitiveness for UMOA econ-omies convinced the UMOA authorities to propose a new approach to regional economic integration, drawing from the existing advan-tages of a common currency. The UMOA heads of state have opted for the BCEAO as the instrument of integration. Two arguments are in favour of the BCEAO for this role. First, it was involved in the multilateral system of payment of the late West African clear-ing house, which has been transformed into the Monetary Agency of West Africa. We believe the change of name is not enough to make it more efficient. Second, it is involved in the programme of harmonization of monetary policy that aims at transforming ECOWAS as the sole integrating scheme of the sub-region.

The UEMOA as a Strategic Path towards Integration

The UMOA strategy for integration can be perceived at the gen-eral principles level and in the practical modalities of implementation. At the outset, it should be stated that the UEMOA was designed by drawing on the lessons from past experiences of integration, namely the UDEAO and the CEAO. The compensation scheme was adjusted so as to share the benefits among members. The basic philosophy is pragmatism and gradualism, relying on a coherent and existing institutional structure.

At the institutional level, the UEMOA scheme of integration is based on member countries agreeing to explicitly transfer to common institutions their sovereignty in major areas of national jurisdiction defined in the treaty. The UEMOA institutional organization is similar to that of the UMOA and in addition it has established institutions closely analoguous to those of the European Union. The conference of the heads of state is the supervising body. The direction of the integrating scheme is under the control of the council of finance ministers of the UEMOA. This council is the same for the UMOA. This option aims at ensuring the compatibility between integration decisions and monetary policy constraints. The UEMOA commission ensures the management of the UEMOA. It is the executive body of the union, much like the European commission. The commission represents the UEMOA in international organ-izations according to instructions from the council of ministers. Commission members act independently and only in the interest of the union, without referring to the government of their country of origin.

The UEMOA also has a court of justice to settle legal disputes among member countries. A court for accounting is established to control all accounting matters. A fully-fledged parliament is projected in the future. Meanwhile, an inter-parliamentary committee of five persons per country, acting on the behalf of national parliaments, must examine the annual report of the commission.

At the financial level, the guiding principles are a real control of the union's spending. More important, the union, learning from the previous lack of commitment regarding arrears in contributions, has proposed *financial autonomy*. According to this principle, the financing of the structures and programmes of the union will be supported by generating revenues through levies that will not depend on individual member states. Moreover, based on the solidarity principle that prevails within the union, any loss of fiscal revenue will be compensated for. Accordingly, five sets of programmes will be implemented:

- the organization of the convergence of national economic policy, namely budgetary policy, by instituting a rigorous multilateral surveillance of national budgetary policy;
- the modernization and harmonization of the legal and regulatory framework of economic activity;
- the harmonization of fiscal policy, especially saving mobilization policy and the design of financial tools that will lead to a subregional financial market;
- the unification of the national economic space in the context of an operational customs union along with a harmonized system of indirect taxes; and
- the conduct of efficient common sectoral policies in vital area of the economies of member countries.

The advent of the UEMOA is quite significant in the West African integration process. It brings within a single framework the CEAO, which attempted to remove trade barriers without much success, and the UMOA, which supports the common regional central bank, BCEAO, and the CFA common currency. However, it is more than a mere merger of the CEAO and the UMOA. It ejects Mauritania, which was a member of the CEAO, from the new scheme and it has the CFA franc as a bedrock. The new scheme has been anchored by France. So how will the European Monetary Union affect the UEMOA?

3.3   THE LIKELY IMPACT OF EUROPEAN ECONOMIC INTEGRATION ON UEMOA SUSTAINABILITY

In the wake of the European Union, especially after the Maastricht accord of 11 December 1991, and the recent devaluation of the CFA franc, the advent of the UEMOA constitutes a major development. M'Bet and Madeleine (1992) put forth alternative exchange rate policy scenarios that the CFA franc may follow. They opted for the pegging of the CFAF to either the ECU as natural anchor or to a basket of the ECU, dollar and yen. A crawling peg rather than a fixed exchange rate was recommended. Indeed, the UMOA countries trade more than 60 per cent with the EU. The question arises as to who will guarantee the CFA if the French franc comes to disappear along with other European currencies according to the Delors agenda. But since UEMOA countries trade more and more with the rest of the world, the authors suggested pegging to a basket in the medium to long term.

But above all there was the worry about the UMOA itself. The speculation before the historic devaluation turned on a possible disintegration of the union. The establishment of the UEMOA brings that issue to a rest. In fact, the UEMOA – which emerged incidentally with the first devaluation – is a signal that France will not use the Maastricht Treaty to pull out of the Franc zone as had been feared in some francophone official circles. Before the UEMOA, among the many regional integrating schemes, the defunct CEAO had a more developed structure of trade harmonization than the larger ECOWAS, helped by a common currency except for Mauritania. The UEMOA resolves the Mauritanian isolated case within the CEAO. The new UEMOA scheme has even more far-reaching goals. As Fine and Yeo (1994) correctly pointed out, the most far-reaching measure is the explicit provision for the multilateral surveillance of macroeconomic policies, especially fiscal deficits, with France acting as the ultimate guarantor. But let Fine and Yeo, in the following long quotation, present UEMOA strength and weakness:

> For the rest of SSA, UEMOA is significant for three reasons. First it comprises a direct challenge to the assumptions behind the Abuja Treaty that have shaped the strategic approach to African regional integration over the past 35 years. UEMOA is incompatible with ECOWAS. The treaty provides for the accession of other African states in addition to the seven original

members ... The new arrangement occurs at a moment when ECOWAS, which has never proved effective, has been badly shaken by Nigeria, its most important member, which reversed years of structural adjustment policies, including trade liberalization.

UEMOA is also significant for SSA in that it may 'establish a unique and unprecedented case that would allow the EU to act as guarantor for other regional arrangements.' If that happens, then UEMOA may become effective and sustainable. The EU specifically supports the formulation and implementation of multilateral economic surveillance that will ensure a better management of the respective economies, in contrast to the previous CEAO. Other parts of the UEMOA package are equally supported by the *Caisse Française de Développement*, and even the World Bank and the IMF.

Like the European Union, UEMOA is motivated by political considerations in addition to economic integration. In fact, regional integration is only likely to succeed if the political benefits complement economic ones. However, analysts shy away from the political component of regional integration in the African context. A successful regional integration scheme requires good management and transparent budgetary procedures. The legal systems of member states must be compatible and comparable in order to quickly settle eventual conflicts. On that ground, UEMOA members present more homogeneity not only at the monetary level but now at the legal and regulatory level. In addition, the harmonization of economic policies will reinforce that coherence if indeed implemented.

When examining regional integration, it is often necessary to distinguish between intergovernmentalism and supranationalism. Supranationalism relates to a system of regional legislation that stands above the national legislation as is the case in UMOA and certainly more with UEMOA. With intergovernmentalism, no regional legislation exists and each member country exercises fully its own sovereignty. This is usually a secretariat that had no independent power of its own and hence can be handicapped by conflicting positions of member states. The ECOWAS integration scheme is of the intergovernmentalism type, like most African integration schemes. Only the schemes in the CFA countries are the exceptions in that they cannot change their own monetary policy. Hence UEMOA presents some chances of carrying out its programmes.

3.4   CONCLUDING REMARKS: REGIONAL INTEGRATION: THE ROAD AHEAD, A SEQUENTIAL APPROACH OR A GLOBAL APPROACH FOR AFRICA?

A look at regional integration in Africa reveals that most schemes have failed. They usually started with grandiose proposals and programmes that could not be implemented. In West Africa, CEAO recorded relative success, at least on the basis of the percentage of traded goods, 8–14 per cent, compared with the 5 per cent in ECOWAS.

The newly established UEMOA has its domain extended beyond the CEAO because of the following objectives:

- rationalization and convergence of macroeconomic policies through a system of multilateral surveillance;
- harmonization of the legal and regulatory framework;
- creation of a single market with free movement of goods, services, persons and capital; and
- establishment of common sectoral policies.

According to Foroutan (1992):

> The emphasis of regional integration in sub-Saharan Africa should shift from the integration of goods markets to the regional coordination of macroeconomic and microeconomic policies, the harmonization of administrative rules and regulations, and the joint provision of public goods. Such steps are likely to make SSA markets more attractive to domestic and foreign investors and to improve economic growth.

The problem we see is that UEMOA countries are also signatories of the Abuja Treaty, which makes ECOWAS the sole integration scheme in West Africa. Although ECOWAS has been plagued with endless problems it constitutes a much more viable market. But the world cannot wait for ECOWAS members to act positively. Moreover, in the UEMOA treaty, arrangements are made so that the UEMOA is open for new member states and the treaty is formulated so as to be consistent with the wider ECOWAS framework. Hence the sequential approach may be an alternative to the global, which has not worked so far. If the sequential approach can be extended gradually to the sub-region, it constitutes an alternative that must be explored through the UEMOA experience.

References

M'Bet, A. and Aissata Camara (1993) 'Groupements économiques et Commerce Intra-Africain: une analyse des obstacles à l'intensification des échanges de produits manufacturés en Afrique de l'Ouest', *Cahiers de CIRES*.

M'Bet, A. and N. A. Madeleine (1992) 'The European monetary integration and the Franc Zone; Phase Two: *Alternative exchange rate policies for the CFA Franc*', AERC Final Report (Nairobi).

Foroutan, F. (1992) 'Regional integration in Sub Saharan Africa; experience and prospects', Working Papers (The World Bank WPS CED).

Fine, J. and S. Yeo (1994) 'Regional integration in Sub Saharan Africa; Dead End or Fresh Start?', paper presented at the AERC Workshop, May.

UEMOA (1996) Traité de l'Union Economique et Monétaire Ouest Africaine, Ouga dougou, Burkina Faso.

4 A UDEAC Case-Study*

Bernard Decaluwe, Dominique Njinkeu,
Lazare Bela and John Cockburn

4.1 INTRODUCTION

The Central African Customs and Economic Union (*Union douanière
et économique de l'Afrique Centrale*, or UDEAC) currently comprises six member states (Cameroon, Chad, the Central African
Republic (CAR),[1] Congo, Gabon and Equatorial Guinea). It is an
outgrowth of an organization, the Equatorial Customs Union (*Union
douanière Equatoriale*, or UDE), that was initially created by former
French colonies in Central Africa in order to facilitate economic
co-operation among themselves. The initial objective was to create
a customs union with a common external tariff and a monetary
union, itself part of the franc zone. For the union to function adequately, it was suggested that co-operation be institutionalized
in other key areas including the harmonization of fiscal and investment codes. Regional and national policies were conceived according
to standard interventionist/protectionist strategies.

In recent years member countries have initiated policy reforms
that aim to create a more market-friendly environment. Key components of the reform include trade liberalization. Because of the
common external tariff, trade policy is not entirely determined by
individual countries. An evaluation of the UDEAC was thus called
for and a structural adjustment programme (SAP) suggested for
the union as a whole, in order to facilitate the implementation of
country-specific SAPs. The design of the regional policy reform also
required an assessment of governance issues. The effectiveness of
the regional integration process was evaluated by the UDEAC's
permanent secretariat and multilateral organizations such as the
World Bank (see UDEAC, 1988). As a result of these evaluations,
a redesign of the integration scheme was deemed necessary.

The objective of this case-study is to contribute to this design,

---

* We gratefully acknowledge helpful suggestions from Richard Baldwin.

focusing on the identification of a better framework for the economic development of member countries and the region as a whole. The reform must learn from past successes and failures and take into consideration current theoretical and practical developments both within and outside the region. The layout of the chapter is as follows: section 4.2 assesses the regional integration experience of the UDEAC with respect to initial objectives and achievements. Section 4.3 presents the economic and political environment that UDEAC member countries currently face and their implications for the future of regional integration.

4.2 REGIONAL INTEGRATION EXPERIENCE IN THE UDEAC[2]

An understanding of the regional integration experience in Central Africa requires knowledge of the structure of member countries and their past and present economic potential. The success or failure of such experiences depends in turn on specific regional integration instruments and institutions. To study regional integration in the UDEAC, we therefore consider the specific conditions of the member countries and the historical background of integration in the region; analyse the conception and implementation of the UDEAC; and evaluate the impact of the UDEAC on economic development in the region.

Background

Description of the Region

The main economic characteristics of the region are described in Table 4.1. The UDEAC comprises six Central African states occupying 14 per cent of subSaharan Africa's (SSA) total land area. Its total population was 25.4 million in 1992, representing 5 per cent of SSA's population, and in 1992, it had a total GDP of US$21.4 bn, unevenly distributed. Gabon had a per capita income of US$4450 while Chad's per capita income was only US$220. Production size and structure and land area vary as well from one state to the other. Agriculture occupies 30 per cent or more of total land in Cameroon, Congo and Chad, and less than 20 per cent in the other states. The lower income countries (Chad, the CAR and Equatorial

Table 4.1   Principal characteristics of UDEAC member countries, 1992 data (1970 in parentheses)

	Cameroon	CAR	Chad	Congo	Gabon	Equatorial Guinea
Population (millions)	12.2	3.2	6.0	2.4	1.2	0.4
Land area (000s km²)	475	623	1284	342	268	28
GDP (US$m.)						
1970	1160	169	302	274	322	n.a.
1992	10 397	1251	1247	2816	5913	n.a.
Per capita GNP (US$)	820	410	220	1030	4450	330
Economic growth						
1970–80	7.2	2.4	0.1	5.8	9.0	n.a.
1980–92	1.0	1.1	5.3	2.4	0.5	n.a.
Production (% GDP)						
agriculture	22 (31)	44 (35)	44 (47)	13 (18)	9 (19)	n.a.
industry	30 (19)	13 (26)	21 (18)	35 (24)	46 (48)	n.a.
manufacturing	22 (10)	n.a. (7)	16 (17)	13 n.a.	5 (7)	n.a.
services	48 (50)	43 (38)	35 (35)	52 (58)	45 (34)	n.a.
Exports (US$m.)	1657	91	194	1284	2303	n.a.
Imports (US$m.)	1344	134	339	1071	913	n.a.
Terms of trade (1987–100)						
1985	139	107	109	145	2303	n.a.
1992	66	61	78	68	913	n.a.
Private consumption (% GDP)	77 (70)	87 (75)	105 (64)	46 (82)	44 (37)	n.a.
Investment (% GDP)	11 (16)	12 (19)	2 (18)	17 (24)	27 (32)	n.a.
Total foreign debt	6554	901	729	4751	3798	n.a.
(US$m.)	(2513)	(195)	(229)	(1526)	(1514)	n.a.
Inflation						
1970–80	9.8	12.1	7.7	8.4	17.5	n.a.
1980–92	3.5	−1.5	0.9	0.5	2.3	n.a.
Principal exports	oil cocoa coffee wood cotton	diamonds coffee wood cotton	cotton	oil wood cocoa coffee	oil wood magnesium uranium	wood cocoa coffee

Source: World Bank (1994b).

Guinea) have very primitive agricultural sectors. The share of agriculture has fallen since the late 1980s in Congo, Gabon and Cameroon, due to increased petroleum production. Agriculture is

Table 4.2 Intra-regional trade in the UDEAC in 1993 (in CFAFm.)

Exporting country	Importing country						
	Cameroon	CAR	Congo	Gabon	Equatorial Guinea	Chad	Total exports
Cameroon		3238	12409	6661	2880	1339	26527
CAR	84		5	8		15	112
Congo	20	463		403			886
Gabon	786	23	151		12		972
Equatorial Guinea							
Chad	6	350	14				370
Total imports	896	4074	12579	7072	2892	1354	28867

Source: General Secretary of UDEAC, *Annuaire du commerce inter-états* (1993).

the principal sector of production in the CAR, Chad and Equatorial Guinea; in all cases, agricultural production is concentrated on two or three primary products.

The wealthier countries (Cameroon, Congo and Gabon) are also petroleum producers. In Congo, the economy relies extensively on oil, which yields 47 per cent of GDP, 72 per cent of total export revenues and 50 per cent of all state revenues. A similar pattern is found in Gabon with, respectively, 44 per cent, 66 per cent and 57 per cent. Cameroon is the only member state that has succeeded in developing its agricultural and industrial bases together with its oil production. Cameroon yields almost half of total UDEAC gross domestic product. Life expectancy is above 55 years only in Cameroon and Congo. Despite its resource base and small population size, Gabon has about an average life expectancy for African countries.

The trade pattern of member states among themselves and with the rest of Africa is very diverse (see Table 4.2). Cameroon, which has the most diversified industrial base, is very closed, in contrast with other members. All member states increased their trade with Cameroon over the period from the creation of the UDEAC in 1966 to 1983[3]; yet, overall, intra-regional trade represented only 4 per cent of total external trade in 1980 (Kitchen and Sarley, 1992), and 8 per cent in 1987 (*Banque mondiale*, 1992). Intra-regional trade increased less than trade outside the region, including the rest of Africa. Trade with ECOWAS[4] countries is more important than intra-regional trade. This pattern is mostly due to the trade patterns of the wealthiest member countries. Gabon trades more with

Nigeria and Côte d'Ivoire than with member states of the union; over 65 per cent of its trade on the African continent is with those two countries. A similar pattern is found for Cameroon, which does 45 per cent of its trade on the continent with Côte d'Ivoire, Guinea and Nigeria combined. Smaller countries – the CAR, Chad and Equatorial Guinea – do at least 90 per cent of their trade on the African continent with UDEAC member states. A consequence of this configuration, as shown later, is the difficulty of setting common policy instruments that allow adequate reaction to external shocks. Some of these shocks, such as oil price hikes, are positive for some member states (the oil producers) and negative for others (oil importers). The different levels of economic development also imply that complicated compensation schemes may be required.

History

The history of regional integration in the UDEAC may be divided into three periods characterized by substantial organizational differences and different memberships. We present successively (1) the colonial period, (2) the post-independence period before the UDEAC and (3) the period since the signing of the UDEAC treaty.

(1) The Colonial Period (1910–59) Between 1910 and 1958, the CAR, Congo, Gabon and Chad were administered by France as a single territory: French Equatorial Africa (*Afrique Equatoriale Française*, or AEF), with Brazzaville as its capital city. The AEF was in charge of economic and social policy in specific domains only; others, such as currency, defence and diplomacy, were the prerogatives of France. Some services were common to the AEF territories (UDEAC, 1988). These included postal and telecommunication services, education, railways and waterways. Property rights for regional infrastructure, located primarily in Congo, were not adequately defined at independence. Some infrastructure built at the time, such as railways constructed in Congo with the assistance of workers from Chad and the CAR, are still considered by some opinion leaders to be AEF's rather than national property.[5]

Cameroon, a former German colony, was put under the mandate of the League of Nations after Germany's defeat in the First World War. It was later placed under the trusteeship of the United Nations and divided into two parts, administered by France and Great Britain. Because of its special status, Cameroon was not part of the AEF. The independence of Cameroon and AEF states was preceded by the signing of different co-operation accords with France. However, political leaders in the respective countries were not in agreement with the process by which these accords were negotiated and signed.

(2) The Equatorial Customs Union (1959–65)   In 1959, on the eve of their independence and before dismantling the AEF, Chad, the CAR, Congo and Gabon signed a treaty in Paris creating the Equatorial Customs Union (*Union Douanière Equatoriale*, or UDE) in spite of the great divergences among African member states and France on the modalities of integration. While all were agreed on the importance of maintaining some form of economic or political integration in the region, differences concerned the form of government and the nature of economic relationships. The CAR and Chad, lacking industrial resources, were in favour of a political federation, which would ensure that they shared in the gains from integration, rather than simple economic integration, which they believed would only make them markets for products originating from other members. Congo, where most of the regional infrastructure and firms created during the AEF period were located, feared that the dismemberment of the AEF would unduly restrict the market for its firms and thus favoured economic integration. In Gabon, which had the best resource endowment in the region, leaders were unwilling to accept a reconstruction of a federation that would exploit their national resources, their minerals and their wood exports, which had served in the past to finance the AEF budget. In France, companies trading in AEF were very much opposed to the idea of a political federation, which they felt would lead to restrictions on their activities. The French government therefore favoured a customs union. The UDE, a customs union, was thus created under pressure from France and its treaty was signed on 17 January 1959 in Paris (CEA, 1981).

(3) The Central African Customs and Economic Union (Union douanière et économique de l'Afrique centrale, *UDEAC, 1966– *) Once the UDE was created, the Gabonese authorities realized that the country's small market size and its resource endowments required that it improve its trade position, as Cameroon had been Gabon's main trading partner for a long time. Cameroon, however, was not a member of the UDE, and Gabon favoured

Cameroon's integration into the union. France also encouraged this development, noting that the members of the UDE and Cameroon shared the same regional central bank, BEAC, as part of the franc zone.

However, Cameroon's admission to the Union faced some opposition. Cameroon was the most industrialized country in Central Africa. Congo, which was the most developed trading country in the UDE, feared competition from Cameroon and was consequently opposed to its admission to the UDE. The CAR and Chad pointed out that circulation of an unlimited number of Cameroonian products, exempted from taxes in the UDE, would jeopardize their own industrialization efforts. In June 1961, a convention establishing a partial preferential trade area was signed between Cameroon and the UDE, and a treaty establishing the Central African Customs and Economic Union (UDEAC) was signed on 8 December 1964. This treaty came into effect on 1 January 1966. Unhappy with the effects the treaty had on their economies, and with the deficient compensation scheme, the CAR – despite the fact that it hosts the general secretariat – and Chad announced their withdrawal from the UDEAC in April 1968. According to the treaty, their decision was to come into effect on 1 January 1969. The CAR reversed its decision on 9 December 1968. In 1985, Chad joined UDEAC at the same time as Equatorial Guinea was being admitted. UDEAC presently comprises Cameroon, the CAR, Congo, Gabon, Equatorial Guinea and Chad.

Other Regional Integration Institutions in the Region

The Franc Zone and the BEAC

UDEAC countries are all members of the franc zone and the Bank of the Central African States (BEAC). Key features of the zone include:

(1) the fixed exchange rate between the regional currency (the CFA franc) and the French franc (FF);
(2) the pooling of foreign reserves in an account at the French treasury; and
(3) full convertibility of the CFAF to the FF, and henceforth to any convertible currency.[6]

Table 4.3 Integration schemes in the region

Regional integration scheme	Membership	Areas of focus
UDEAC (1964)	Congo, Chad, CAR, Gabon, Cameroon (1966), Equatorial Guinea (1985)	Customs union
BEAC (1961)	Congo, Chad, CAR, Gabon, Cameroon, Equatorial Guinea	Monetary union
CEAC (1983)	Congo, Chad, CAR, Gabon, Cameroon, Equatorial Guinea, Zaire, Burundi, Rwanda, São Tomé	Economic community
Lake Chad Basin Commission (CBLT)	Cameroon, Nigeria, Chad, Niger	Lake Chad water management
CAPTAC	Afrique Centrale	Telecommunications co-operation

Member states and France jointly determine the overall monetary policy, namely foreign exchange allocation, money creation, interest rates and credit policy. Some key policy decisions – for example, exchange rate modifications – are considered jointly for the entire zone.

These arrangements have the advantage of ensuring policy credibility, which unfortunately comes at the cost of policy flexibility; the Banque de France is the lender of last resort for the member states. It also has the added advantage of credibility. Availability of an internationally convertible single currency is an advantage for regional integration. As such, monetary and financial developments in individual countries are linked to those of France and other African members of the zone. The difficulty in the UDEAC's recent history is the insolvency of the banking and financial sectors.

Other Regional Integration Schemes

Other integration accords in the region are listed in Table 4.3. The most ambitious is the Central African Economic Community (*Communauté Economique d'Afrique Centrale*, CEAC). The CEAC comprises all UDEAC members countries and other central African states. It was created within the Lagos Plan of Action but has not been operational because of lack of funding. Member contributions have not been paid.

Conception and Implementation of UDEAC Accords

The preamble of the 1964 treaty, revised in 1974 and 1992, stipulates that the member states aimed to:

(1) establish an ever-closer union among their populations in order to strengthen regional solidarity;
(2) promote the gradual and progressive establishment of a Central African Common Market;
(3) remove barriers to trade among states so as to contribute to the expansion of existing national markets and the improvement of the living standards of their populations; and
(4) strengthen the unity of their economies and ensure their harmonious development through the adoption of measures that take into account the interest of each and all while adequately compensating, through appropriate measures, for the special situation of the economically less-developed countries, particularly through the harmonization of community projects and the co-ordination of the development programmes of the various productive sectors.

These objectives were to be achieved through the following measures: a reduction of taxes on intra-regional trade through the establishment of a reduced single tax (*taxe unique*, or TU) on industrial goods; the adoption of a common external tariff (CET); the creation of a solidarity fund as a compensatory mechanism within the region; the harmonization of investment codes and internal taxes;[7] and the co-ordination of transport policies[8] and regional development programmes. The establishing of free trade of manufactured products is at the centre of the integration strategy of the UDEAC, and the common external tariff and *taxe unique* are the two instruments of the UDEAC that have been most widely used.

The following sections present the governing institutions and the various regional integration instruments provided for in the UDEAC accords, among which the TU plays a predominant role.

Governance

Regional institutional organization and decision-making processes are important for the evaluation of the performance of and appreciation of future prospects for regional integration in the UDEAC. Its decisions are taken by the council of heads of state based on recommendations by a management committee composed of ministers from each member country. The management committee can refer issues to an 'experts' committee for recommendations.[9] The management committee and the experts committees can also request from the general secretariat specific studies on the basis of which they can make their recommendations. All decisions, whether in the council of heads of state, the management committee or the experts committees, are made by consensus on a one-state, one-vote basis, so that consensus-building is always required. Each country is responsible for the application on its territory of the decisions taken at the regional level.

Lack of regional monitoring of the implementation of decisions has greatly weakened UDEAC performance. Initially, the role of the secretariat was important. France used it to facilitate co-ordination with its former colonies. A Frenchman, the secretary general of the AEF, became secretary general of the UDE and held the post until the UDEAC was created. However, three years later, when management was turned over to UDEAC nationals, the UDEAC directing organs limited the functions of the secretariat to the preparation of dossiers (CEA, 1981), purportedly to avoid possible conflicts of interest. Consequently, the 1974 treaty states that the secretariat may not take initiatives. Nor is it authorized to make suggestions on topics without due request from the relevant decision-making organs. For example, to draw up a consulting experts directory for the UDEAC, the secretariat had to be mandated (issue no. 519 of December 1987).

Consensual decision-making and equal voting power to member countries have favoured the pursuit of national interests (in particular, the balance of trade) at the expense of the collaboration that is necessary for the UDEAC's sustained and equitable development. In Table 4.4, we see that decisions on certain issues may be postponed eight or more times, to 'be studied in depth', particularly when the issue is contentious. In 1986, for example, 27 new issues were discussed, among which the decision was postponed for analysis on six. Four issues were at their eighth appearance on

A UDEAC Case-Study

Table 4.4 Number of management committee debates on an issue and the result obtained

| | | No. of debates | | | | | | | | |
Year	Result	1	2	3	4	5	6	7	8 or more	Total
1980	A	20	10	3		1	1	2	2	39
	P	6	4	2	1	1	2		2	18
	W	1		1						2
	Total	*27*	*14*	*6*	*1*	*2*	*3*	*2*	*4*	*59*
1987	A	30	8	3	2	2		2	2	49
	P	9	5	1	3		2			20
	W	2	1							3
	O	3	1							4
	Total	*44*	*15*	*4*	*5*	*2*	*2*	*2*	*2*	*76*
1988	A	7	4	1		2	1	1	4	20
	P	5	2	3	1			1	4	16
	W	2							1	3
	O			2		1				3
	Total	*14*	*6*	*6*	*1*	*3*	*1*	*2*	*9*	*42*
1989	A	17	7	1						25
	P	4	2		1				1	8
	Total	*21*	*9*	*1*	*1*	*0*	*0*	*0*	*1*	*33*
1990	A	20		3	1		1		5	30
	P	8								8
	W	5								5
	O	1								1
	Total	*34*	*0*	*3*	*1*	*0*	*1*	*0*	*5*	*44*
1991	A	1		2	1					4
	Total	*1*	*0*	*2*	*1*	*0*	*0*	*0*	*0*	*4*
1992	A	6	1		1	2	2		1	13
	P				1	1				2
	Total	*6*	*1*	*0*	*2*	*3*	*2*	*0*	*1*	*15*
1993	A	2				1	1			4
	P			1						1
	Total	*2*	*0*	*1*	*0*	*1*	*1*	*0*	*0*	*5*
1994	A	3			1					4
	P	1			1					2
	Total	*4*	*0*	*0*	*2*	*0*	*0*	*0*	*0*	*6*
Total	*1986–94*	*153*	*45*	*23*	*14*	*11*	*10*	*6*	*22*	*284*

the management committee meetings' agenda, among which the decision was further postponed on two issues, while a decision was made on the other two. As we will see further on when we consider the *taxe unique*, resolving conflict is particularly important in relation to the reduction of barriers to intra-regional trade. In other areas, such as the harmonization of fiscal, legal and accounting principles, where national interests do not conflict with regional interests, the requirement for consensus is less problematic.

The UDEAC's decision-making process contrasts with the practice in the BEAC, the region's central bank, which currently has exactly the same member countries. The BEAC's council makes decisions on a majority basis. In addition, the council is composed of 13 representatives of member countries, the number of representatives reflecting the relative size of the member countries: four representatives for Cameroon, two for Gabon, one each for the other four states and three for France. The relative performances of the two institutions are quite different. As we shall see, regional monetary policy co-ordination by the BEAC has been more successful than regional integration in the UDEAC (see World Bank, 1994a).

UDEAC leaders are more concerned with mercantilistically maximizing their country's gains than with ensuring the UDEAC's success. Member country representatives, whether they be experts, ministers or heads of state, use their veto right whenever their country's interests are at stake. The management committee is often unable to formulate a consensual recommendation and therefore refers the issue to the council of heads of state.[10]

The members of experts committees, principally senior civil servants, generally have very short-term preoccupations, as these committees are created on an *ad hoc* basis. Given the discretionary basis for choosing experts, their competence is not always guaranteed. Consequently, debates, instead of being technical, often become political even though the experts have no political authority. To make matters worse, during a negotiation delegates are free to reverse their positions on a decision on which a consensus was reached previously. At the staff level, the preparation of studies and dossiers is often marred due to the clientelistic process by which staff are hired and assigned to duties in the general secretariat. Employment in the general secretariat and other UDEAC institutions is allocated to member states and positions are mostly filled according to political considerations rather than competence. Posts are shared among the member countries and each country appoints whomever it wants to the post that it has been attributed. The person appointed can be replaced at any time. Consequently, studies are often of poor quality. Indeed, most dossiers are postponed because the background studies were too badly carried out for appropriate decisions to be taken.

In addition, the relatively high remuneration of participants in UDEAC reunions has numerous perverse effects on the decision-making process. Staff members, with the complicity of the delegations of their countries, put issues on the agenda in order to allow the expert to attend the heads of state summit even if they know that the studies were poorly carried out. At one point, UDEAC missions had the reputation of being the best paid. Civil servants in the member states and members of the general secretariat staff therefore endeavoured to be involved in these missions. Staff members could ensure their own attendance at these reunions by submitting the dossiers they have prepared on practically any pretext.

In sum, while there was a consensus in favour of the principle of integration within the UDEAC, institutional arrangements work against the process. In combination with the requirement of consensual decision-making, this has led to a stagnation of integration initiatives. To make matters worse, the UDEAC accord does not specify any transfer of sovereignty to the regional authority, which essentially leaves the door open to blockages of all sorts in both decision-making and implementation. In contrast, the transfer of sovereignty on monetary policy within the BEAC is quasi-complete, which helps explain the relative success of the latter.

Regional Integration Instruments

Regional integration aims primarily to increase trade among member countries. To do so, intra-regional trade barriers must be reduced or eliminated and, ideally, barriers to external trade need to be harmonized to avoid external goods destined to the region being imported through the countries where the external barriers are lowest. The TU mechanism was meant to progress toward free trade, whereas the common external tariff, supplemented occasionally at the national level by quantitative restrictions, aimed to harmonize external trade barriers in the region. These policies clearly create winners and losers and, consequently, require compensatory mechanisms to ensure the adhesion of the losers. Harmonization in domestic taxes and the reduction of barriers to factor mobility were also seen as necessary elements of regional integration in the UDEAC. We shall now present each of these regional integration instruments, focusing on their initial conception, their actual implementation and an analysis of failures and successes.

The Common External Tariff (CET)

External-regional trade is regulated in UDEAC by a common external tariff and various non-tariff barriers such as quantitative restrictions. Non-tariff barriers are under national jurisdiction and, in 1990, they covered less than 1 per cent of products listed in the customs code, although they represent a substantial share of manufacturing production (see World Bank, 1991a). Consequently, our analysis of extra-regional trade regulations is limited to the CET.

The CET was established at the UDEAC's creation and reformed in 1994. It concerned only import duties, as Article 34 of the UDEAC accord specifies that export taxes are of national jurisdiction. Before the reform, the CET had four components: (1) a customs duty, (2) an entry duty, (3) a turnover tax and (4) a complementary tax; only the complementary tax was of national jurisdiction. The other three taxes were set, by UDEAC authorities, at the same level for all countries. Given the importance of customs duties in the public revenues of member countries, often representing 50 per cent, and the large initial divergences in individual rates, the complementary tax aimed to compensate member countries temporarily for lost tariff revenues due to harmonization of the other customs duties. Consequently, the complementary tax rate varied among countries, but the UDEAC management committee had to be informed of any decision concerning it. Eventually, complementary tax rates were to be harmonized.

The essential flaw in the conception of the CET was the possibility given to member states of adjusting their complementary tax rate and other taxes not covered by the CET, thereby ensuring differential protection. Although this possibility was meant to be temporary, no date was set for its removal. As member states were more concerned with national interests than regional integration, substantial variations in rates arose. For example, the total tax rate (duty plus entry plus turnover plus complementary) on electric batteries was 94 per cent in Cameroon, 69 per cent in the CAR and 59 per cent in the other states, where the divergences are due to differences in the complementary tax rate. Table 4.5 presents the structure of legal and effective import taxes in the early 1990s as a percentage of import tax revenues.

In addition, discretionary decision-making had a substantial impact on duty collection rates. While average legal tariff rates are comparable in the region (with the exception of Equatorial Guinea, which only recently joined the UDEAC) the effective rates are much lower – never more than 50 per cent of the legal rate – yet the variance is considerable regardless of the category of imports (see Table 4.5).

The Single Tax (TU)

Intra-regional trade is a key component in the success of the regional integration process. Like most developing countries, UDEAC countries adopted industrialization as their principal objective in the 1960s. Countries hoped to expand national production so as to supply the local markets and to export – a target export market being that of the region. The *taxe unique* was put in place at the creation of the UDE; it aimed at fostering regional industrial production and trade in manufactured goods by reducing domestic and import taxes on regional goods relative to extra-regional goods. The TU regime was eliminated in the 1994 UDEAC reform.

The TU regime had the following characteristics:

(1) The TU replaced all other domestic indirect taxes and import duties for industrial products sold in the region by registered firms; this is why it was called the single tax. It was paid at the frontier by the importer. For domestic sales, it was paid directly by the producer. To export within the region, firms were required to have TU status.[11] All UDEAC member states were obliged to allow goods produced by TU-registered firms to circulate freely, as long as the TU was paid, while applying the common external tariff on imports of regional goods produced by non-TU firms.

(2) *Taxe unique* rates were restricted to be lower, often significantly, than the CET, which applied to extra-regional imports and regional imports from non-TU firms. The rates were meant to become uniform for all goods, firms and countries of destination within the region; this objective, as we shall see, was never attained.

Table 4.5 Legal and effective tariff structures

Year	Country	All imports	Essential consumer goods	Raw materials and capital goods	Other consumer goods	Consumer goods to be subject to excise taxes
(A) Average legal rates (%)						
1987/88	Cameroon*	59	33	58	58	159
1990	CAR	52	43	50	54	150
1990	Chad	48	44	51	55	73
1990	Congo	51	43	49	54	153
1989	Equatorial Guinea*	44	32	44	49	90
1989	Gabon*	54	34	50	55	210
(B) Effective rates (%)*						
1987/88	Cameroon	23	6	14	41	45
1990	CAR	12	33	6	24	127
1990	Chad	7	0	4	13	10
1990	Congo	16	25	7	25	54
1989	Equatorial Guinea	17	7	11	24	24
1989	Gabon	25	10	20	40	100

Notes:
* Weighted by the value of each category of imports.
† Unweighted
‡ Revenues from taxes on imports/c.i.f. value of official imports; not to be confused with the effective rate of protection (ERP), which measures the variation in value-added due to protection and which is presented in Table 4.21.

Source: World Bank (1991b).

(3) Registered firms also benefited from tax-free purchases of some or all of their material inputs, with the condition occasionally that they be imported from within the region.

(4) To be registered, existing or newly-established firms were required to present a feasibility study to the government of the country of establishment and the government would in turn present the project to UDEAC. The decision on admission was made by the management committee. These decisions specified the TU rates to be charged on each product of the firm and varied according to the country of destination within the region. No specific guidelines – such as the origins of the owners, management and workers of the firm, the degree of transformation, value-added, and so on – existed for these decisions.

The *taxe unique* was a very discriminatory regime. Rates varied from firm to firm, country to country and product to product.[12] As we shall see below, numerous strategic considerations, emanating from disparities in the conditions of member countries and the existence or non-existence of competitive industries in the importing country, were taken into account when determining the TU rate. In effect, tariff rates for the same products often vary in the same country. For example, in December 1972 in Gabon, soap produced by CCC (Cameroon) was taxed at a rate of 14 per cent, while soap produced by SICPAD (CAR) was subject to a 15 per cent rate. Fortiori, lorry coachwork, manufactured in Gabon by two Gabonese companies, is taxed at different rates, 6 per cent (ACAE) and 10 per cent (CMG).

In this section, we conduct a numerical evaluation of admission to and rate-setting in the regime before making a strategic assessment. Establishing the failure of the TU regime carries over to that of the regional integration process. We do so by establishing that the TU rates were not uniform among products, firms and countries, and therefore created a distorted incentive structure.

Mytelka (1975) counted 115 firms producing 673 products that were subject to the TU during the first five years of the regime (1966–70). Most of these firms already existed before the regime was established. Her analysis, however, is based on 106 of these firms producing a total of 635 products.[13] Mytelka studied 635 decisions setting the TU rates on products: 46.6 per cent of these decisions concerned products from Cameroon, 21.4 per cent from the CAR, 18.1 per cent from Congo, 2.8 per cent from Gabon and 11 per cent from Chad.

From 1966 to 1990, when new agreements were suspended, Bela (1992) counted 1524 decisions and 208 firms. The distribution of firms is as follows: 106 in Cameroon (51 per cent), 20 in the CAR (10 per cent), 35 in Congo (17 per cent), 36 in Gabon (17 per cent), 11 in Chad (5 per cent) and none in Equatorial Guinea. The distribution of decisions on products is as follows: Cameroon 49 per cent, CAR 14 per cent, Congo and Gabon 13 per cent, and Chad 6 per cent. Many decisions concerned the same product, as rates were modified. Consequently, the 1524 decisions studied by Bela concerned only 255 products.

In addition to the limited number of products subject to the regime, one notes the constantly growing hegemony of Cameroon, which manufactured 46.6 per cent of the products in 1970 and 49 per cent in 1990. The CAR's share fell from 21.4 per cent to 14 per cent, Chad's from 11 per cent to 6 per cent. Congo remained at 18 per cent, while Gabon increased its share from 2.8 per cent to 13 per cent. The decrease of the CAR's and Chad's shares (both countries were initially afraid of being mere trade outlets for the products of the other member countries), the rise in Gabon's share (a country that favoured the expansion of its commercial relations because of its small market size relative to its resource endowments), and the decline of Congo's share (Congo was against the admission of Cameroon, its principal competitor) clearly bring to light the effects foreseen by the initial member countries. The admission of Cameroon to the union and Gabonese industrial growth made Congo lose the dominant role it had in the UDE and radically modified the structure of competition within the region.

There is a lot of competition and duplication in the range of goods covered by the TU regime. Of 255 products subject to the TU in 1990, 151 were manufactured by firms that were first registered between 1966 and 1970; 67 new products were added from 1971 to 1984 and 37 more from 1985 to 1990. These figures confirm the narrowness of the industrial base and the slowness of industrial diversification in the region. In effect, enterprises that were newly admitted to the regime generally produced the same goods as existing enterprises.

Out of the 255 considered, Cameroon manufactures 194, the CAR 90, Congo 88, Gabon 97 and Chad 46. According to Table 4.6, 77 per cent of products manufactured in the CAR are also made in Cameroon; 36 per cent of products manufactured in Cameroon are also made in the CAR. Nearly all the products manufactured in

Table 4.6 Percentage of country A's products (rows) manufactured by country B (columns)

A\B	Cameroon	CAR	Congo	Gabon	Chad
Cameroon	100	36	37	37	20
CAR	77 (64)	100	44	39	28
Congo	81 (79)	45	100	47	27
Gabon	73 (82)	36	42	100	31
Chad	85 (75)	54	52	65	100

Note: 1968 figures, in parentheses, are from Mytelka (1975, p. 148).

Chad are also made in other member countries. Individually, the enterprises of other member countries cannot threaten Cameroonian enterprises; however, put together, they are a real threat. Out of 194 Cameroonian products, 124 are produced in other member countries. Thus, Cameroon has the monopoly of the manufacturing of 65 products out of 194, while the CAR monopolizes the production of 19 out of 90, Congo 12 out of 88, Gabon 20 out of 97 and Chad 2 out of 46.

Nonetheless, harmonization and reduction in taxes on intra-regional imports is noted. In 1966, before the establishment of the TU regime within the UDEAC, the import tax rates were low in Cameroon and relatively high in the former UDE countries. After two or three years of the TU regime, the margin between these rates was reduced in view of harmonizing, as rates increased in Cameroon and declined in other member countries. The same phenomenon occurred in 1985 when Chad rejoined the union, and when Equatorial Guinea was admitted to the UDEAC. Adjustments are made as new enterprises are admitted, the new rates being applied to new enterprises.

A Strategic Analysis of the TU

The original objective of the TU was to tax all regionally-produced goods at the same rate in all the member countries. This objective was not attained, as rates varied importantly between firms, products and consuming countries. This section analyses the flaws in the conception and the implementation of the mechanism that led this trade expansion instrument to become an instrument of protection.

The determination of TU rates was a highly complicated process, which, we shall argue, was dominated by innumerable strategic considerations. Although the rate structure for each firm, each good

Table 4.7   *Taxe unique* rates on electric batteries

Firm (country)	Date of decision setting TU rate	Consuming countries' TU rates (%)				
		Cameroon	CAR	Congo	Gabon	Chad
PILCAM (Cameroon)	18/12/73	8.5	20	25	15	
SOGAPIL (Gabon)	18/12/73	15	20	25	8	
SOCADEP (Cameroon)	23/ 7/80	8.5	20	25	15	
SAPEC (Congo)	26/ 7/85	15	20	8	25	49.5
PILCAM (Cameroon)	15/ 7/86	8.5	20	15	15	25

and each country of destination was defined by the UDEAC's management committee, the requirement for consensus meant that, in practice, each country defined the rate that was applied on its territory. These individual rates were set according to a series of strategic considerations motivated largely by the absence of an adequate compensatory mechanism within the UDEAC. In general, on its own territory, the producing country set a lower TU rate on national products relative to products originating in other member countries, indicating national protectionism. The rates it applied on competing products or products it did not produce depended on retaliatory, co-operative (reciprocity) or fiscal strategies.[14]

The example of batteries gives a good introduction to the strategies adopted under the TU regime. They are produced by three countries (Cameroon, Congo and Gabon), and the CAR is an importer. There are two producing firms in Cameroon, but only one (PILCAM) exports batteries to other UDEAC countries. Table 4.7 shows for each consuming country (columns), the TU rates applied on the batteries produced by different firms (rows). Cameroon, Gabon and Congo apply lower rates on domestically-produced batteries (8.5 per cent in Cameroon and 8 per cent in Gabon and Congo) than on intra-regional imports (15 per cent in Cameroon and 15 per cent and 25 per cent, respectively, in Gabon and Congo), reflecting protectionist motivations. In 1973, the rate (15 per cent) imposed on Gabonese batteries in Cameroon was the same as that imposed on Cameroonian batteries in Gabon, indicating reciprocity. In retaliation, Gabon applied in 1985 the same rate (25 per cent) on Congolese batteries as Congo had earlier applied on Gabonese batteries. However, the rate applied on Congolese batteries by Cameroon was 15 per cent instead of the 25 per cent applied by Congo on Cameroonian batteries. Congo rewarded this concession,

Table 4.8 Producing-country distribution of acts fixing a UDEAC-wide uniform TU rate on a given product

Producing country	1971–84			1985–90		
	No.	*Total*	*%*	*No.*	*Total*	*%*
Cameroon	82	237	35	28	150	19
CAR	28	58	48	3	7	43
Congo	56	82	68	20	35	57
Gabon	61	115	53	12	68	18
Chad				9	24	37
Total	*227*	*492*	*46*	*72*	*284*	*25*

by subsequently imposing a 15 per cent rate on PILCAM's (a Cameroonian firm) products when it applied in 1986 for a modification in its TU rates. Thus, Gabon discriminated in favour of Cameroonian batteries over Congolese batteries, indicating that all member countries were not treated equally in any given market. Since it does not produce batteries, the CAR had no discriminatory rates for firms that produce batteries.

In general, these conflicting strategies prevented the establishment of a uniform rate for each product irrespective of the producing firm and country, which was the initial goal – to be achieved by 1972 – of the TU regime. According to the data in Table 4.8, 46 per cent of the 492 decisions taken from 1971 to 1984 fixed the same rate on a given product in all countries, whereas on 25 per cent of the 284 decisions taken from 1985 to 1990 did so. This leads to the conclusion that the objective of establishing a uniform rate became more and more difficult to achieve. Indeed, excluding Chad, the percentage of acts setting the same rate in all member countries decreased in the period 1985–90 as compared to the period 1971–84 for each member country. However, the pursuit of uniformity always remained an objective of the TU regime. Indeed, once a uniform TU rate was imposed on a product, later modifications were supposed to keep rates uniform in all the member countries. In 69 per cent of the cases, the decision imposing a uniform rate was the last one to be taken.

If we look briefly at each producing country in Table 4.8, we first note that a uniform rate applies more often on Congolese and Gabonese products than on goods from other countries. This result is partially explained by the fact that Cameroon, and to a lesser extent the CAR and Chad, are more protectionist and thus set a very low rate for national products. In effect, non-uniformity is usually caused by the low rate applied in the country of origin. Reciprocity also leads to non-uniformity. For example, Gabon does not discriminate much against imports; reciprocally other member countries apply a low rate on Gabonese products. For fiscal reasons, Congo imposes a high rate even on its own goods and never grants preferential treatment to goods made in Cameroon and Gabon. We shall now study the role of protectionist, retaliatory, co-operative (or reciprocal) and fiscal motivations in determining the TU rate structure.

Protectionism Member countries have used the TU as an instrument of protection against intra-UDEAC imports by applying, on their respective territories, lower rates on nationally-produced goods than on goods produced in other member countries. In the batteries example (Table 4.7), Cameroon, Congo and Gabon each applied lower rates on nationally-produced batteries relative to batteries produced in other UDEAC countries. Consequently, intra-regional exports face discrimination unless there is no local producer in the importing country (the case of Chad in the batteries example). This deviation from an initial objective of encouraging regional trade is exacerbated by the fact that competition is primarily local or of UDEAC origin. According to a 1990/91 survey of 186 firms with 20 or more employees carried out by the national directorate of statistics in Cameroon, 45 per cent of Cameroonian entrepreneurs declare that their main competitors are other entrepreneurs from within the UDEAC, and only 15 per cent Nigerian enterprises and 12 per cent French firms. This protectionism not only explains in part the non-uniformity of TU rates, but it also helps explain the low level of regional trade, as discussed later.

This is particularly the case for Cameroon, which protects its market by applying low rates on goods produced by its own firms (see Table 4.9). The rates on Cameroonian products were strictly the lowest in Cameroon in 49 per cent of the decisions that concerned them between 1985 and 1990, the rate often being half of that set in other member countries. Given the size of Cameroon's market, it can impose lower rates on its products, regardless of the rates fixed by its partners. In effect it has less to gain from increased access to its partners' markets than its partners have to gain from access to Cameroon's market. Gabon, which is more liberal, applies relatively moderate (often the lowest) rates on both local and

Table 4.9 Decisions where the rate in the producing country is strictly smaller

Country	1971–84			1985–90		
	Frequency	*Total decisions*	*%*	*Frequency*	*Total decisions*	*%*
Cameroon	117	237	49	88	150	59
CAR	17	58	29	3	7	43
Congo	10	82	12	5	35	14
Gabon	29	115	25	35	68	51
Chad				6	24	25
Total	*173*	*492*	*35*	*137*	*284*	*48*

Table 4.10 TU rates on cheese by country of sale

Firm	Date	Cameroon	CAR	Congo	Gabon	Chad
CAMLAIT (Cameroon)	26/7/85	5	5	5	10	49.5
SLIGA (Gabon)	14/7/87	10	5	5	5	10

imported goods from its other partners. In effect, Gabon from the beginning conceived its industrialization only through regional integration. As we will see in the following section, the behaviour of the CAR, Congo and Chad is less motivated by protectionist objectives than by fiscal objectives. They therefore protect their enterprises less and apply high rates on all goods. Indeed, Congo and Chad never apply the lowest on imports. Table 4.9 shows that rates on products by firms in Congo and Chad are rarely smaller than those applicable on imports in their partner countries.

Retaliation/Dissuasion The role of retaliation/dissuasion is introduced by Bela (1992). Cameroon, an important exporting country, is also an important potential importer. The possibility of having the same low rates on imports in Cameroon may prevent its partners from fixing very high rates. For example, Chad can be affected if Cameroon, through high tax rates, prevents Chad's products from being sold on the Cameroonian market. To avoid such a situation, it therefore adopted reasonable tax rates on Cameroonian goods even though it imports a lot of products from Cameroon. A country that wants to avoid reprisals on its exports thus needs to reduce rates on imports. An example of the retaliatory mechanism is the case of cheese (Table 4.10). To protect SLIGA, which had just

Table 4.11   Frequency of uniform rates according to no. of
producing countries, 1971–90

	1	*2*	*3*	*4*	*5*	*Total*
No. taxed uniformly	30	25	18	14	12	99
Total	120	63	35	24	13	255

been constructed, Gabon imposed a 10 per cent rate on CAMLAIT products (from Cameroon) instead of 5 per cent in retaliation, Cameroon later imposed a 10 per cent on SLIGA's products.

This process favours TU uniformity when there are multiple producing countries (competition) as seen in Table 4.11. Overall, 39 per cent (99/255) of the products were taxed at a uniform rate between 1971 and 1990. Of these, 25 per cent, 40 per cent, 47 per cent, 61 per cent and 92 per cent of goods manufactured respectively by one, two, three, four and five countries, were taxed uniformly. It is clear that the uniform rate became more frequent as the number of producers increased.

Reciprocity/Co-operation   There are also cases of reciprocity. By applying a low rate on imports, a country's regional exports receive preferential treatment in return. For example, Cameroon applied a lower rate than Gabon on Congolese batteries in 1985. Consequently, Cameroonian batteries were taxed less than Gabonese batteries in Congo and less than Congolese batteries in Gabon. From 1971 to 1990, 92 products manufactured in two or more countries were not taxed at a uniform rate in Cameroon, the CAR, Congo and Gabon. For 78 of these products (85 per cent), there was reciprocity of rates between at least two producing countries, as shown in Table 4.12.

There is reciprocity between Cameroon and the CAR, for five out of the 32 products they both manufacture, and 55 out of 83 between Cameroon and the rest of UDEAC. Reciprocity is most frequent between Cameroon and Gabon (53 per cent of the products manufactured by both countries), Cameroon and Congo (44 per cent), Congo and Gabon (36 per cent), the CAR and Congo (22 per cent). It is to be noted that these are all pairs of countries with common borders and, consequently, greater trade relations. In all, 72 per cent of the Congolese goods have reciprocal rates with at least one member; the figures are 70 per cent for Gabonese

Table 4.12   Frequency of bilateral reciprocity rates (no. of products)*

	CAR	Congo	Gabon	Chad	Total	Cumulative %
Cameroon	5 (32)†	18 (41)	31 (59)	1 (14)	55 (83)	66
CAR	–	5 (23)	3 (23)	1 (11)	14 (35)	40
Congo		–	12 (23)	1 (9)	36 (50)	72
Gabon			–	1 (13)	47 (67)	70
Chad				–	4 (18)	22

Notes:

*That is, products for which the rate applied by country A on imports from country B is identical to the rate applied by country B on imports of the same product from country A.

† No. of products simultaneously manufactured by these countries is given in parentheses.

Table 4.13   Frequency of uniform and non-uniform rates in non-producing countries

Country	Same rate	Variable rates	No. of products
Cameroon	3	6	9
CAR	32	25	57
Congo	21	21	42
Gabon	18	7	25
Chad	13	61	74

products, 66 per cent for Cameroonian products, and 40 per cent and 22 per cent for CAR and Chadian products, respectively.

In general, Cameroon never imposes a higher rate on a product from the CAR than the rate imposed on the Cameroonian products in the CAR. The CAR and Congo make few concessions to each other. Concessions made by Cameroon and Gabon to the CAR are generally rewarded in multilateral exchange. The CAR never applies a lower rate on a Congolese product than it applies on a product from Cameroon or from Gabon, as there is no reciprocity in the former case. Indeed, products from Congo, a country that makes no concessions to other member countries, are generally at a disadvantage in regional markets, contrary to their Cameroonian and Gabonese counterparts.

For a given product, non-producing countries, Gabon and the CAR in particular, often apply the same (relatively high) rates regardless of the origin of the product (see Table 4.13). For example, batteries are taxed at 20 per cent in the CAR, a non-producing country, regardless of the producing firm. Non-producing countries, however, may also be guided by a strategy of reciprocity. A country may discriminate in favour of a firm from a country that has favoured it in another way, for example in relation to another product it does produce. Cameroon manufactures almost all products sold in the region and thus is not to be considered. Congo is unusual, as it discriminates according to a product's origin as often as not. Chad appears to be highly discriminatory in setting rates on products it does not produce.

Fiscal Constraints   Strategic considerations alone cannot justify the difference between the rates from one country to another. One explanation for the rising TU rates observed between 1966 and 1970 is the fiscal requirements which were not met by the very low initial rates (Mytelka, 1975, p. 149). While Cameroon, which produces most products traded in the region, applies low rates on products it produces, for fiscal reasons other member countries cannot do the same. The CAR and Chad export very little and thus are particularly motivated by fiscal considerations. Accordingly, their rates are much higher. Countries which do not produce a good in question are particularly motivated by fiscal objectives, as they need not fear direct reprisals.

Conclusion   To sum up, the initial objective of the TU regime to stimulate the creation and growth of firms in the region which could produce and substitute for imports has not been achieved. The industrialization policies in the region have not, however, addressed the concerns expressed by member countries when the UDEAC was established. The hegemony of Cameroon prevails and no real compensation scheme has been conceived and implemented, as we shall see in the following section. As a result of the inadequacies of the compensatory mechanisms and the ambiguities in the TU regime, member countries used the regime as a substitute for compensation. Rates were negotiated on a case-by-case basis.

The TU regime has thus encouraged the establishment of existing industries in other countries within the region, thereby reducing regional trade and, probably, the exploitation of scale economies. Consequently, most firms subject to the TU do not export. The tax appears simply to protect them against import competition. When these firms are first established, they generally benefit from privileges granted by an investment code regime. These privileges, which are limited in time, consist in importing equipment duty free. They then apply for admission to the TU regime, which exonerates packing-cases, wrappings and imported raw materials for an unlimited period.

To make matters worse, the rules of origin are very lax and do not ensure that any gains obtained from the regime actually benefit the region. This contrasts with the situation in other regional integration schemes. In West Africa's economic community, ECOWAS, to qualify for the generalized preferential tariff, at least 60 per cent of inputs used or 40 per cent of value-added generated by the firm must originate from within ECOWAS. A similar clause exists in the CEAC according to which a product is defined as regional by 'the rule of origin' if nationals from the region hold a minimum of 30 per cent of the capital of the firm, if a maximum of 45 per cent of materials needed for its manufacturing are of outside-union origin, and a minimum of 45 per cent of value-added is local. Although it is part of the CEAC, the UDEAC refused this clause. In 1987, the draft of the Act defining the notion of 'products of origin' according to the CEAC criteria was abandoned because many of the products that were subject to the TU could not satisfy the CEAC criteria. Considering the fact that a product of outside origin cannot be admitted to the regime, UDEAC brought down the minimal level of capital control to 10 per cent.

However, as TU status is granted only upon a unanimous management committee decision, access to it is not necessarily easy. Discontented with decisions made or delays caused by this process, a number of countries have consequently set up local alternatives to the TU regime, such as the domestic production tax (*taxe intérieure à la production*, or TIP) in Cameroon and domestic consumption taxes (TIC/TCI) in the CAR, Gabon and Congo. These regimes provide comparable privileges to firms, but access to them is much easier because it is determined by the national government. To illustrate the similarity of privileges, in the case of Pilcam, the TU rate in Cameroon in December 1973 was the same as the TIP rate applied since October 1972. For Sincatex, a firm subject to the TIP in May 1972 and to the TU in December 1973, the TU rate was similar to the TIP rate in Cameroon. In some cases the alternative regime gives even better protection than the TU.[15]

The impact of the regime is thus difficult to assess. Although it represented the main explicit and effective instrument for industrial co-operation in the UDEAC, the incentive potential of the tax was mitigated. Member states, incapable of harmonizing their conception of the TU regime and the union in general, have not adopted precise rules that can regulate it. Negotiations were undertaken whenever they were needed. Current negotiations depend on the past and the future decisions. The TU rates were fixed so as to limit trade flows that could grant gains to some countries at the expense of others. The *taxe unique*, like the treaty of the union, is a compromise between strictly national interests and the regional interest. It prevents integration in the absence of an appropriate mechanism to ensure a fair distribution of gains.

Compensatory Mechanisms

The decision to adhere to or remain[16] in a regional trade association should, in principle, be based on the expected gains accruing to members compared to the likely losses from non-membership. The problem is more acute in the presence of asymmetric preferences, which is the case in the UDEAC (see Mytelka, 1975).

UDEAC member countries are characterized by differences in resource endowments and in the initial levels of development that induced different assessments of the relevant policy choices for regional integration. Wealthier members gain more from integration, especially with respect to firm location and hence job creation and improvement in welfare. This result arises from scale economies and demand externalities as firms tend to locate close to other firms with whom they trade. Also, in order to save on distribution cost, firms prefer to locate in areas where a larger demand exists for their products. The relatively strong performance of Cameroon noted earlier can be linked to favourable initial conditions that influenced firm location.

Free market operation does not ensure a fair distribution of gains from integration and thus, in the absence of a specific compensatory mechanism, the winners do not compensate the losers and integration is slowed or halted. A compensatory mechanism thus needs to be put in place. Indeed, the success of current reform and the prospects of UDEAC depend on the reconciliation of the interests of existing and potential partners.

The conception of the integration scheme may address this compensation issue by (1) letting each member assume equal costs and benefits; or (2) allowing some proportional allocation of these costs and benefits, a possible allocation being that poorer members get a larger share of the benefits. Both approaches have been used in the UDEAC. The UDEAC treaty preamble underlines the necessity of compensating, through appropriate measures, less-developed countries. Essentially, two compensatory mechanisms were identified at the UDEAC's creation: the establishment of a solidarity fund and the fair distribution of regional projects.

The Solidarity Fund   The origins of UDEAC's solidarity fund can be traced to the AEF and the UDE. The AEF disposed of a federal budget financed principally by export taxes on minerals and wood from Gabon. In order to allow the inland importing countries to receive an adequate share of customs duties subsequent to the creation of the common external tariff, a solidarity fund and a common customs service were established in Congo, the CAR and Chad by the UDE treaty in 1959. The CAR and Chad, in particular, hoped to maintain this federal financial mechanism at the time of independence instead of counting on less-solid national finances. Under this treaty, the solidarity fund was financed by 20 per cent of import taxes collected by the common customs service. Because of the insufficient communication network, there was no significant trade between Gabon and the rest of the community. As a result, Gabon kept a separate customs service, a concession that exonerated this country from any important contribution to the UDE solidarity fund. Through the solidarity fund, UDE had a secure source of revenues, contrary to current practice of UDEAC.

The 1964 treaty creating the UDEAC aimed to compensate inland countries for tariff revenues lost on extra-regional imports transiting by the coastal countries, subsequent to the establishment of the CET. Contrary to the UDE solidarity fund, which had its own sources of finance, the UDEAC solidarity fund was financed by fixed lump-sum contributions from each country, the amount of which was determined annually by the council of heads of states. Delays in these contributions created discord as to the proper sharing of the receipts from the common customs services, which were consequently eliminated. The current mechanism is inadequate, as the beneficiaries claim that the amounts accorded to them are insufficient, while contributors find their contributions excessive and therefore delay them. A mercantilistic outlook on the part of member countries, and the absence of a clear analysis of the gains from integration (aggravated by the suspension of data collection on intra-regional trade in 1983), have therefore undermined the impetus for regional integration in the UDEAC.

Initially, the fund served its stated purpose, namely to ensure solidarity and compensation of losers. The system worked to everybody's advantage. Imports into Chad went through the CAR, hence the CAR received less than Chad because of lesser compensation. Gabon was paying as much as Congo. This equity did not last; solidarity was abandoned and the main exporters (Cameroon and Congo) became the main contributors to the fund. The common customs services also disappeared.

According to the UDEAC treaty of 1968, the CAR is not required to contribute as of 1969. When Chad left the UDEAC, the rules were kept, and likewise when it returned in 1985. The total contribution went to the CAR before 1985 but has had to be shared between the CAR and Chad since. Table 4.14 presents the structure of solidarity fund financing between 1966 and 1991. Contributions by member states were initially stable; up until 1985, no country had yet failed to contribute. However, beginning in 1988, contributions by other members became irregular: Gabon paid only part of her due in 1988; in 1989 and 1990 only Cameroon paid; and in 1991 none of the three did. In 1992, a decision by the council of heads of states cancelled all arrears with the fund. Although the solidarity fund is still in the revised 1992 treaty, it is no longer operational.

The Regional Distribution of UDEAC Investment Projects   The question of the distribution of industries in the region was first posed when the AEF was dismembered into sovereign nations with independent policies. In 1975, UDEAC member countries proceeded with a distribution of industries throughout the region to ensure gains for all. The bauxite–aluminium industry was attributed to Cameroon, chemicals to Congo, petrochemicals and cement to Gabon, pharmaceuticals and clock/watch-making to the CAR. Chad had just withdrawn from the union at that time and Equatorial Guinea had not yet joined.

In reality, the bauxite-aluminium industry has existed in Cameroon since the colonial period. Chemicals are produced more in Cameroon than in Congo. The three oil producers (Gabon, Congo and Cameroon) each have their own oil refinery. Cement is produced in Gabon and Cameroon (the joint property of Cameroon and Chad), although only the latter exports (to Chad and the CAR). This deliberate industry distribution was aimed principally to favour the CAR, the least-industrialized country in the region at the time. Yet, it is in the CAR that it has had no impact. Private enterprises produce pharmaceutical products in Cameroon, whereas UDEAC

Table 4.14   Structure of solidarity fund financing (in CFAF m)

Year	Country	Dues	Payments	Revenues received from the fund
1966	Cameroon	300	300	–
	CAR	300	300	665
	Congo	500	500	57
	Gabon	500	500	2.85
	Chad	300	300	1 175.15
1967	Cameroon	500	500	–
	CAR	300	300	630
	Congo	500	500	
	Gabon	200	200	
	Chad	300	300	1 170
1969	Cameroon	150	150	
	CAR	0	0	400
	Congo	150	150	
	Gabon	100	100	
	Chad*			
1984	Cameroon	400	400	
	CAR			1 000 000
	Congo	300	300	
	Gabon	300	300	
	Chad			
1985	Cameroon	400	400	
	CAR			600
	Congo	300	300	
	Gabon	300	300	
	Chad			400
1989	Cameroon	400	400	
	CAR			200
	Congo	300	0	
	Gabon	300	0	
	Chad			200
1990	Cameroon	400	392	
	CAR			196
	Congo	300	0	
	Gabon	300	0	
	Chad			196
1991	Cameroon	400	0	
	CAR			0
	Congo	300	0	
	Gabon	300	0	
	Chad			0

Note:
* Chad had left the UDEAC in 1969 and rejoined in 1984.

projects for the CAR have never obtained financing. Nothing was done to establish clock/watch-making production in the CAR.

Faced with the failure of these two compensatory mechanisms, inequalities among the member countries remained and even increased. Consequently, Chad abandoned the UDEAC for 17 years and the CAR threatened at one point to leave. Both were unhappy about being only trade outlets with very few local industries. The TU regime became, *de facto*, the main compensatory mechanism. Through it, countries were free to apply differential TU rates and exemptions in an attempt to ensure that no gains in other countries were made at their expense. A new framework needs to take all these into account if better prospects for integration can be contemplated.

Fiscal Harmonization

Distortions in production and trade may arise from trade policy, as analysed above, or domestic taxation. Domestic taxes include taxes on goods and capital. In a monetary union, if countries adopt a common external trade regime but do not co-ordinate their domestic tax regimes, member countries will have incentives to expand their deficits and thereby eliminate the gains expected from integration. Co-ordination is therefore also required in the field of domestic taxation. Efforts to harmonize domestic taxation include the adoption of common accounting principles and uniformity of fiscal and statistical declarations.[17] Taxation of capital is also co-ordinated via the harmonization of investment codes and the activities of the BEAC.

Before the 1994 regional fiscal reform, five types of indirect tax instruments were used in the UDEAC: import taxes, export taxes excise taxes on domestic goods and services, and sales taxes on domestic goods and services, and specific taxes especially on petroleum products. Import and export taxes were discussed above, and so this section focuses mainly on harmonization of domestic indirect taxes.

The relative importance of both trade and domestic indirect taxes for each UDEAC member country is presented in Tables 4.15–4.17. We note in particular that indirect taxes yield between 62 per cent and 94 per cent of non-petroleum government revenues, with the highest rates occurring in the least-endowed country, Equatorial Guinea, which is somewhat of an outlier. Import taxes represent between 29 per cent and 53 per cent of total indirect taxes.

Table 4.15   Indirect taxes*

Year	Country	Indirect taxes/total non-oil tax revenues	Import taxes/total indirect taxes	TU on sales of local products/total indirect taxes†	Other taxes on local sales of products/ total indirect taxes)‡	Turnover tax (TT) on services/total indirect taxes	Transactions tax/total indirect taxes	Specific taxes on petroleum products/ total indirect taxes	Other indirect taxes/total indirect taxes
1990/91	Cameroon	0.75	0.32	0.17	0.06	0.09	–	0.19	0.17
1990	CAR	0.69	0.36	0.15	0.01	0.07	0.05	0.21	0.15
1990	Chad	0.77	0.29	0.09	0.09	0.08	0.01	0.20	0.24
1990	Congo	0.62	0.53	0.18	–	0.08	0.11	0.09	0.01
1990	Equatorial Guinea	0.94	0.30	–	–	0.07	–	0.39	0.24
1989	Gabon	0.65	0.49	0.02	0.03	0.16	0.05	0.12	0.13

Notes:
* All import taxes, the TU/TIP/TCI, the turnover tax (TT), stamp duties and export taxes (expect on petroleum products).
† TT on sales of local goods plus TIP/TCI/TIC.
‡ Mainly export taxes, stamp duties and other miscellaneous indirect taxes and parafiscal levies.

Source: World Bank (1991b).

Table 4.16   Burden of indirect taxes (%)

Year	Country	Weighted average effective import tariff rate*	Average rate of the TU/TIP/TCI on local sales of goods	Average rate of TU on intra-UDEAC imports	Average burden of indirect taxes on imports and local sales†	Average effective tariff rate on non-exempt imports
1990/91	Cameroon	14	18	38	10	52
1990	CAR	13	29	35	16	42
1990	Chad	7	11	19	8	73
1990	Congo	16	18	–	18	52
1990	Equatorial Guinea	15	–	–	15	62
1989	Gabon	25	8	22	23	62

Notes:

*Receipts from taxes on imports/c.i.f. value of recorded imports.

†Import and indirect tax receipts on local sales/c.i.f. value of recorded imports plus value of local sales of goods net of taxes.

‡Receipts from import taxes/c.i.f. value of non-exempt imports.

Source: World Bank (1991b).

Table 4.17   Import taxes by type* (% of total import tax revenues)

Year	Country	Customs duty	Entry duty	Import turnover tax (ITT)	Complementary tax	Other†	Total (billions CFAF)
1990/91	Cameroon	17	39	22	15	6	59.0
1990	CAR	12	38	16	13	21	8.5
1990	Chad	19	47	19	7	9	6.4
1990	Congo	29	35	19	17	–	25.8
1990	Equatorial Guinea	–	–	–	–	8	1.5
1989	Gabon	17	41	20	20	2	60.7

Notes:
*Excluding specific taxes on petroleum products.
†TU on intra-UDEAC trade, statistical levies, and so on.

Source: World Bank (1991b).

Table 4.18   Regional institutions in the UDEAC

Institution	Objectives
BEAC	Development Bank
ISTA	Training in project management
ISSEA	Training of statisticians
Ecole Inter-Etats de douanes	Training of customs officials
CEBEVIRA	Co-operation in livestock and animal husbandry

Other Areas of Co-operation

Factor mobility is key to successful integration, but this issue, particularly labour mobility, is politically charged in the region. Contrary to capital, which may move freely within the region, several barriers reduce labour mobility. Visa requirements exist, except in the CAR and Chad, and there is almost no preference given to nationals of the UDEAC region. Because of these visa requirements most immigrants from the region have illegal status and can be sent home any time, especially following political disagreements.[18] Current negotiations aim at allowing mobility for some categories of skilled labour.

Co-operation in other areas such as joint research facilities, training, transport and transit (see Table 4.18) can contribute to reducing regional production costs and foster regional integration. In the field of transportation and transit procedures, co-operation is particularly important. As stated above, land-locked countries such as Chad and the CAR rely on the facilities existing in other member countries for their international trade. A country like Cameroon has reached acceptable food self-sufficiency and can supply other members with food products. At issue here are the lack of an appropriate transportation network and the differences in transit procedures. The inter-state transit accords, or TIPAC (*Transit Inter-Etats des Pays de l'Afrique Centrale*) aim at improving transit and transport of goods in the region. This requires that a road network be identified and given priority for funding.

Member states are also required to harmonize their legislation regarding customs practices. Member countries, in co-operation with donor agencies, agreed in 1991 to give priority to investment in transportation network infrastructure to those projects that would

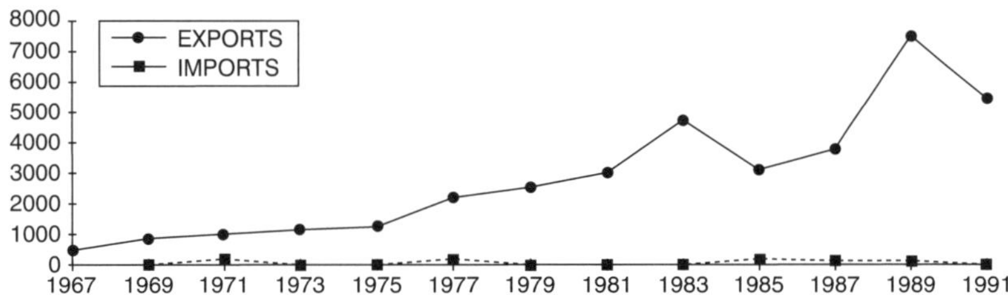

Source: The National Directorate of Statistics and National Accounts (Cameroon).

Figure 4.1   Cameroon's trade with the CAR (billions of CFAF)

benefit at least two UDEAC member countries. Likewise, harmonization has been initiated in transit formalities. The process here follows that currently prevailing in accounting practices. The agreement is to have individuals operating in transit formalities monitored and accredited by the UDEAC. In turn, a single transit official will file the required documents for all member countries, instead of the previous system where officials in each country requested similar information. This new system saves money and time and can foster regional integration.

Evaluation of the Economic Impact of UDEAC on the Region

Table 4.2 shows that, except for Cameroon, exchange among other member countries is very limited and is mostly based on TU products. After France, Cameroon is the second supplier for member countries. It buys very little from other UDEAC members, especially since it started producing oil and stopped its oil imports from Gabon in 1978. Cameroon trade patterns with UDEAC as a whole and the CAR individually are illustrated in Figures 4.1 and 4.2. Because countries became too inward-looking after the 1974 treaty revision, larger firms have not been created. Firms have developed behind protectionist walls, so that they produce mostly, if not exclusively, for domestic markets, even in the case of many TU firms, as discussed above. Manufactured products represent 80 per cent of the intra-UDEAC exchanges (*Banque Mondiale*, 1992). In nominal value, Cameroon imports in 1989 (CFAF 2223 m.) were at their 1969 level; considering inflation, this represents a drop in real value.

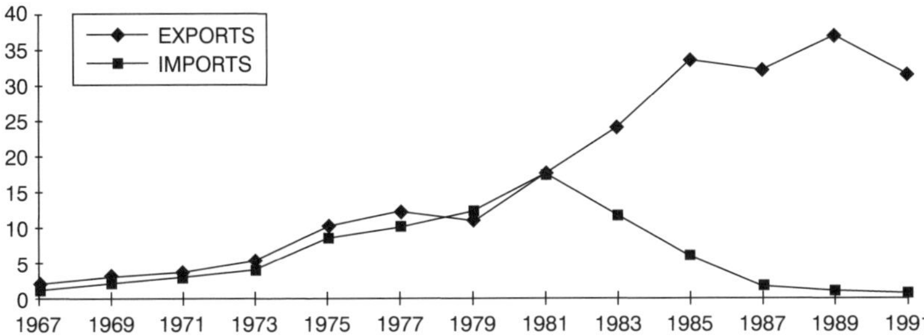

Source: The National Directorate of Statistics and National Accounts Cameroon.

Figure 4.2   Cameroon's trade with the UDEAC (CFAF bn)

Exports have not increased much. Congo was the main supplier of the UDE. There was trade creation with the expansion of the UDE into the UDEAC. As illustrated by a 1988 publication by the CAR statistics department, imports essentially come from France (42 per cent) and Cameroon (12 per cent). In UDEAC, the CAR imports 30 times more than it exports. This imbalance is due to sizeable imports from Cameroon. The CAR trades more with Zaire and Sudan (extra-UDEAC countries) than with Gabon and Chad.

The protective use of the TU has restrained trade creation and may even lead to trade reduction. For example, international brands of beer, which were previously exported from Cameroon to Gabon, are now bottled in Gabon. Where trade exists, it is because the producer is the joint property of the trading countries (the case of cement exports from Cameroon to Chad produced by a firm that is the joint property of Cameroon and Chad) or a regional monopoly (for example, Cameroonian exports matches, for which it has a monopoly in the UDEAC).

Smuggling of external imports further reduces intra-regional trade. Bela (1994) examines cases where local competition (beer, soap), or fraud (cloth), substantially reduce protection. Real effective protection is often negative on the main goods traded in the UDEAC. Indeed, smuggling has led some firms in the clothing and textile activities to bankruptcy.

Potential for intra-regional trade can be based on comparative advantage analysis, as measured below by domestic resource cost

Table 4.19   Domestic resource cost of important products in Cameroon
exports in the UDEAC

	1975/76	1985/86	1990/91
Aluminium (plank/sheet)	–	*	*
Beer	0.17–0.19	1.61	8.6 (0.51)
Matches	0.85	1.84	*
Soaps	0.89	2.34	0.85 (0.39)
Batteries	1.53	*	*
Cement	0.14	*	0.53
Cloth	1.97	*	* (0.78)

Notes:
* negative value-added.
   Figures in parentheses take local competition into account.

Sources: For 1975/76, Banque Mondiale (1991); for 1985/86, Maxwell Stamp
Associates (1987, p. 49); for 1990/91, Bela (1994, p. 35).

ratios in the case of Cameroon (Bela, 1994). Aluminium by-products
are the main Cameroonian exports in the UDEAC. Cameroon used
to export iron sheets, but it now sells planks that serve in the
manufacturing of iron sheets in other member countries. Table 4.19
indicates that, at world prices , value-added in this activity is negative. This may be due to distorted inter-firm pricing, as Cameroonian
production is generated by a multinational firm (Maxwell Stamp
Associates, 1987), but it may also indicate a lack of comparative
advantage. If this is the case, given the predominance of aluminium
in Cameroon's exports, one can conclude that the gains from
integration are mainly illusory.

   The performance of Cameroon's two main export products,
aluminium by-products and beer, is determined by the strategies
of multinationals, which can strongly affect production decisions in
the UDEAC. As trade in manufactured products based on comparative advantage has not yet materialized, we can conclude that
the potential is great in that domain.

   In summary, with respect to its objectives and instruments, the
UDEAC has attempted to set mechanisms for policy harmonization in fiscal, industrial, monetary and trade policies. As most of
these mechanisms have not worked properly, the UDEAC has therefore not fostered the industrialization of less-endowed partners and
has not improved intra-regional trade. Most institutions have not
functioned adequately. Attention has concentrated on gains shar-

ing rather than gains creation. A mercantilistic assessment of the process would conclude that Cameroon is a net gainer and accordingly has financed a larger share of the secretariat budget. Because the general secretariat is not allowed to take initiatives, and personnel are appointed without regard for competence, all the mechanisms put in place failed to foster regional integration.

4.3 CHANGING CONDITIONS AND THEIR IMPLICATIONS FOR REGIONAL INTEGRATION

Prospects for regional integration in the UDEAC depend on its environment and, in particular, on its coherence with national objectives and policies and other regional integration schemes both in Africa and outside. National policies are dominated by structural adjustment efforts and, in relation to international trade, a move toward trade liberalization. Such a move has implications for policy design at the national and regional levels. The redesign of regional integration schemes and other international co-operation mechanisms worldwide also have direct and indirect implications for the UDEAC. We address these changing conditions before presenting and assessing the current reform of UDEAC institutions and instruments. We first focus on conditions within the member countries.

National Policies

Each UDEAC member country experienced significant shocks over the 1970s and 1980s. These shocks included declines in international primary commodity prices, fluctuations in oil prices and interest rates, and natural disasters. Although the effects of these shocks were not the same in all countries, because of their production structure, the reaction in each was less than satisfactory. Reasons for such a poor reaction include weak domestic resource mobilization, a narrow government revenue base, a vulnerable current account due to an insufficiently diversified export sector, a very distorted incentive structure, an inefficient public sector and a distressed financial sector.

A combination of stabilization and adjustment measures was necessary and each country turned to both multilateral and bilateral institutions for financing. A summary of stabilization policies in each of the countries, presented below, highlights the difficulty of country-specific adjustment and underscores the need for a regional adjustment programme. Given membership in the franc zone and the extent of disequilibrium in key macroeconomic indicators, regional adjustment was insufficient, as only internal adjustment could be contemplated. We shall thus consider both the CFA devaluation of January 1994 and the franc zone participation in the analysis.

Structural Adjustment

Over the period 1970–9, UDEAC economies generally experienced strong economic growth with rates greater than those in the rest of SSA (see Table 4.20). GDP grew at an average 6.4 per cent rate per annum in real terms. Investment relative to GDP was quite high and inflation was under control: an average 11 per cent annual inflation rate as compared to about 25 per cent in the rest of SSA and close to 20 per cent for other low-income countries world wide. International competitiveness was better than that of the rest of SSA, as the real exchange rate was at a sustainable level. The terms of trade (TOT, base: 1980 = 100) were, on average, above 100 in all countries except for Gabon, whose TOT were less than 55 until the 1973 oil boom. As a result, the annual export growth rate (7 per cent) was higher than that of other low-income countries.

Beginning in the early 1980s, growth performance deteriorated and adjustment (internal and/or external) was needed. The adjustment strategy depends in such cases on the available policy instruments and the perception (temporary or permanent) made with respect to the shocks the economies are experiencing. In theory, internal adjustment is called for if the shocks are small or perceived as temporary; otherwise a combination of both internal and external adjustment is required. The 1980s may further be divided into two periods, the first over which internal adjustment could be relied upon to secure growth, and the second, starting in 1986, when both internal and external adjustment were required.

Over the period 1980–5, the average annual GDP growth rate was 7.35 per cent and terms of trade increased from an average 124 to 131 between 1970–9 and 1980–5, especially due to oil price shocks and the relative importance of oil-producing countries – Cameroon (since 1976), Congo, Gabon. The second oil boom was a positive shock for oil-exporting countries, but negative for the other three UDEAC members. In Gabon, the TOT almost doubled, increasing from 80 to 152. Gross national income per capita increased from \$1583 to \$1910 on average, and from \$691 to \$1035 in Cameroon. Yet, in neither the oil-exporting nor the oil-importing countries did the government adopt the right policy mix. Because oil-exporting countries interpreted the shocks as permanent, large investments were made in non-reversible areas such as public employment.

Given the extent of currency over-valuation in the late 1980s, with temporary shocks internal adjustment could still be relied upon in the earlier part of the period. Although GDP growth and the real total investment to GDP ratio fell, they were still high compared to those in other countries at the same level of development. Shocks in international markets (fluctuations in the US \$, devaluation of the Nigerian nara, declines in commodity prices, an increase in international interest rates) were so important that internal adjustment was no longer sufficient to restore growth.

Hence, growth performances deteriorated after 1985, particularly in the oil-rich countries. Overall, GDP fell by 1.5 per cent per annum, and has fallen even more in recent years. Internal adjustment did not succeed in reducing aggregate demand to levels compatible with current economic conditions. In fact, it seems to have reduced the level of domestic investment. Total and long-term debt increased in the region. These results, when compared to those of other SSA countries, suggest the need for exchange rate adjustment over that period (see Devarajan and de Melo, 1990).[19] We consider developments in key sectors.

The objectives of the stabilization programmes in each country consisted, in the short and medium run, of obtaining a sustainable balance of payments, with stable prices that do not jeopardize long-term perspectives. The stabilization measures were associated with adjustment measures in order to yield, in the long run, a neutral incentive structure. The contents of country-specific SAPs are very similar in the UDEAC; Table 4.20 below summarizes IMF-supported SAPs performance in the region. For each performance indicators, we show in the second column the frequency of programmes that improved *vis-à-vis* the preceding year's results. The third column gives the frequency of programmes that led to improvement after one year of implementation and the last column reports those that met their stated objectives.

According to Table 4.20, 64 per cent of IMF-supported programmes aimed at a higher growth rate than the rate of the

Table 4.20　Evaluation of IMF-supported SAPs in the UDEAC

	Objectives of the programme/preceding year's result*	Current year's result/preceding year's result†
Growth	64	64‡
Inflation	43	82
Current account balance (in units of GDP)	58	61
State revenues (in units of GDP)	71	75
State expenditures (in units of GDP)	60	53
Wages/revenues	66	52
Budget deficit (surplus) (in units of GDP)	60	61
Debt/GDP	33	31
Foreign arrears	59**	64
Debt services/exports	56	70
Domestic credit (growth rates)	57	44
Credit to the government (growth rates)	36	50
Credit to the economy (growth rates)	67	56
Money supply (growth rates)	57	50
Liquidity rate	50	55
Savings (in units of GDP)	56	47
Investment (in units of GDP)	31	52

Notes:
* Frequency of adjustment measures *vis-à-vis* preceding year's performances.
† Frequency of programmes with improvements *vis-à-vis* preceding year's performances.
‡ Frequency of programmes that met objectives.
** Results based on a smaller sample of 13 programmes.

Source: Mohammed (1994).

preceding year. Given the restrictive monetary policy followed by BEAC, inflation is not much of a concern and was an objective in 43 per cent of the programmes. Improvement in the ratio of current account of the balance of payments to GDP was an objective in 68 per cent of the programmes, compared to 71 per cent for the ratio of total balance of payments to GDP. Public finance came high on the agenda; 50 per cent of the programmes targeted the ratio of total revenues to GDP, 83 per cent the expenditure to GDP ratio, 66 per cent the wage bill, and 60 per cent total budget deficit reduction.

The aims were long-term economic growth, which could only be obtained when investment and technological know-how were forthcoming in all sectors. In order to secure long-term economic growth, the short-term conditions must be appropriate. Accordingly, policies for the long, medium and short term should be co-ordinated. Medium-term and short-term policies are in the arena of macroeconomic policy, especially aggregate demand management and exchange rate policies.

The need for region-wide stabilization stems from the rigidity of available instruments, and the limited extent of adjustment that can be made with the instruments under the control of national authorities. The desirability and feasibility of a region-wide SAP should be considered on both economic and political grounds. The economic aspect concerns the feedback mechanisms between regional and national reform efforts. Before 1994, as in other African franc zone (AFZ) members, adjustment in UDEAC countries was limited to internal measures. However, on 12 January 1994, an important currency devaluation was carried out, changing the exchange rate from its 1948 level of CFAF 50 to CFAF 100 per FF. It is expected that such a significant devaluation will improve competitiveness and rapidly create conditions to meet internal and external equilibriums. To reach that objective the governments in individual countries have designed temporary accompanying measures that include price monitoring, an increase in rural population income,[20] the protection of vulnerable income groups in rural areas and, progressively, the settlement of internal debt.

Trade Policy

As in other developing countries, the overall framework on which trade policy was set in the UDEAC led to heavy protection of local firms and active government involvement in production activities. Government involvement in trade policy includes quantitative and qualitative restrictions, price controls and homologation on internal markets. The industrial sector was protected via:

(1) loopholes provided by the investment codes through which fiscal concessions were granted to firms on a discretionary bases;
(2) rigid labour codes through which the government could intervene in setting wages and/or firing; and
(3) creation of (often unnecessarily) heavily subsidized parastatal enterprises, often enjoying quasi-natural monopoly privileges.

An activist development policy relies on quantitative restrictions, price controls and close monitoring of economic activities. A non-activist development policy keeps government intervention to a minimum and is non-discriminatory. In the latter case, trade policy instruments include market-friendly tools such as tariffs, subsidies and taxes applied so as to be neutral *vis-à-vis* resource allocation. The incentive structure leads to an allocation of domestic resources that reflects comparative advantage. The analysis of TU initiatives and the overall decision-making process in the UDEAC, coupled with the structure of indirect taxation, as presented above, illustrates the complex policy environment and the ensuing distortions to incentives.

National reform, as we have shown, aimed at creating a neutral incentive structure without bias in favour of the production of importable over exportable goods, or in favour of sales on domestic markets over those on foreign markets. The expected advantages of such an incentive structure include the alignment of domestic prices with international levels, more competitive production and a sustained, poverty-reducing growth. The reform was designed in relation to constraints facing each government in promoting economic growth. These constraints included the need for fiscal revenues, protection of domestic firms, balance of payments equilibrium and income distribution. It was then necessary to determine the tools that were most appropriate for meeting each of these constraints.

By and large, the aim of foreign trade reform was to liberalize imports and exports by eliminating quantitative restrictions and suppressing the direct taxation of exports. The overall process started in all member countries, but some reversals have also taken place in all countries. In Cameroon, reforms were supposed to take place between 1989 and January 1991, yet they are still in process. Import licences were due to terminate by June 1989 but relevant legislation is still awaited. Some policy decisions have even been reversed, and other policy reversals are possible. The direct taxation of exports, lifted in 1991/92, has been reinstated on some products, such as bananas, cocoa and coffee.

Trade policy reform is limited by UDEAC accords, as it requires common external tariff and TU reform. Including trade policy reform in regional accords has the added advantage of partially freeing national authorities from local lobbying while submitting them to peer pressure from other member countries to respect national trade policy reform obligations. This gives national trade policy reform a credibility it would not otherwise have.

Fiscal Policy

Fiscal adjustment is necessary for macroeconomic stability and sustained growth. Reductions in tariffs, often included in trade reforms, generally increase existing budget deficits, with direct adverse effects on the entire economy, unless appropriate measures are taken in other key policy arenas. A co-ordination of tariff and tax reforms is therefore necessary for successful adjustment, while separation of these two reforms can easily lead to policy reversals and compromise the credibility of the entire reform process. Requirements for such co-ordination are more binding in a regional integration scheme, such as the UDEAC, as some tax instruments are controlled at a regional jurisdiction level and decision-making is not supported by objective criteria.

Macroeconomic adjustment in member countries, individually or collectively, relies extensively on fiscal adjustment. Because of the rules of the franc zone, a link between the rate of growth of domestic credit and the growth of the nominal demand for money has to be maintained. Higher growth of domestic credit is possible only when inflation in the rest of the world is important, when real income growth is high and when money demand is income elastic. Almost ruling out a devaluation, as is the case in the franc zone, puts great pressure on fiscal discipline. In the case of currency overvaluation, the cost of devaluing the exchange rate in terms of output and employment is very high, as illustrated by Devarajan and Rodrik (1991).

When a country that has a fixed exchange rate, and a strong commitment to maintain it, experiences a fiscal deficit, reliance on internal adjustment takes time. Adjustment is even longer when prices are sticky. An analysis of the mechanism ensuring fiscal discipline in the region is thus called for. The principal issue is to determine the extent to which quasi-fiscal deficits can be used by member states, as BEAC constraints are limited to the fiscal deficit.

National Political Conditions

The feasibility and form of the regional integration scheme may be examined within the framework presented by Grossman and Helpman (1994). The evolution in the region since the late 1980s is toward multi-party politics, with stronger labour unions and other forms of interest group co-ordination. A consequence of this evolution is that politicians will be exposed to more diversified lobbies. The decision on any key economic issue will thus take into consideration the political future of an incumbent government and existing interest groups. A member state's stance with respect to the future of regional integration depends in this case on the relative political power of existing interest groups and the requirements of other multilateral and bilateral agreements.

In individual countries, interest groups indicate their opinions on each policy question and influence election campaigns. Politicians decide by reconciling existing viewpoints and assessing impacts on overall welfare. At the regional level, a two-stage decision-making process operates. In the first stage, national governments reconcile national interest group positions to come up with their own policy preferences. In the second stage, national governments make deals in which sufficient compensation is obtained to deter opposing views. Clear identification of costs and benefits, losers and gainers is therefore important.

With respect to the level of economic development, there are substantial differences in preferences. In this case a preference asymmetry effect operates and can undermine the integration process. The preference asymmetry effect leads to difficulties in reconciling opposing lobbies and the possibility of policy reversals. The analysis presented above illustrated these possibilities in the case of TU decision-making and effective functioning of the general secretariat.

One way to enhance the process is to penalize individual members who fail to follow the rules. Such penalties may be the denial to these members of certain privileges available to those that abide by the rules. An adequate institutional set-up for this is required.

Monetary and Financial Policies and the Franc Zone

In the beginning of the current economic restructuring, monetary and financial policy in each UDEAC country shared many characteristics of developing countries: prevalence of credit controls, weak bank supervision and direct and indirect intervention in interest rate determination, a limited number of financial institutions and instruments, and high concentration of deposits in a few banks. To foster both national and regional adjustment efforts, reforms aimed at reducing impediments to free competition were contemplated. We shall review developments in key areas and stress the implications for regional reform; areas include monetary policy, credit policy and monetary and financial supervisory bodies.

With respect to monetary policy, the aim is to secure low inflation and acceptable levels of economic activity via the real interest rate. The BEAC, as the region's central bank, has the authority to print money. A non-inflationary policy is supposed to create just enough money to satisfy the transaction demand for money. The levels of inflation and seignorage are low and even declined over the 1980s, both in the BEAC and other AFZ countries (See World Bank, 1994a). Inflation in 1990–1 fell by 11.6 per cent as compared to the 1981–6 period.

Over the structural adjustment period, interest rate policy in the BEAC zone was changed in order to make it more flexible. Three specific objectives were adopted: the liberalization and simplification of the structure of interest rates; an increase in the profit margins for commercial banks; and the maintaining of a positive rate differential with foreign partners within and outside the franc zone. Consequently, interest rates were adjusted according to economic and financial developments.

More flexibility was put into the system by allowing the BEAC governor to adjust the rate according to internal and external positions facing the zone. Interest rates were raised in October 1988. Less than a year later, on 3 February 1989, the interest rate structure was liberalized and significantly simplified, reducing the number of lending rates from more than 20 to four. On 17 October 1990, another modification in the interest rate structure was made. The preferential discount rate was cancelled, but state-owned enterprises, in the process of restructuring, could be granted concessional rates on a case-by-case basis. Several rates were simultaneously increased; the discount rate went from 10 per cent to 11 per cent and the rate charged on advances to national treasuries rose from 4.5 per cent to 5.5 per cent with a one-point increase every six months beginning in March 1991 until parity with the ordinary discount rate is reached.

Concerning credit policy, as above mentioned, state intervention is present through the setting of interest rates, the creation of specific purpose banks and direct credit allocation. The board of directors of the BEAC determines a maximum amount of credit that a member state can obtain. In turn, the BEAC determines a maximum credit level for banks and enterprises. This ceiling policy is supplemented by a discount rate policy. The discount policy leads to the determination of a normal rate, a preferential rate and a penalty rate. These rates change depending upon the economic conjuncture. Until

September 1991, the BEAC credit council determined the maximum refinancing to the economy based on the levels of deficits resulting from the comparison of revenues and expenditures appearing in each state's bank balance sheet. Credit policy reform sought to change this practice. Currently, monetary programming is used to establish a maximum amount of BEAC assistance to banks, using target monetary aggregates. These targets take into account the trends in economic activities (GDP growth potentials), balance of payments and public finance as consolidated in the State Flow of Funds Table (*tableau des opérations financières de l'état*, or TOFE).

For a long time, an informal money market functioned among commercial banks within the BEAC zone. A money market covering the whole BEAC zone – on the agenda since 1986 – has been in effect since July 1994, and is limited to banks. One of the objectives of this inter-bank market is to secure the optimal mobilization of internal resources in the presence of massive capital flight. It is expected that the creation and implementation of a money market within the BEAC zone will preserve the free movement of funds within the zone, improve the control of monetary policy and attract capital generated both within and outside the zone. In that respect, it can favour regional integration, especially with appropriate bank supervision and payment legislation.

Until 1993, bank supervision was carried out by individual member states of the BEAC, based on three instruments: a liquidity ratio, a risk coverage ratio and rules for the risk sharing. This structure did not prevent bank insolvency, which led to a distressed banking and financial sector in the region. COBAC (*Commission Bancaire d'Afrique Centrale*) was thus set up in October 1990 to harmonize bank supervision and counter such situations. Henceforth, the liquidity ratio was to be determined monthly, rather than every three months, based on a formula that incorporates all items that can affect bank liquidity. In this new framework, the risk coverage indicator is a weighted average of risky activities in the bank's portfolio. Coverage is made uniform for all member states. The creation of COBAC is expected to reduce risk and improve bank management, as the political pressure on decision-making is reduced.

A similar structure is being put into place in the insurance sector. In each member state of the BEAC, insurance supervision is carried out by the ministry of finance, which supervises the legality of operations as well as the level of risk. For political and other reasons the process has not worked. On 10 July 1992 most francophone African countries created a regional supervisory body, the CIMA (*Conférence Interafricaine des Marchés d'Assurances*). Member countries are to be covered by the same insurance code and control, carried out by a regional commission (*Commission Régionale de Contrôle des Assurances*, CCAR). The prospects for this organization depend on the ability of the governments in individual countries and the financial institutions to continue the reforms.

The implications of these changes for integration in the UDEAC region are important. Regional integration can succeed only if natives of the region can set up multinational corporations. These corporations need a sound financial market where risk is low. Flexibility in interest rates and their adjustment to capital scarcity will limit capital flight, which has prevailed in recent years. Addressing the issue of financial repression was necessary. Multinational corporations with investment originating in the region cannot function without appropriate financial institutions. Continuation of reform in these areas is therefore crucial to the success of regional integration. These reforms need to be supplemented by international agents: private banks, foreign investors, multinational agencies and foreign governments. The form of the relationships with these bodies can hinder regional integration.

Other Regional and Global Integration Schemes

The nature of the relationship with the rest of the world is important for the success of a regional integration scheme. As suggested by Collier and Gunning (1994, p. 15), 'Free trade within a trading bloc can achieve for its members all the gains of global free trade if the composition of the bloc spans the global range of production.' UDEAC members, overall, have similar endowments and hence, the reduced level of intra-regional trade described above. To span the global range of production, reciprocal trade with another bloc is necessary. Candidates in that matter depend on the following complementary factors: the extent of existing and potential trade, culture and history. Possible candidates for the UDEAC include: other African regional integration schemes, France, the European Union (EU), the USA, Japan.

Despite the efforts to create an African economic community, it would not span the world trade pattern given the similarity of production on the continent. Recent experience suggests that African countries cannot form coalitions in which members are both threat-makers and threat-receivers. The USA and Japan have neither significant trade with the region nor important cultural and political interests in the region. France, as the former colonial power, meets all the above requirements. It is also a member of the EU, which is the largest trading bloc that has deep historical, cultural and economic relations with each member state. The EU is preferable to France alone, as the feeling of external political interference is diminished. In any case, France would gain almost as much from such a multilateral accord as it would from a bilateral accord with the UDEAC.

UDEAC's interest in free trade with the EU is thus twofold: it might achieve virtually all the gains expected from global free trade, and it can enhance credibility as it reduces the power of anti-free trade lobbies within individual countries (Collier and Gunning, 1994). Reciprocal discrimination between the two groups is compatible with Article XXIV of the GATT if the abolition and/or reduction of protection among countries is based on rules of origin and the common external tariff rates are no higher than before.

Economic Rationale for Regional Integration in the UDEAC

Before analysing the recent reforms of the UDEAC, we shall examine briefly the standard economic rationale for regional integration.

Regional integration aims at eliminating all discrimination between domestic goods and services among member countries and between them and the rest of the world. It can be presented as a four-stage process that includes:

(1) the creation of a free trade area;
(2) the establishment of a common external tariff against non-member countries, or the creation of a customs union;
(3) the establishment of a common market in which factor movement is free; and
(4) the creation of an economic union in which national economic policies are harmonized and co-ordinated by a supranational authority.

Arguments for regional integration are numerous (see Langhammer and Hiemenz, 1991, for a summary survey, or Lyakurwa et al., 1993). These including the following.

- *The infant industry argument and market size and economies of scale argument*   Regional integration opens up a larger market to domestic firms. In an enlarged market these firms can increase production and reduce unit production costs. As the World Bank (1991 a) points out, however, we should not overestimate the economies of scale argument as it is more relevant to heavy industries than small-scale firms.
- *The resource allocation and availability argument*   Within a larger market, firms are more prone to use resources based on comparative advantage within the entire region; also, transaction costs are reduced and informal and inefficient trade is replaced by formal and efficient trade.
- *The industrialization argument*   Regional integration can increase competition and efficiency in the region by widening the size of all products and factor markets; the argument here is to be distinguished from that related to import-substitution policy, which widens the market only to a few privileged firms protected via high tariff or quantitative restrictions. The industrialization argument also identifies the possibility of trade creation and trade diversion.
- *The joint production of public goods argument*   It is a truism that economic development will come only when the infrastructural network is adequate. Most of the time such infrastructure can be provided by the state, and regional integration may create facilities for producing such infrastructure at lower cost. In UDEAC, telecommunications are co-ordinated on a regional basis; training in some fields (computer sciences, statistics and planning, customs) is also provided under regional institutions.
- *The protection against worsening terms of trade argument*   Instead of exporting raw materials to industrialized countries, some manufacturing and sales within the region will limit the negative impact of terms of trade shocks. Also, a group of countries is in a better position to influence their external terms of trade.

A strong case may be made against regional integration based on the negative results of regional integration so far obtained in SSA, and especially in the UDEAC, as we shall see below.

Mild progress in regional integration may be related to: (1) the multiplicity of regional integration schemes to which the country belongs; (2) lack of political commitment in individual member states; (3) weak institutional framework; (4) insufficient involvement of the private sector and civil society.

The success of regional integration thus requires actions at national, regional, continental and international levels:

(1) At the national level there is need for increased political commitment, the assessment of the costs and benefits of belonging to existing schemes, a co-ordinating body linking partners in the integration process, including participants of the informal sector, the dissemination of necessary information, the acceptance of a supranational institution in charge of regional integration.

(2) At the regional level there is need for harmonizing legal frameworks of alternative integration schemes, merging superfluous schemes, involving alternative partners of which the informal sector, accepting multi-speed approaches, accepting the principle of subsidiarity, adopting an efficient compensation scheme, and allowing the regional body to generate some of its revenues.

(3) At the continental level regional integration should be compatible with the Abuja Treaty, aiming at establishing the Africa Economic Community (AEC), and actions by organizations such as the African Development Bank (ADB).

(4) At the international level, regional integration should be compatible with interventions by multilateral and bilateral organizations.

If regional integration should continue, it is necessary to point out how it fits into the current policy framework characterized by a market friendly environment. The main argument arises from recognition of the fact that regional integration has to be complementary to domestic policy in each member state. Another reason for pursuing policy reform within a customs union such as UDEAC is related to the near impossibility of interest groups forcing the government to reverse itself from previous reforms (see Panagariya and Findlay, 1994). Policy reform needs to be credible, sustainable and time-consistent with other policy decisions. Collier and Gunning (1994) provide directions for analysing credibility. According to their arguments, regional integration within the UDEAC region with reciprocal discrimination with the EU is preferable to unilateral liberalization in four ways:[21]

(1) It allows the region to earn the most gains from global trade liberalization.

(2) Provided there are adequate institutional reforms, it will establish credibility of trade reform in individual member states.
(3) It can serve a defensive purpose that allows the smoothing and beneficial application of GATT rules.
(4) Given the political will for regional integration, it will be politically easier to implement trade reform imposed by the regional framework. An important component of this research is to investigate the likelihood of reforming UDEAC so that regional integration reinforces policy reform by individual state; we return to this below.

Current Reforms of UDEAC Accords

Current reform of the UDEAC aims to address the issues that led to the failure of the regional integration process and to take into account developments in member countries, the region and the rest of the world. Past failures of the UDEAC to foster regional integration are blamed on poor governance, inappropriate integration instruments and duplication with other initiatives. We address each of these issues and analyse the compatibility of the current reform in relation with developments in international trade institutions such as the GATT.

Governance

The new approach to regional integration (see UDEAC, 1988) attributes the poor results obtained so far to the lack of a fixed schedule for specific objectives, micro-nationalism, deficient institutionaal arrangements and required unanimity in decision-making. The proposed reform includes the principle of a restrictive list of questions for which unanimity rule is necessary. A deadline would be attached to each decision.

The approach proposes the creation of a court of justice with jurisdiction over conflicts among member countries. Presently, this duty is incumbent upon the council of heads of state in which each member has veto power. Also the principle of an autonomous general secretariat has been accepted. Equal contributions are still required of all member countries, but the principle of penalties in the case of non-payment has been introduced despite the reservations of Equatorial Guinea. Staff positions are no longer allocated among member states. Staff are to be recruited solely on the basis of their competence given predefined job profiles.

Instruments for Regional Integration

The Common External Tariff and Quantitative Restrictions   Before the regional reform, the common external tariff (CET) was mainly determined according to budgetary preoccupations. A non-UDEAC product was subject to four taxes, the cumulative rate of which was unduly high and which differentiated by products within and between countries. Tables 4.3 and 4.15 give, respectively, the legal and effective tariff structure and the indirect tax structure in the early 1990s. Except for consumer goods that were subject to excise taxes, average nominal rates are comparable between countries. This pattern changes when effective rates are considered, mainly because of exemptions granted on a discretionary basis. Current tax reform has removed these taxes and reduced the number of rates in order to simplify their administration and reduce distortion.

Within the framework of the regional reform, the CET comprises two taxes: a customs duty and a tempory surcharge tax. Concerning the customs duties, products are classified in either of four groups, representing successive levels of product transformation. Group I products include essential goods and has the lowest rate. Group II includes primary goods and equipment. Group III includes semi-finished goods and Group IV comprises consumption goods. The rates fixed per category rae 5 per cent, 15 per cent, 35 per cent, 50 per cent. Only Equatorial Guinea implemented these rates. The other member states took advantage of the rise in prices caused by the CFA devaluation on 11 January 1994 to lower these rates to 5 per cent, 10 per cent, 20 per cent and 30 per cent, respectively.

The second component of the common external tariff is the temporary surcharge tax. It was put into place to substitute for the protection formerly provided to firms via non-tariff barriers. It is thus temporary and its rate varies but may not exceed 30 per cent. All quantitative restrictions are to be abolished by 30 June 1996 and the rate for the temporary tax should reach zero by 1999.

The Single Tax (TU)   The TU is replaced by the generalized preferential tariff (*tarif préférentiel généralisé*, or TPG). The TPG represents 20 per cent of the common external tariff and is applied on sales of all products satisfying the rules of origin. The rate should be zero in 1998 at the latest, and is already zero on local textile products. The replacement of the TU regime by a uniform reduction in tariff rates for all intra-regional trade, as established in the recent UDEAC reform, puts an end to the complicated strategies noted earlier, which, in general, are inimical to the overall aim of regional integration and growth.

Compensatory Mechanisms   The solidarity fund, financed by lump-sum contributions determined by the council of heads of state, is maintained. All these undertakings overlook the lack of equity in gains sharing, which has undermined regional integration in the UDEAC in the past.

Fiscal Harmonization   Tax collection activities were heavily affected by both internal and external shocks in the late 1980s and early 1990s. Standard characteristics of developing country tax systems are present: the number of tax sources is limited and most tax income comes from foreign trade activities based on very unstable prices that are determined by international markets, especially as fara as exports are concerned. In recent years, as balance of payments problems increased and trade liberalization took place, the tax base eroded even more and its reform became necessary.

Tax reform, carried out within UDEAC reform, aims in the short run to correct fiscal imbalances and in the medium run to improve resource allocation and ensure sustainable economic growth. Tax reform aims to broaden the tax base and reduce the level and number of tax rates. In the process, such a reform is expected to lead to uniform corporate and personal income taxes. Thus, the tax structure will become simple, easy to administer, less distorted and horizontally equitable.

One approach is to make sure that each of the measures included serves only one purpose. For example, tariffs could be used exclusively for protection purposes, while domestic taxes could be used for revenue collection. Lack of this property was the main deficiency of the former UDEAC common external tariff structure.

Domestic indirect taxes have two components: a turnover tax (the *taxe sur le chiffre d'affaires*, or TCA) and an excise tax. Both the TCA and the excise taxes respond to budgetary concerns. The turnover tax applies to imported as well as locally produced goods and services. For imported goods the tax base is the sum of the c.i.f. value, the customs duty and the excise tax. For locally-produced goods and services the tax base is either the ex-factory price or the market price, net of other taxes. The TCA has two rates, a normal rate and reduced one, the latter being applicable for products of first necessity. The TCA is comparable to a value-added tax. The rates are freely fixed by each member state between 3 per cent and 6 per cent for the reduced rate, and between 7 per cent and 18 per cent for the normal rate. In July 1994, the rates fixed were 5 per cent and 15 per cent in Cameroon, 5 per cent and 10 per cent in the CAR, and 5 per cent and 12 per cent in Congo and Equatorial Guinea. Gabon opted for the value-added tax instead of the TCA. Chad had not yet implemented the TCA as of June 1994. The list of products exempted from the TCA is fixed by the UDEAC authorities; it comprises pharmaceutical products, books, medical and surgical equipment, manufacturing equipment, and so on. The TCA paid on raw materials is deductible when the finished products are sold.

The excise tax, supplemented by temporary surtaxes, is essentially budgetary and its rate is freely set by each member country at a rate that ranges from 0 per cent to 100 per cent. The list of products subject to this tax is adopted at UDEAC level. For cigarettes and alcohol, the rate must be non-zero. The rate is 25 per cent in Cameroon. It is 20 per cent on alcohol and 30 per cent on tobacco in the CAR, with 2 per cent levied on goods as a contribution to the various UDEAC organisms. The objective of the temporary surtaxes is to protect national industries against dumping, smuggling or tax fraud. They are requested by manufacturers and should be eliminated by the year 2000. Each country determines in applicable rates at the national level within the range of 0 per cent to 30 per cent. The likely impact of the regional reform is described in Table 4.21.

4.4　CONCLUSION

In this chapter we have analysed integration in the UDEAC region since its creation in 1964 in order to assess future prospects. In terms of achievements, the UDEAC has succeeded in some areas: establishment of a common external tariff and harmonization of internal fiscal codes and accounting practices. UDEAC member states belong to the franc zone, which has strict monetary management clauses. Accordingly, monetary, financial and fiscal policy records are satisfactory, compared with those of other developing countries, especially for the period ending in 1985.

Despite the existence of a common external tariff and a common

Table 4.21   Post-reform effective rate of protection* (simulation)

	Cameroon		Congo		Gabon		Equatorial Guinea		CAR		Chad	
	A	C	A	C	A	C	A	C	A	C	A	C
(A) Post-reform structure of import duties (%)												
Average rate on final products (Rates applicable on category III products)	59	31	31	19	47	25	28	16	38	21	11	8
Average rate on inputs (Rates applicable on category II products)	8	10	5	8	7	10	3	4	3	5	4	4
(B) Post-reform ERP by level of value-added (%)												
Value-added (% of sales, world prices)												
0.05	1028	430	525	228	807	310	503	244	703	325	144	84
0.20	263	115	135	63	207	85	128	64	178	85	39	24
0.30	178	80	92	45	140	60	86	44	120	58	27	17
0.40	136	63	70	36	107	48	66	34	91	45	22	14
0.50	110	52	57	30	87	40	53	28	73	37	18	12
0.65	86	42	45	25	69	33	41	22	57	30	15	10

Notes:
*The scenarios A and C denote alternatives hypotheses about world value-added based on average effective rates of protection of categories I and II products in each country. Differences in ERP between countries are due to prevailing exemptions.
*Calculations based on the Corden formula.

Source: World Bank (1991b).

convertible currency, regional integration in several areas has had mixed results: intra-regional trade is low; joint facilities created to foster integration have not functioned; the TU, a mechanism aimed at fostering industrialization, has been turned into a protection scheme; regional training institutes have almost been closed down in recent years.

These setbacks are mainly due to the decision-making process. Deficiencies in decision making have surfaced in recent years due to the economic crisis. Structural adjustment programmes have been implemented in each member country and now in the UDEAC as a whole. Key elements in the regional reform programme include: determination of a fixed schedule for specific objectives, restriction of areas in which unanimity in decision-making is required in order to reduce micro-nationalism, and institutional reforms. A court of law with jurisdiction over conflicts among member countries is being contemplated. The common external tariff has also been restructured to separate instruments with budgetary concerns from those aimed at providing protection.

From the presentation above, regional integration offers interesting possibilities for economic growth in the UDEAC region. These possibilities include: the scale economies argument; efficiency in resource allocation, with the driving force being comparative advantage; and the creation of an environment for designing and implementing policy with less probability of reversals. Whether these possibilities will lead to economic growth depends on (1) the resource endowment of member states and their level of development; (2) the existence and form of organization of interest groups; and (3) regional dependence on regional markets, and their access to alternative markets.

Notes

1. The colonial name for the CAR was Oubangui-Chari.
2. This section uses data gathered for a study, financed by the *Réseau sur les politiques industrielles en Afrique*, CODESRIA, on industrial competitiveness in the UDEAC, presented in Bela (1992, 1994), Bela and Amvouna (1993).
3. This pattern most probably continues beyond this period, but sustaining data are very fragmentary.
4. Economic Community of West African States, the UDEAC's counterpart in West Africa.

5. During a recent independence anniversary TV programme in the CAR (8 August 1994, 'Independence Memoirs' by the political leaders of that time on the eve of the anniversary date), a pre-independence political leader claimed that the Congolese railway network is joint property. This resentment, probably shared in Chad, has its roots in the fact that the death rate during the construction of the railway was 600 per cent convicts in 1925 in Congo, against 30 per cent in Côte d'Ivoire (Buell, 1928) and 61.7 per cent in Cameroon (Mbembe, *Le Monde Diplomatique*, no. 373, April 1985). Moreover, in Congo, victims were mainly natives from the CAR and Chad.

6. In August and September 1993, two decisions were taken that indirectly restrict convertibility. The August decision restricted the physical exchange of CFA to foreign currency notes only within the African CFA zone countries, and the September decision made it impossible to exchange Central African CFA notes in West African CFA zone countries, and vice versa.

7. Statistical and fiscal declaration documents were harmonized by Act no. 13/77-UDEAC-260. Accordingly, accounting and fiscal practices have been harmonized throughout the region.

8. Bilateral accords in the co-ordination of transports between Cameroon and the CAR and Chad, respectively, have been more effective than the regional initiative.

9. The word 'expert' here refers to a title and not to a qualification.

10. More than once, the council of heads of state of UDEAC has criticized the management committee for sending too many issues to their arbitration, issues that had already been sent by the expert committee to the management committee for arbitration. In addition, secretariat staff members are more responsive to their governments than to their superiors at the UDEAC (see UDEAC, 1988).

11. The only exception was agricultural products.

12. The name 'single tax' refers to the fact that it replaces all indirect taxes for a registered firm. This name does not imply that a single tax rate applies to all goods in all countries.

13. Mytelka identifies as a separate product every decision fixing TU rates on a product. Frequent changes in the TU rates on a given product therefore led to double counting. Bela (1992) distinguishes products and decisions.

14. Although the TU rate applied on any given firm's products is determined by the governing bodies of the UDEAC, this rate is proposed by the country in which the firm is located, principally taking into account the structure of national industry.

15. Because of these flaws, fiscal reform has eliminated these alternative taxes as part of the new approach to regional integration (see Part 4.3 below).

16. Given the political conditions in the region, at least at the conception of the UDEAC, it is arguable that any decisions were really made by member states. But whether or not the behaviour of officials in member states forsters the process is compatible with their stance on this issue.

17. Accountants receive their certification from the UDEAC, which allows them to work anywhere in the region.
18. An illustration is the January 1995 decision by the Gabonese government to send home thousands of African workers, most of them from the UDEAC. This is not unusual for Gabon. As an underpopulated and very rich country, Gabon needs foreign workers. But it attracts too many job-seekers, most of them illegal.
19. The CFA was devalued in January 1994, a move that is expected to restore growth. Its impact on regional integration is assessed below.
20. See Tamba (1994).
21. See also Yeats (1994) for the analysis of the importance of OECD trade with Africa.

References

Banque Mondiale (1992) 'Coopération régionale et ajustement structurelle: programme de réformes de la politique fiscalo-douanière pour les Etats membres de l'Union Douanière et Economique de l'Afrique Centrale (UDEAC)'. (Washington, DC).

Banque Mondiale (1994) *Rapport sur le développement dans le monde 1994* (Washington, DC).

Bela, L. (1992) 'Identification des Industries Compétitives dans les Pays Membres de l'UDEAC', research report submitted to the Réseau sur les Politiques Industrielles en Afrique (July).

Bela, L. (1994), 'Efficacité comparée en 1991 des firmes camerounaises et centrafricaines agréées au régime de la taxe unique en UDEAC', research report submitted to the Réseau sur les Politiques Industrielles en Afrique.

Bela, L. and A. Amvouna (1993) 'Calcul des indicateurs de protection et d'avantage comparatif des entreprises camerounaises agréées au régime de la taxe unique en UDEAC', research report submitted to the Réseau sur les Politiques Industrielles en Afrique.

Buell, R. L. (1928) 'The native problem in Africa' 1, report to the committee of international research of Harvard University and Radcliffe College, vol. 1 (Macmillan).

CEA (same as ECA) (1981) 'Mission d'évaluation de l'UDEAC et possibilités d' élargissement de la coopération économique en Afrique du centre: rapport à la conférence annuelle du Conseil des Chefs d' Etats de l' UDEAC', Libreville, 17–19 December.

Collier P. and J. Gunning (1994) 'Trade Policy and Regional Integration: Implication for the Relationship Between Europe and Africa', CEPR Discussion Paper no. 1012.

Devarajan, S. and J. de Melo (1990) 'Membership in the CFA Zone: Odyssean Journey of Trojan Horse?', in A. Chibber and S. Fischer (eds), *Economic Reform in Sub-saharan Africa* (World Bank).

Devarajan, S. and D. Rodrik (1991) 'Do the benefits of fixed exchange rates outweigh their costs? The franc zone in Africa', NBER Working Paper. Cambridge, MA.

Grossman, G. M. and E. Helpman (1993) 'Trade Wars and Trade Talks, Working Paper no. 4280 (National Bureau of Economic Research). Cambridge, MA.

Grossman, G. M. and E. Helpman (1994) 'The Politics of Free Trade Agreements', CEPR Discussion Paper no. 908. London.

Kitchen, R. and D. Sarley (1992) 'Industrial efficiency and policy reform: the Central African Customs and Economic Union (UDEAC)', *Industry and Development*, January, pp. 57–80.

Langhammer, R. J. and U. Hiemenz (1991) 'Regional Integration Among Developing Countries: Survey of Past Performance and Agenda for Future Action', UNDP–World Bank Trade Expansion Program, Occasional Paper no. 7.

Lyakurwa, W., A. McKay, N. Ng'eno and W. Kennes (1993) 'Regional Integration in Sub-Saharan Africa: A Survey of Experiences and Issues', Framework Paper, AERC.

Maxwell Stamp Associates (MSA) (1987) 'Etudes Techniques: Assistance en vue de l' Elaboration d' un Plan Directeur d'Industrialization au Cameroon', mimeo.

Mohammed, A. B. (1994) 'Le Fonds Monétaire International et les PAS en Afrique Subsaharienne: Analyse Comparative des Expériences d'Adjustement des Pays Membres de la BEAC', Thesis, University of Yaoundé II.

Mytelka, L. K. (1975) 'Fiscal Politics and Regional Redistribution: Bargaining Strategies in Asymmetrical Integrative System', *Journal of Conflict Resolution*, **19** (1).

Panagariya, A., and R. Findlay (1994) 'A Political–Economy Analysis of Free Trade Areas and Customs Unions', Policy Research Working Paper 1261 (Washington, DC: World Bank Trade Policy Division).

Tamba, I (1994) 'Les Mesures d'accompagnement de la dévaluation de janvier 1994', Finance et Developpement

UDEAC (1988) *Proposition d'une Nouvelle Stratégie d'Intégration Economique et Sociale de l'UDEAC* (Bangui: UDEAC).

World Bank (1991a) 'Intra-Regional Trade in Sub-Saharan Africa', Report no. 7686–AFR (Economics and Finance Division, Technical Department, Africa Region).

World Bank (1991b) 'Coopération Régionale et Ajustement Structurel: Programme de Réformes de la Politique Fiscalo–Douanière, pour les Etats Membres de l'UDEAC' (Industry and Energy Division, Department of West and Central Africa).

World Bank (1994a) *Adjustment in Africa: Reforms, Results and the Road Ahead* (Washington, DC: World Bank).

World Bank (1994b) *Rapport sur le développement dans le monde 1994*, (Washington, DC: World Bank).

Yeats, A. J. (1994) 'What are OECD Trade Preferences Worth to Sub-Saharan Africa?', Policy Research Working Paper no. 1254 (Washington, DC: World Bank, Trade Policy Division).

5 Regional Integration and Economic Liberalization in Eastern and Southern Africa

Louis A. Kasekende and
Nehemiah Ng'eno*

5.1 INTRODUCTION

Regional integration (RI) in eastern and southern Africa dates back to the early part of the twentieth century. The region indeed boasts two of the oldest regional integration schemes: the South African Customs Union (SACU) dates back to 1910 and the origins of the former East African community can be traced to 1917, when free trade was established between Kenya and Uganda. Even the former federation of Rhodesia and Nyasaland, formed in 1953, predated the European Economic Community, established in 1957. However, almost all the current regional integration schemes in the region, except SACU, were established after 1970 (Lyakurwa *et al.*, 1993).

The Lagos Plan of Action (LPA) and the Final Act of Lagos of 1980 provided a framework through which the regional groupings in subSaharan Africa could evolve into an African Economic Community (AEC) by the year 2000. The four sub-regional blocs were the Economic Community of West African States (ECOWAS); the Economic Community of Central African States (ECCAS); the Preferential Trade Area for Eastern and Southern African States (PTA); and the Arab Maghreb Union in Northern Africa.

The Abuja Treaty of 1991, recognizing the difficulties of estab-

---

* Dr Louis A. Kasekende is Executive Director of Research & Policy, Bank of Uganda, and Dr N. K. Ng'eno is Chief Economist, Office of the President, Kenya. The views expressed in this paper are those of the authors and do not in any way represent the view of the institutions they work for.

lishing a continent-wide common market by the year 2000, extended the formation of an African single market to 2025.

The subSaharan Africa countries have joined one regional integration group or another with the hope of addressing common problems in a collective and co-ordinated manner. One objective has been enhancement of growth and development through a collective effort. Regional economic co-operation has been considered as a means of promoting increased intra-regional trade and economies of scale by pooling small and fragmented domestic markets to support industrialization strategies.

The eastern and southern Africa region currently has the highest number of regional integration groupings (De la Torre and Kelly, 1992). The Common Market for Eastern and Southern Africa (COMESA) and the Southern Africa Development Community (SADC) are the major groupings in the region. The others are SACU, the Indian Ocean Commission (IOC) and the Rand Monetary Area. Rwanda and Burundi, while members of COMESA, also belong to a Central African grouping, the Economic Community of the Countries of the Great Lakes (CEPGL), which in turn is a member of ECCAS. The former East African Community is also in the process of being revived. Some countries of the region also belong to two other regional organization, namely: the Kagera Basin Organization and the Inter-Governmental Authority on Drought and Desertification (IGADD).

Regional integration schemes in SSA have on balance failed to achieve their stated objectives. This is mainly a result of incompatibility of the original goals with the political and economic realities of the day. Many regional groupings set up before independence either collapsed or have remained weak. A good example is the East African Community, which collapsed in 1977 after about 60 years of existence. The Federation of Rhodesia and Nyasaland collapsed because its objectives were inconsistent with the realities of the independence era. The regional integration schemes established in the post-independence era have equally foundered for political and economic reasons. This contributed to the loss of enthusiasm for regionalism in the 1970.[1]

There has, however, been renewed interest in regionalism in recent years. De la Torre and Kelly (1992) concluded that this has been spurred by the difficulties in concluding the Uruguay Round of multilateral trade negotiations. The movement towards a single market in the European Union and the creation of the North

American Free Trade Agreement (NAFTA) involving Mexico, the USA and Canada has rekindled fears that countries outside these trading blocks might be excluded from those markets. The creation of new regional blocks can be viewed as a defensive mechanism, with countries afraid of being locked out of the markets of the new regional blocks applying to join or hurriedly forming their own.

Baldwin (1993) had called this response a 'domino effect' of increased regionalism. The conversion of the Southern African Development Co-ordination Committee (SADCC) into a community and the re-emergence of the Eastern Community in the form of East African Co-operation would appear to be a result of the frustrations of the slow pace of the development of the PTA and a sense that nations closer together and with common interest are better placed to take advantage of regional co-operation.

This chapter reviews the prospects of regionalism in SSA, with emphasis on integration in eastern and southern Africa. A number of contradictions and inconsistencies that have arisen out of attempting to implement structural adjustment programmes *vis-à-vis* the aims and objectives of the regional organization are also highlighted.

5.2   PROBLEMS OF INTEGRATION IN SSA

Regional integration schemes have historically been viewed as a means to faster development through co-ordinated industrial development. Member countries expected increased industrial output to be sustained by increased regional trade resulting from removal of trade barriers. Consequently, inward-looking industrial strategies were coupled with intra-regional trade liberalization.

Conflicts between the inward-looking industrial strategies and trade liberalization among regional integration schemes have been well documented in De la Torre and Kelly (1992), OECD (1993) and Lyakurwa *et al.* (1993). The conflicts have always arisen from attempts to remove trade barriers, allocate industries, establish common external tariffs and implement rules of origin. In addition, attempts to encourage factor mobility, especially labour, have been a source of serious recrimination among the countries in the groupings.

The initial conditions prevailing in many of these countries, especially the different levels of development, and in particular differences in the stages of industrial development and levels of macroeconomic stability, have led to problems in policy implementation and co-ordination. These problems have slowed the pace of regional economic co-operation and in some instance have caused the collapse of some regional integration schemes. Deeper understanding of the origins of these problems is necessary if future and current integration schemes in SSA are to succeed.

The polarization effects of integration schemes have been greatest where regionalism has been used as an instrument for import-substitution industrialization (ISI) policies. This has been especially so where some of the members of the regional grouping have been more industrialized than others. This situation has tended to create two basic problems:

(1) in the more industrialized countries, vested interest groups in the protected industries have resisted intra-regional trade liberalization;
(2) poor countries have resisted faster trade liberalization, in the form of lower tariffs, for fear of revenue loss.

Furthermore, the poor countries view the protection of industries of the more advanced countries within a custom union as a disadvantage to them in the absence of a mechanism that distributes benefits equitably. Trade liberalization in this instance is stalled by divergent views on the impact of intra-regional liberalization.

The anti-export bias of ISI policies, associated with past integration schemes, proved to be the most important mitigating factor against intra-regional trade liberalization. For instance, the restrictive trade practices, such as import licensing and other quantitative restrictions, contributed to unfavourable external balances which were invariably dealt with through exchange controls coupled with fixed exchange rate regimes. This in turn contributed to the overvaluation of regional currencies. The consequence is that the region found it cheaper to rely on imports of intermediate inputs instead of developing local sources. Moreover, the shortage of foreign exchange meant that countries had to look for markets that could offer the best credit facilities. These markets were often those outside the region and, most importantly, in the North. It is not surprising therefore that, as a means of promoting trade, regional integrations designed payment arrangements intended to reduce the use of foreign currencies and offered implicit credit facilities. A good example is the PTA clearing house, where member countries are encouraged to quote in their respective currencies.

The deterioration in internal balance also contributed to poor intra-regional trade. Large budgetary deficits resulting from unsustainable increases in public expenditure made it difficult to reform the economies of the region. For example, budget deficits contributed to inflation and overvaluation of regional currencies and therefore to making exports uncompetitive. Budget deficits also made the scope for trade liberalization difficult for revenue reasons.

Another drawback to regional integration in subSaharan Africa is that countries with few or no common interests have united. Many of the countries have little trade among themselves and indeed, have well-established trading links with countries outside the region. For many countries, production structures developed during the colonial period have not changed and often do not favour intra-regional trade. Attempts to increase intra-regional trade in these circumstances have proved difficult.[2]

Ideological differences and lack of political commitment to implement integration policies, though not normally acknowledged, have also played a significant role in the failure of these groups. Countries have been unwilling to cede national sovereignty where regional decisions are perceived as being against national interests. This has been common with policies related to customs regulation, movement of labour and redistribution of industries. Even where countries have actively participated in the drafting of the protocols of regional integration groupings, in the end they lack commitment to ratify the protocols. It is indeed not unusual even for heads of state to take actions contrary to earlier decisions.

The speedy manner in which countries in SSA have rushed to form regional groups of one form or another reflects the lack of seriousness.

Among other factors, it is often argued that the implementation of structural adjustment programmes has contributed to the weakening of regional integration groups. Almost all countries in the PTA region are implementing structural adjustment programmes in which multilateral trade liberalization dominates. These programmes require the rationalization and lowering of tariffs by the participating countries. The problem facing integration arrangements in Africa is that the present reform agenda and the structural adjustment programmes do not necessarily take into account the regional integration dimension. It is not generally correct, how-ever, to argue that unilateral trade liberalization has weakened regional integration. With the elimination of over-valued curren-cies and non-tariff barriers, the environment for trade is improved and the objective of trade-based integration enhanced (Collier and Gunning, 1994; Langhammer and Hiemenz, 1991). The issue then becomes one of according preferences to members of the regional groups. It should be stressed from the outset that regional integra-tion is not a substitute for efficient macroeconomic management of the domestic economies.

Another problem is that member countries have failed to ration-alize co-operation arrangements within the region. Regional groups have been established with little regard for the necessary initial conditions for integration,[3] not only diverting attention from the wider goal but in many cases leading to wasteful duplication of activities. The best example is COMESA, which brings together over 22 countries, ranging from Angola in the south to Eritrea in the north. It groups the relatively more-industrialized – Mauritius, Zimbabwe and Kenya (and potentially South Africa) – and the least-industrialized – Somalia, Uganda, Djibouti and Ethiopia.

Moreover, COMESA encompasses about five other regional groups, with some members belonging to the three associations. In addition to COMESA, Tanzania also belongs to SADC and EAC, and Lesotho, Namibia and Swaziland are members of SADC and SACU (Lyakurwa *et al.*, 1993). Potential for conflicts of interests exists. It is already evident that arriving at the consensus necessary for the implementation of regional integration policies within COMESA is often difficult. Proliferation and duplication of func-tions give rise, at the regional level, to conflicts over mandates and to divided loyalty among governments. At the governmental level, they impose heavy financial and administrative burdens. The insti-tutions' budgets are invariably too small for the tasks governments assign to them. Insufficient funding thus prevents these institutions from making meaningful contributions towards the objectives of regional groupings. The contra view being raised now is that smaller regional bodies are more viable in the short run. It is argued that such smaller but well-functioning units would then form a bigger block in the long run. Indeed, some SADC member countries have expressed their desire to break away from COMESA.

5.3   ECONOMIC INTEGRATION IN EASTERN AND SOUTHERN AFRICA

Economic Co-operation in East Africa

Economic co-operation started in East Africa with the formation of a customs union between Kenya and Uganda in 1917. Tanganyika joined in 1927. The union was relatively advanced, with a common external tariff, free trade, free movement of labour and capital, and a single authority for collection of import duty. Customs revenue was allocated to members states according to the ultimate destination of imports. A common currency was used in the union and there was joint administration of transport and communication and other common services. The union had no legislative or administrative organization. It was run by the colonial governors, who met at least once a year to deliberate on issues covering tariffs, railway rates and scientific research. The governors, however, had no legal or constitutional power to pass legislation affecting the activities of the union. Although the governors acquired these powers with the establishment of the East Africa High Commission (EAHC) in 1948, the customs union had little impact in promoting interterritorial development. This was because the Commission had no independent source of revenue, leaving its activities to be financed from limited contributions by the member states.

The perception that the EAHC failed to contribute to the development of the members states led to the appointment of the Raisman Commission, which was also charged with the duty of examining the longstanding view by Uganda and Tanaganyika that the Union benefited Kenya the most. The commission reported in 1961 and recommended ways of raising independent sources of revenue and the establishment of a mechanism of fiscal redistribution among the member states.

The East Africa Common Services Organization (EACSO) replaced EAHC in December 1961. EACSO had more authoritative legislative and administrative bodies. Its source of revenue, as recommended by the Raisman Commission, was the distributable pool. Under this scheme, 6 per cent of customs and excise revenues and 40 per cent of revenues from income tax on company profits in the manufacturing and finance sectors were to be allocated to the pool. The activities of EACSO were to be allocated 50 per cent of the funds from the pool and the rest were to be distributed equally among the three countries. The redistributive effect of the arrangement was that, while Kenya would be the largest source of funds *to* the pool, each country received the same amount *from* the pool.

Despite the existence of the distributable pool, the perception by Uganda and Tanganyika that the common market did not favour them continued. The two countries argued that the tax redistributed through the pool was not large enough to offset the disparity in economic development, which was perceived to be disproportionately higher in Kenya. There was also disagreement about the allocation of industries and the movement of labour. An attempt to address these problems was made with the Kampala Agreement of 1964. This endeavoured to encourage increased export from trade deficit countries to surplus countries. It also aimed to persuade firms in Kenya and Uganda to relocate to Tanzania. Import quotas were also allowed to be imposed on Kenyan goods by the deficit countries where productive capacity existed in these countries. Although the quota arrangements of the agreement were implemented, no progress was made in the allocation of new industries.

The failure of the common market's industrial policy led to Tanzania's decision to establish its own central bank and currency in 1965, which also contributed to the weakening of EACSO.

The East African Community (EAC)

In an effort to save the common market, the Philip Commission was set up; its recommendation formed the basis for the Treaty of East African Co-operation signed in June 1967. The treaty established the East African Community. The objective of the EAC was 'to strengthen and regulate the industrial, commercial and other relations of the partner states to the end that there shall be accelerated, harmonious and balanced development and sustained expansion of economic activities the benefits whereof shall be equitably shared' (Treaty of the EAC, 1967). It is evident that the treaty emphasized a development programme whose benefits would be equitably distributed among the member states.

The treaty, also recognizing the importance of free trade, called for the removal of all trade barriers. The community had a common external tariff and common excise duties. The taxation and fiscal policies were to be used to promote industrial development. Commercial laws, transport and economic development policies were to be harmonized. There was to be free exchange of currency and uninhibited movement of current-account payments in the common market. The treaty, however, did not fully address the issue of the movement of factors of production across the member states; in fact, it recognized the right of each country to restrict the movement of certain categories of capital.

The treaty provided specific and clear guidelines on the redistribution of the gains from the common market. The main instruments for the purpose were:

- the establishment of the East African Development Bank (EADB), whose main objective was to promote industrial development in the community;
- the establishment of the tax transfer system to be used to redistribute industries directly in the community; and
- the replacement of the distributional pool with the distribution of common services among the member states as a means of income and employment distribution.

The redistributive role of EADB was construed as promotion of balanced industrial development. Although the contributions to the bank's capital from each member state were the same, the investments of the bank were to be 38.75 per cent in Tanzania and Uganda and 22.5 per cent in Kenya. Moreover, the bank's redistributive role was limited by the mandate that it had to finance only viable projects. This led to a large share of investment funds being channelled to Kenya during 1971–3 (Kim, 1979). Kim also argued that the absence of co-ordinated industrial planning by the member states limited the effectiveness of EADB.

The direct distribution aspects of the EAC treaty were effected through the decentralization and the transfer of the headquarters for the common services, which were previously all in Kenya. The East African Railways and Harbours was spilt into two, the harbours headquarters moved to Tanzania, while the railways remained in Nairobi. Tanzania also got the community headquarters and Uganda was allocated the regional headquarters of the East African Post and Telegraphs and the newly-created EADB. The headquarters of the East African Airways remained in Kenya. Although the decentralization move was done as a means of redistributing the components of the common services that generated income and employment, it was acknowledged that some losses in efficiency, especially those related to administrative economies, would occur.

The most important aspect of the treaty with regard to the distribution of industry was the transfer tax system. The transfer tax was a policy instrument granted to the less-developed members of the common market to protect their industries from those of the more-developed partners. The transfer tax was essentially a tariff and was imposed by a country on the imports from a country with which it had a deficit in intra-territorial trade in manufactures. The deficit country could levy the tax only if it had a production capacity to produce the product within three months after the imposition of the tax, of a least 15 per cent of domestic consumption of the good or an output value of £100 000. The transfer tax imposed on a partner country was not to exceed the trade deficit on manufactured goods of the taxing country with respect to the partner country. The tax was also not to exceed 50 per cent of the common external tariff on the commodity and was not to be in effect for more than eight years.

If a transfer tax caused a significant deviation of trade away from goods originally from partner states to goods from the rest of the world (for example, if a tax on a partner country's exports increased prices of the partner's goods relative to world prices and therefore reduced imports from the partner country) steps had to be taken to minimize this effect. The treaty also forbade selling goods to partner countries at prices lower than those in the domestic markets. At the time the treaty was signed, Tanzania had a trade deficit with both Kenya and Uganda, and Uganda had a trade deficit with Kenya. Tanzania was therefore to impose transfer taxes on Kenya and Uganda, and Uganda was to impose taxes on Kenyan goods. Kenya could not impose any transfer taxes on the goods from the other two partner countries. The transfer tax system was intended to reduce the advantage Kenya had in the location of industries.

The use of the transfer tax as an instrument of redistribution of industrial development in East Africa would not have been possible had it not been accepted that there was historically an unequal distribution of industries in the common market. The importance of the transfer tax therefore lies in how effective it was as a mechanism of industrial development in the common market.

The community also had a legislative assembly with nine appointed members from each country plus the EAC ministers and other ministerial committee and council members. The East African

Community Legislative Authority (CLA) passed Bills that, before being enacted, had to be approved by the authority. The community institutions, the authority, the councils, the secretariat and the legislative assembly worked relatively well until 1971. The minor problems that occurred during the first few years of the community resulted from increased economic nationalism in the common market. Kenya made aggressive efforts to attract foreign capital, thus impinging on the work of the transfer tax system. Uganda imposed exchange controls on other partner states and started expelling other nationals employed in Uganda. Tanzania leaned more towards China for its imports. These problems were immediately intensified after General Idi Amin took over power from Dr Milton Obote in a military *coup de'état* in 1971. President Nyerere's refusal to recognize Amin severely reduced the role of the authority in community affairs.

The imbalance in inter-regional trade was a major factor in the treaty's emphasis on the redistribution of industries in East Africa. Industrial redistribution was intended to increase inter-state trade in manufactures from the less-developed members of the common market to Kenya. The change in the pattern of inter-regional trade, especially in the manufactures, in the common market after 1967 is supposed to indicate the impact of the treaty in industrial redistribution. This is particularly important when dealing with the impact of the transfer tax, because this tax was primarily aimed at redistributing industries.

Kim (1979), using inter-regional trade data for the years 1964–73, shows that the treaty actually increased the unequal distribution of benefits from the common market. During this period, Kim shows that Kenya's share of intra-regional trade declined from 22 per cent to 13 per cent. He argues that East African economic integration was not geared to deal with the inability of the less-developed partners of the common market to overcome the inequality in the production of manufactured goods. Kim also argues that the transfer tax was not an effective method of increasing inter-state trade in the common market. He notes that the tax was designed to protect the partner's domestic import-competing industries and therefore did not lead to the development of complementary industries in the common market. He supports his proposition by showing that for the period 1969–73 the volume of traded goods transfer taxed as a percentage of total imports on the average accounted for about 15 per cent for Tanzania and about 10 per cent for Uganda. Such low percentages of taxed goods, Kim suggests, show how the transfer tax system played an insignificant role in reducing the inequality of inter-regional trade.

Hazelwood (1975) is more optimistic than Kim as far as the impact of the treaty on inter-regional trade is concerned. He shows that the value of inter-regional trade in manufactures of East African origin was 24 per cent greater in 1973 than in 1967. The shares of the increased inter-regional trade in manufactures, however, differed among the states. Tanzania's increase in exports within the common market is shown to be smaller than Kenya's but proportionately higher than its share in 1967. Kenya's export of domestic manufactures to its partners in 1973 was half what it was in 1967, but Tanzania's had doubled over the same period.

Hazelwood argues that the inequality in inter-regional trade in manufactures in absolute terms was greater in 1973 than in 1967, in the sense that Uganda and Tanzania had larger regional trade deficits in 1973 than in 1967, while Kenya had a larger trade surplus. Using the treaty's criterion of equality of trade, Hazelwood argues that Tanzania moved closer to balance in inter-regional trade in manufactures, but Uganda's trade was less balanced. More precisely, he argues that 3 per cent of Tanzania's manufactured imports from Kenya were taxed, while 8 per cent of Uganda's imports from Kenya were taxed. He also shows that the flow of the goods from Kenya that were under the transfer tax in Tanzania increased faster than that of the untaxed goods. On the other hand, the flow of taxed goods from Uganda to Tanzania and from Kenya to Uganda declined, while those that were untaxed increased. There appears to have been no correlation between the tax transfer and the change in the pattern of trade in the taxed products. Under these circumstances it would be difficult to determine the influence of the transfer tax on intra-regional trade from trade flow data, at least in the first few years of the common market. This is complicated by the fact that the transfer tax ceased as an effective tool in 1973.

It would be very difficult to pinpoint a major cause for the collapse of the EAC. The problems that faced the East African corporations, and the failure to arrive at concrete and honest solutions to these problems, certainly paved the way. There was no political commitment to deal with the difficulties that riddled the corporations. (The corporations with the major problems were the East African Railways, East African Airways and, to a lesser extent, East African Harbours.) It is safe to say, however, that there was a lack of political will by the East African leaders to ensure the continuity of the EAC.

Short-run narrow economic nationalism was allowed to override the greater long-run economic benefits of the community. The refusal by President Nyerere to recognize Amin and the failure of the East African Authority to meet and transact community matters weakened the functions of the EAC. The closure of the Kenya–Tanzania border precipitated the collapse of the community. Tanzania's dissatisfaction with the EAC occurred because of its impatience with the trade imbalance and the unequal industrial development in the community, which were perceived to have favoured Kenya.

For its part, Kenya seemed too eager to see the community collapse, and as it did so was willing and ready to devise what it claimed would be an acceptable formula to share the assets of the community. Having lost faith in the EAC, Kenya argued that viable East African economic integration had to include more than three partner states. Kenya called for a larger economic community, from Sudan to Mozambique, with the belief that if one partner state took a different stance on a policy issue it would not paralyse the union. Kenya argued strongly that ideological differences should have no effect on the success of an economic union.

At least in the last years of the EAC, Uganda cannot be blamed for the downfall of the community. Amin had ravaged Uganda both politically and economically. As it struggled for economic survival, its financial contributions to the community dwindled. Although Amin's constant disagreements with Nyerere reduced the effectiveness of the authority, a well-designed economic integration should survive personality or even ideological differences between leaders of nation states.

East African Economic Co-operation

The collapse of the EAC dealt a heavy blow to regionalism in Africa, because it had been seen as a model for the way toward an African Economic Union. The collapse also occasioned the disruption of economic and social affairs among East Africans. The closure of the border with Kenya and Tanzania led to a drastic reduction in official trade between the two countries and practically halted the movement of persons across the borders. This state of affairs remained until 1984, when Tanzania agreed to re-open the border.

The improvement of relations between Kenya and Tanzania

followed the signing of the East African Community Mediation Agreement of 1984, which resolved the problem of the division of assets and liabilities of the former EAC. The agreement also allowed for the operation of certain institutions, namely the EADB, the East African School of Librarianship, the Inter-University Council of East Africa, the Soroti Flying School and the Eastern and Southern African Management Institute, to continue to operate as joint institutions or common services of the three states. The agreement also opened a window for future co-operation through Article 14.02 of the agreement, which allowed for the exploration and identification of further areas for future co-operation, and for concrete arrangements to be worked out for such co-operation. One the basis of the mediation agreement, the heads of state of the three countries met in Nairobi on 15 July 1986 and agreed to establish a follow-up mechanism for renewed regional co-operation. A tri-partite summit of officials, which met on 21 June 1986, was formalized to work out the modalities of renewed co-operation.

After a series of meetings at head of state and official levels, it was finally agreed at a summit meeting in Nairobi on 22 November 1991 that co-operation among the three East African countries should be re-activated. A committee of the foreign ministers of the three states was appointed to work out in detail the form the co-operation should take and the areas it should cover. The recommendations of the committee were ratified by the three heads of state when they signed the 'Agreement to Establish the Permanent Tripartite Commission for East African Co-operation' and the 'Declaration on Closer East African Co-operation' at a meeting in Arusha on 30 November 1993. The meeting agreed on the following areas for co-operation: industry, science and technology, trade, transport and communication, security immigration, tourism, health and animal disease control, education and culture, and institutional matters. The Arusha summit was followed by a meeting of the heads of state in Kampala on 26 November 1994 at which the 'Protocol to Establish the Secretariat for East African Co-operation' was signed. The meeting decided that the EAC secretariat was to be operational by 1 March 1995.

The Kampala meeting considered and endorsed the recommendations of the Permanent Tripartite Commission report. The report outlined the priority areas for co-operation as transport and communications; trade and industry; investment promotions; and immigration and security. The summit agreed that institutions responsible for transport and communications in the region should meet and prepare mechanisms for the implementation of the recommended means of co-operation. On trade, industry and investment, it was agreed that private sector joint ventures and enterprises would be encouraged; tariff rates and customs procedures would be harmonized through regular consultations and exchange of information; standards for goods would be harmonized and rationalized; investment promotion policies would be harmonized; and the cross-border initiative would be adopted and implemented, especially the removal of tariff and non-tariff barriers to trade. To encourage the free movement of citizens of the three countries across the borders, it was agreed that standard travel documents for East African nationals would be introduced and that existing travel documents would be recognized; separate counters for East African nationals would be introduced at international airports, and all countries would issue national identity cards to their citizens; and more border crossing points would be opened, to be manned by officials with adequate mandates to deal with cases arising. On security, the meeting agreed to increase co-operation on border security, exchange of information, training and co-ordination of security operations. The heads of state also agreed that expulsions or deportations of citizens of any country should be done after appropriate consultations with the diplomatic missions concerned in the host country. They also agreed to strengthen co-operation and co-ordination of law enforcement activities to fight and eradicate drug-trafficking in the region.

Some progress on economic co-operation has been achieved since the renewal of the East African Economic Co-operation. The most important have been in the areas of trade, customs, fiscal and monetary co-ordination, exchange and payments systems, and immigration. There have also been extensive consultations and effective co-operation in transport and communications. This is especially true of the railways systems, where co-operation has included shared use of wagons on a rental basis. On the payments system, the three governments have made attempts to increase capital flows in the region by allowing quotation of currencies in local money markets and relaxing the flow of investments to the East African countries.

The biggest setback to the new co-operation, however, was the failure of the secretariat to take off as scheduled on 1 March 1995. This was a result of the failure by Kenya to nominate the executive secretary of the secretariat, largely because of political differences between Kenya and Uganda. The stalemate has clearly reduced the momentum for the implementation of the decisions of the EAC, which has been built up within a short period of time. The impasse demonstrates that regionalism in Africa is dictated by other than economic issues.

The Preferential Trade Area of Eastern and Southern Africa (PTA)

Introduction

In accordance with the Lagos Plan of Action, the East and Southern African countries created the Preferential Trade Area (PTA) in 1982. The objective of the PTA as defined in the PTA treaty are:

> The promotion of co-operation and development in all fields of economic activity, particularly in trade, customs, industry, transport, communication agriculture, natural resources and monetary affairs; with the overall aim of raising the standard of living of its people, of fostering closer relations among its member state; to create a common market by the year 2000 which would allow free movement of goods, capital and labour within the sub-region, and contributing to the progress and development of African countries.

The functioning and development of the PTA was to be reviewed in accordance with the provisions of the treaty with a view to establishing an Economic Community for Eastern and Southern African States. Indeed, in December 1993, a Common Market for Eastern and Southern Africa (COMESA) was formally established as a first step toward this goal.

The COMESA currently covers most of the countries in Eastern and Southern Africa with a total population of 207 million people and GDP of US\$62 bn. Its current membership is 22 countries: Angola, Burundi, Comoros, Djibouti, Eritrea, Ethiopia, Kenya, Lesotho, Madagascar, Malawi, Mauritius, Mozambique, Namibia, Rwanda, Seychelles, Somalia, Sudan, Swaziland, Tanzania, Uganda, Zambia and Zimbabwe. Three potential members, Botswana, South Africa and Zaire, are yet to join.

The region has immense diversities in economic size, per capita income, level of industrialization and cultural background (See Tables 5.1 and 5.2). Six of the member countries have a population size of fewer than 2 million people while four countries, Sudan, Kenya,

Table 5.1   SSA population and income diversity

	Gross domestic savings		Population (millions), 1992	GNP per capita (US$), 1992
	1970	*1992*		
Angola	—	—	—	—
Burundi	4	–2	5.8	210
Comoros	—	—	—	—
Djibouti	—	—	—	—
Ethiopia	11	–1	54	110
Kenya	24	15	25.7	310
Lesotho	–32	–39	1.9	590
Malawi	11	2	9.1	210
Madagascar	—	—	12.4	230
Mauritius	11	25	1.1	2700
Mozambique	—	–19	16.5	60
Namibia	—	2	1.5	1610
Rwanda	3	–1	7.3	250
Seychelles	—	—	—	—
Somalia	7	—	8.3	—
Sudan	15	—	26.5	—
Swaziland	—	—	—	—
Tanzania	20	5	25.9	110
Uganda	16	–1	17.5	170
Zimbabwe	21	10	10.4	570

Source: World Bank, *World Development Report*, 1994.

Ethiopia and Tanzania, account for about 60 per cent of the population of the region. About 40 per cent of the GDP of the region is generated in Kenya, Ethiopia and Zimbabwe. The income per capita ranges from as low as US$60 for Mozambique to as high as US$2700 for Mauritius; only five members states have per capita income of over US$300. By and large, the countries in the region are very poor, with minimal potential to support large trade flows in differentiated products. This view is supported by studies using gravity models that find no evidence that countries in sub-Saharan Africa trade less with each other than would be expected given their low trade potential.

On the other hand, subSaharan Africa produces most of the world's gold, diamonds, platinum, chrome and manganese. It has 300 billion tons of coal, over 170 billion cubic metres of natural gas, over 200 billion metric tonnes of petroleum, and large quantities of uranium, nickel, copper and cobalt. The PTA, therefore, has great

Table 5.2 SSA economic indicators

	Average annual rate of inflation (%)		GDP growth rates (%)		Overall deficit	Overall surplus	Merchandise trade Imports Exports*	
	1970–80	1980–92	1970–80	1980–92	1992 (%)	1992 (%)	1992	1992
Angola	–	–	–	–	–	–	–	–
Burundi	10.7	4.5	4.2	4	–3.9	–	72	221
Comoros	–	–	–	–	–	–	–	–
Djibouti	–	–	–	–	–	–	–	–
Ethiopia	4.3	2.8	1.9	1.2	–4.5	–	169	799
Kenya	10.1	9.3	6.4	4	–4.6	–2.8	1339	1713
Lesotho	9.7	13.2	8.6	5.4	–3.7	–0.3	–	–
Malawi	8.8	15.1	5.8	2.9	–17.3	–1.7	383	718
Madagascar	9.9	16.4	0.5	1.1	–	–	–	–
Mauritius	15.3	8.6	6.8	6.2	–10.4	–0.8	1336	1774
Mozambique	–	38	–	0.4	–	–	–	–
Namibia	–	12.3	–	1	–	–6.9	–	–
Rwanda	15.1	3.6	4.7	1.4	–1.7	–7.2	–	–
Seychelles	–	–	–	–	–	–	–	–
Somalia	15.2	49.7	4.8	2.4	–	–	40	150
Sudan	14.5	42.8	5.8	–	–33	–	412	892
Swaziland	–	–	–	–	–	–	–	–
Tanzania	14.1	25.3	3	3.1	–8.4	–	400	1200
Uganda	–	–	–	4.5	–3.1	–	164	405
Zambia	7.6	48.4	1.4	0.8	–20	–	1100	1300
Zimbabwe	9.4	14.4	1.6	2.8	–11.1	–6.7	1235	2306

* US$ millions.

Source: African Development Bank. African Development Report, 1995 (Abidjan) and World Bank. World Development Report, 1994. (Washington, DC).

potential for restructuring its economy into a self-sustaining region. Now South Africa has overcome its political problems, it should provide the necessary industrial leadership to accelerate the growth and development of this region.

Measures Implemented by the PTA

Institutions   Since its establishment, the PTA has created specialized institutions to co-ordinate the development and integration process of the member states. Its major achievements include the establishment of the Trade and Development Bank for Eastern and Southern Africa (the PTA Bank), the PTA clearing house and the PTA Federation of Chambers of Commerce and Industry to enable the private sector to participate effectively in PTA programmes for development. To resolve trade disputes, the commercial arbitration centre was established in Djibouti and a PTA tribunal was instituted to settle disputes among member states arising from the interpretation or implementation of the treaty and common decisions.

Most success has evidently been achieved in the area of monetary co-operation, through the well-functioning clearing house and the PTA bank. The bank was established on 6 November 1985 as a financial wing of the economic integration arrangement. It is charged with providing financial assistance to promote economic and social development and trade, plus co-operating with other institutions engaged in promoting development of region.

The clearing house, which began operations on 1 February 1984, was set up by the member states in order to promote inter-PTA trade liberalization and expansion.

Its objectives include:

- to promote the use of national currencies in the settlement of all transaction among member states;
- to establish adequate machinery for the settlement of payments among the member states;
- to economize on the use of foreign exchange by the member states in their inter-state transactions;
- to encourage the member states to promote and liberalize trade among themselves; and
- to promote monetary and financial co-operation among the member states and closer relations among banks throughout the PTA sub-region as to contribute to the expansion of trade and economic activity among the member states.

The method of achieving trade liberalization through the use of the clearing house is the convertibility of all member countries' currencies into one another. This is attained through the commitment of the member central banks to discharge their respective foreign currency obligations as notified by the clearing house promptly at the end of the transaction period.

Instruments   The PTA bank has, since 1988, introduced a number of instruments through its trade window for the benefit of its member states. The primary objective of these schemes is to promote intra-PTA and extra-PTA trade. These include pre-shipment and post-shipment advances, bills discounting, export credit guarantees, export credit insurance, an export revolving fund and forward exchange cover. The economic sectors financed by the bank include: agriculture, mining, manufacturing and industry, tourism, transport, and energy. The bank plans to borrow from multilateral sources to boost its lending operations.

The regional grouping also adopted a unit of account, the UAPTA, which is equivalent to the SDR of the World Bank. Exchange rates for each of the local currencies *vis-à-vis* the UAPTA are worked out to facilitate the recording of transactions, especially by the clearing house and the bank. In August 1988, PTA member states launched PTA travellers' cheques, which are managed by the PTA bank on behalf of a committee of the PTA central bank governors. The cheques are only valid within the PTA/COMESA region and can only be converted into one of the local currencies of the region.

Other measures introduced to facilitate intra-PTA trade include:

- road customs transit declaration document
- PTA customs bond guarantee scheme
- simplification and harmonization of trade documents and procedures
- harmonized commodity description and coding system for customs purpose
- the PTA regional ASYCUDA/EUROTRADE centre
- the PTA trade information network (TINET)
- common vehicle insurance through the 'Yellow Card'.

Tariff reduction   The most important objective of the PTA was to promote intra-regional trade by way of trade liberalization measures. The PTA trade liberalization programme started in 1984 and was expected to be completed by the end of September 1992. The initial tariff reductions were to be effected as follows:

- luxury goods – 10 per cent

- manufactured goods (excluding luxury items)
  - highly competitive consumers goods – 30 per cent
  - non-durable goods – 35 per cent
  - durable goods – 40 per cent
  - consumer goods of particular importance to economic development – 70 per cent

- raw materials
  - agricultural – 50 per cent
  - non agricultural – 60 per cent

- intermediates – 65 per cent

- capital goods (excluding transport equipment) – 70 per cent

These tariff reductions were to followed by reductions of 25 per cent every two years.

Under the treaty, quantitative restrictions and other non-tariff barriers were to be relaxed and eventually removed by 1992. The programme for removal of these restrictions was, however, not fully defined.

High tariff reductions on capital goods, intermediates and raw material signified the importance attached to industrial growth in the region. The potential for trade liberalization was, however, blunted by limiting the preferential treatment to a prescribed number of goods in a common list. There were only 232 goods in the original list. The treaty stipulated that goods could be added to the common list only if they met the conditions laid down under protocols or the rules of origin. The treaty specified that goods could only qualify for preferential treatment if: they were produced by enterprises with majority management by nationals; at least 51 per cent of equity was held by nationals, parastatals or governments of the member states; and the c.i.f. value of the imported components of the goods did not exceed 60 per cent of the total cost of production or the value-added was not less than 45 per cent of the ex-factory cost. This rule was intended to promote the development of an indigenous industrial sector and increased use of local resources. The rule, however, came to be viewed as a tool for limiting the participation of foreign-owned firms, especially in Kenya and Zimbabwe, in intra-regional trade.

Protocols   A number of protocols have been signed under the PTA umbrella. These include protocols on reduction and elimination of trade barriers, customs co-operation, the rules of origin, re-export of goods, transit trade and transit facilities, clearing and payments arrangements, transport and communications, simplification and harmonization of trade documents, and procedures on standardization and quality control. The other areas of co-operation are designated as industry, agriculture, monetary affairs and natural resources.

The Common Market for Eastern and Southern Africa (COMESA)

At its inception the PTA was programmed to be transformed to a common market by the year 2000. In January 1992 the PTA Authority adopted recommendations to transform the PTA to the Common Market for Eastern and Southern Africa. (COMESA). The treaty establishing COMESA came into force in December 1994, after it was ratified by the required number of members states.

The COMESA treaty specifies the areas of co-operation as: trade liberalization and customs; transport and communication; industry and energy; monetary and finance; agriculture, and economic and social development. The major departure from the PTA treaty is that the countries agreed to adhere to specified fundamental principles, notably those related to recognition, promotion and protection of human rights; the rule of law; good governance; and economic justice and popular participation in development.

The treaty calls for the establishment of a customs union through the removal of all trade barriers and establishment of a common tariff and rules of origin. Co-operation in monetary and financial matters, not covered by the PTA treaty, was introduced to allow for macroeconomic policy co-ordination within COMESA. This is seen as necessary in an environment of free movement of services and capital and a movement towards convertibility of currencies. Co-operation in these areas is also considered as a step towards the establishment of a monetary union.

Co-operation in economic and social development addresses the issue of the redistribution of the benefits from integration. This issue was not addressed by the PTA treaty. The COMESA treaty stipulates that special programmes and projects will be promoted towards the development of the least-developed countries in the region. Regional policies will be used to promote equitable and balanced development within the common market.

Assessment of Regional Integration Experience in the PTA Region

Implementation of Treaties and Protocols

The implementation of PTA/COMESA treaties/protocols has had mixed results. The most important of the protocols are those related to trade. According to the protocol on reduction and elimination of trade barriers, tariffs and non-tariff barriers were to be reduced and eventually relaxed by 1992. Compliance with the protocol was so behind schedule that the terminal years was shifted to 1998. By the end of 1994, only Kenya, Sudan and Zambia were on schedule and most countries were more than a year behind. This implies that the goal of achieving a common market by the year 2000 is doubtful.

The protocol on the rules of origin defined the goods that could be given preferential treatment in the region as those produced by enterprises with majority management by nationals, parastatals and governments of member countries and those goods whose c.i.f. value of imported components does not exceed 60 per cent of the total cost of production or the value-added in the process of production is not less than 45 per cent of the ex-factory cost. Although the original common list had only 769 items, the more industrialized countries of PTA found the conditions of the protocol too restrictive. After a few years of debate, the list was abolished.

The protocol on co-operation in the field of industrial development aimed to promote the sector in the region through a multilateral industrial enterprises (MIE) charter. The charter was intended to regulate the locale, minimum capacity, ownership and management, and quality and standards of goods of multinational companies engaged in the industrial sector. The charter also specified that for an enterprise to benefit from the incentives provided under the charter it had to engage in a joint venture between two or more states or nationals from two or more states. Most states found the MIE charter to be in conflict with their emerging investment programmes and the PTA/COMESA was forced to re-examine the objectives of the charter. Indications are that the whole idea will be shelved.

The protocol on the gradual relaxation and elimination of visa requirements was intended to be implemented in two phases. The first phase for called relaxation of visa requirements for the residents of PTA/COMESA states. Most countries have ratified this phase. The second phase would enable nationals of COMESA to enter the other COMESA states freely. Not all countries have ratified this phase of the protocol.

The protocols on trade facilitation, customs co-operation, and transport and communication have largely been ratified and implemented. There have, however, been various difficulties at the implementation stages.

The Performance of the Eastern and Southern African Trade and Development Bank

The cumulative approved financing by end December 1994 was UAPTA 65.98 m. in support of 34 loans, two mixtures of loans and equity, and one equity and participation.[4] This was mainly accounted for by projects in the manufacturing sector (50.8 per cent) followed by the infrastructure and energy sector (22.5 per cent). Agro-industry and tourism accounted for 11 per cent and 8.6 per cent, respectively. Most of the projects approved have been concentrated in Zambia, Ethiopia, Uganda, Kenya and Zimbabwe, jointly they accounted for 91.8 per cent of approved financing for projects.

In addition, the bank has been very active in financing trade. The cumulative trade finance approvals as of end-December amounted to UAPTA 165.08 million of which UAPTA 96.3 million were extended in 1994. The instruments used in financing trade include the pre-shipment and post-shipment loan, the commercial paper programme and the gold loan. Under the trade finance window, the PTA Bank has supported exports in agricultural, textiles and mining sectors and arranged letters of credit for the importation of beverages as well as petroleum products.

Performance of the Clearing House

The total value of intra-PTA trade transacted through the clearing house steadily increased from US$441 m. in 1989. Since, then, there has been a declining trend in the use of the clearing house, falling to US$330 m. by 1991 (See to Table 5.3). The decline in gross

Table 5.3   Clearing house performance, 1984–91

	(1) Volume (UAPTA m.)	(2) Change %	(3) Net % settlement in foreign exchange	(4) Total intra-PTA trade (UAPTA m.)	(5) (1) as % of (4)
1984	74.6		74.6	895.4	8.3
1985	98.1	31.5	85.7	795.4	12.3
1986	118.8	37.2	51.7	822.0	14.5
1987	175.8	48.0	54.8	760.3	23.1
1988	283.1	61.0	50.1	830.6	34.1
1989	441.0	55.8	46.9	903.8	48.8
1990	389.0	−18.8	42.3	854.5	45.5
1991	330.0	−15.2	33.7	n.a.	n.a.

Source: PTA Secretariat.

trade transacted through the clearing house is a cause for concern; this has been caused by a number of factors, most of which arose from the liberalized system of foreign exchange, and which include the following.

- With liberalization, travellers and importers can very easily access dollars from the market, which is certainly a preferred mode of settling payments compared to the more bureaucratic UAPTAs.
- The retention of export proceeds in foreign currency encourages exporters to trade outside the clearing house.
- There is often a problem of depreciating currencies – exporters prefer to invoice in foreign currencies like the US $ to avoid such losses.
- There are some central banks in the clearing house payments mechanism. It also true that some central banks have deliberately limited their imports through the clearing house to ensure that they do not run substantial net debit balances, which they may fail to settle in foreign convertible currency settlement date.

The yearly net positions of the monetary authorities participating in the clearing facility indicate that Burundi, Malawi, Rwanda, Uganda and Zambia have been large substantial debtors in the mechanism, while Kenya, Swaziland and Zimbabwe have been mainly large creditors (see Table 5.4).

Table 5.4   Net position (UAPTA m.)

	1984	1985	1986	1987	1988	1989	1990	1991
Burundi	—	0.01	–0.18	–0.96	–4.29	–8.48	–7.27	–7.71
Comoros	—	—	—	–0.02	–0.01	–0.004	–0.002	—
Djibouti	—	—	—	—	—	—	–0.02	–0.001
Ethiopia	0.55	0.73	–3.76	–2.78	–2.95	–6.38	–3.39	–0.98
Kenya	—	0.52	3.56	20.13	34.68	34.98	23.74	20.42
Lesotho	—	0.014	0.0	–0.16	–0.06	–0.22	–0.07	–0.29
Malawi	1.14	–15.32	–16.69	–14.92	–13.78	–8.61	–9.96	–9.15
Mauritius	0.003	0.01	0.07	–0.66	–2.82	–4.69	–4.11	–1.74
Rwanda	—	—	–1.63	–13.69	–24.25	–20.02	–19.65	–18.43
Somalia	—	—	–0.27	–0.27	—	—	—	—
Sudan	—	—	—	—	—	—	—	–0.68
Swaziland	5.02	6.36	1.36	2.93	3.12	10.82	14.89	12.67
Tanzania	—	—	–0.50	–0.29	4.10	6.52	5.38	5.11
Uganda	—	–0.09	–1.67	–1.03	–5.99	–16.84	–9.24	–7.84
Zambia	–25.97	–26.80	5.65	–4.96	–16.26	–21.53	–23.95	–4.03
Zimbabwe	19.25	34.59	10.67	11.07	19.64	19.86	25.76	38.37

Source: PTA Secretariat.

Performance of Intra-PTA Trade

The share of the PTA trade in world trade was 0.56 per cent as of 1982; by 1993, the share had dropped to 0.4 per cent – its lowest in 10 years. The figures further indicate that slightly over 94 per cent of the PTA trade is with third countries. The share has barely changed over the 11-year period since 1982. Specifically, intra-PTA exports as a percentage of total PTA exports declined from 7.0 per cent in 1982 to 6.6 per cent in 1992, and intra-PTA imports as a percentage of total PTA imports stagnated at only 4.7 per cent over the period (See Table 5.5).

A number of earlier studies, especially from the PTA secretariat (Bingu-wa-Mutharika 1994), have demonstrated the prospects for higher levels of intra-PTA trade. An example quoted shows that of the US$15 bn worth of goods imported in 1991, only 4.4 per cent was purchased within the PTA, and of the US$11 bn worth of goods that were exported in 1991, only 6 per cent were sold to PTA countries. In other words, more than US$24 bn worth of business is transacted with countries outside the PTA. It has been estimated that goods worth about US$1.8 bn that are exported by the PTA countries to non-PTA countries, are on the other hand imported by other PTA countries from non-PTA countries.[5] It is therefore disappointing that the share of intra-PTA trade in total PTA trade,

Table 5.5 PTA external trade indicators

	1982	1983	1984	1985	1986	1987	1988	1989	1990	1991	1992
Intra-PTA exports as % of total PTA exports	7.02	6.28	5.76	5.59	5.92	5.93	6.08	6.03	5.80	6.62	6.63
Intra-PTA imports as % of total PTA imports	4.72	4.56	4.55	3.96	4.43	4.20	4.65	4.12	4.20	4.70	4.72
Total intra-PTA trade as % of total PTA trade	5.65	5.28	5.08	4.63	5.07	4.91	5.27	4.90	4.87	5.50	5.51
Intra-PTA exports as of PTA exports to third countries	7.55	6.70	6.11	5.92	6.29	6.30	6.47	6.42	6.15	7.09	7.10
Intra-PTA imports as % of PTA exports to third countries	4.96	4.78	4.77	4.12	4.64	4.38	4.88	4.30	4.39	4.93	4.95
Total intra-PTA trade as % of total PTA trade with third countries	5.98	5.58	5.36	4.86	5.34	5.17	5.56	5.15	5.12	5.82	5.84
Total PTA trade as % of total world trade	0.56	0.54	0.52	0.50	0.46	0.44	0.43	0.42	0.43	0.40	0.40

Note: This table includes all 22 PTA member states.

Source: PTA Secretariat.

which stood at 5.65 per cent in 1989, declined to 5.51 per cent by 1992 despite extensive promotion of intra-PTA trade. It seems that more efficient third countries have taken advantage of the ongoing multilateral trade liberalization to increase their trade with PTA countries, much more than have the PTA countries between themselves. However, comparing trade figures of 1982 to those of 1992 hides certain key developments in the intervening years. The total PTA trade declined by 6.4 per cent between 1982 and 1985. However, intra-PTA trade declined by over 23 per cent over the same period, which results in a drop in the share of intra-PTA trade in total PTA trade from 5.65 per cent as of 1982 to 4.63 per cent by 1985. The period 1985 to 1992 witnessed a recovery in intra-PTA trade from US$851 m. (1985) to US$1651 m. (1992).

However, intra-PTA trade as a percentage of total PTA trade is yet to recover to the 1982 level (see Table 5.5).[6] If there is any claim of success in exploiting trade opportunities, the recovery in intra-PTA trade is worth mentioning. The fact that the level of the share of intra-PTA trade in total trade attained in 1982 is yet to be exceeded is, however disappointing.

An analysis of intra-PTA trade by country between 1982 and 1992 reveals that most of the increase in intra-PTA imports is accounted for by Zambia, Somalia, Mozambique, Mauritius, Malawi, Madagascar and Kenya. On the other hand, the increase in intra-PTA exports is accounted for by Burundi, Madagascar, Malawi, Mauritius, Swaziland, Tanzania and Zimbabwe. Madagascar, for example, increased its export to the region from US$0.9 m. to US$101.9 m. The figures also reveal that Kenya, Zimbabwe and Madagascar, out of 22 member states, account for almost 70 per cent of total intra-PTA exports (see Table 5.6).

The evidence could be interpreted as reflecting gains from preferential trade, but the gains are concentrated in a few members of the regional group. It is clear that some countries within the region, especially those with a relatively more-developed manufacturing sector, export a significant part of their products to other PTA countries that are relatively more dependent on agricultural products and do import heavily from other PTA countries. As an example, Uganda in 1992 sourced goods worth US$100 m. or 22 per cent of her imports from the PTA sub-region. Ugandan exports to the PTA countries, on the other hand, were only US$2 m., or 1 per cent of her total exports. Kenya and Zimbabwe imported only about 3 per cent from other PTA countries, but their share of exports to the PTA

Table 5.6   Intra-PTA trade by country, 1982–92 (as a % of total intra-PTA trade)

	Imports				Exports			
	1982	1986	1990	1992	1982	1986	1990	1992
Angola	0.71	0.59	0.83	1.25	0.00	0.00	0.00	0.01
Burundi	6.09	6.01	2.70	3.97	0.18	1.80	0.87	1.01
Comoros	0.83	0.87	0.64	0.65	0.02	0.11	0.01	0.01
Djibouti	8.21	4.26	2.91	2.83	3.37	3.07	3.39	3.37
Ethiopia	1.57	2.48	1.26	1.32	6.83	5.55	3.79	3.90
Kenya	4.50	4.98	8.68	5.93	43.43	52.93	33.36	32.66
Lesotho	0.05	0.04	0.29	0.18	0.05	0.02	0.04	0.11
Madagascar	0.26	1.10	1.51	1.57	0.16	0.64	12.08	12.34
Malawi	6.48	3.32	4.75	7.54	3.25	4.95	4.15	3.65
Mauritius	1.82	2.05	3.57	3.43	0.58	0.80	2.74	3.31
Mozambique	4.96	10.17	11.85	9.28	7.50	1.14	0.86	1.33
Namibia	0.34	0.15	0.11	0.40	0.04	0.02	0.01	0.02
Rwanda	7.36	10.80	4.40	6.16	0.37	0.93	1.77	0.04
Seychelles	1.50	0.55	0.70	0.76	0.04	0.02	0.01	0.02
Somalia	3.83	3.56	4.81	4.41	0.62	0.23	0.09	0.08
Sudan	7.12	9.23	5.02	4.75	0.16	0.08	0.10	0.08
Swaziland	0.42	0.04	0.67	0.34	1.73	1.16	3.51	3.80
Tanzania	7.49	5.15	5.14	5.57	4.06	1.67	2.34	6.19
Uganda	18.10	23.19	12.86	13.25	0.53	0.32	0.27	0.36
Zambia	8.53	8.62	20.70	19.50	8.42	3.94	4.66	4.61
Zimbabwe	9.83	2.84	6.60	6.90	18.66	20.62	25.98	23.00
Total	*100*	*100*	*100*	*100*	*100*	*100*	*100*	*100*

Source: IMF, *Directory of Trade Statistics Year Books*, 1986, 1991 and 1992.

sub-region amounted to 19 per cent and 13 per cent of their total exports, respectively. In fact, the share of manufacturing in GDP exceeded 10 per cent in 1994 in Kenya, Mauritius, Zambia and Zimbabwe. It was about 8.0 per cent in the case of Tanzania. These countries account for a very high share of intra-PTA exports. The issue of sharing costs and benefits in the PTA sub-region needs to be addressed. Member countries who benefit most from the regional group must compensate those that are deriving little or even suffering costs. The promise of benefits to be derived from economic development of the region alone is unlikely to promote compliance with the PTA protocols.

The fact that significant trade existed before the formation of the PTA and full implementation of the PTA protocols, weakens the arguments for the regional as a means to promote trade. In addition, trade has been extensively liberalized in a number of the PTA member states. Administered allocation of foreign exchange to finance trade has been replaced by market-based systems. The foreign exchange constraints have also eased in a number of these countries. Currently, the private sector has a free choice in sourcing imports. The PTA producers will be preferred to the extent that they have a comparative advantage over suppliers in third countries. The trade strategy should therefore have a component of improving efficiency in production to promote effective completion. To the extent that PTA producers are preferred because of administrative control on foreign exchange utilization and licensing, trade liberalization is bound to constrain intra-PTA trade. Indeed, this is one of the reasons for the declining use of the PTA clearing house and UAPTA travellers' cheques.

Performance of the PTA Travellers' Cheques

The total sales of PTA travellers' cheques between 1988 and 1994 amounted to UAPTA55.73 m. (see Table 5.7) Almost 80 per cent of the sales were accounted for by four countries: Zimbabwe, Burundi, Malawi and Zambia. It is interesting to note that countries with alternative arrangements that facilitate convertibility to the local currencies have negligible records of sales. These include Swaziland, Lesotho, Mauritius, Comoros and Djibouti.

Sales of the cheques increased by 49 per cent in the first two years of operation, from UAPTA8.071 m. in 1989 to UAPTA12.034 m. in 1991. Since then, sales have dropped by about 23 per cent, to UAPTA8.179 m. in 1994. A number of countries scaled back sales to UAPTA cheques as the foreign markets were liberalized. The most dramatic drop was recorded by Zambia, where sales declined from UAPTA6.277 m. in 1991 to UAPTA0.526 m. in 1994. Zimbabwe also recorded a drop in sales of about 72 per cent between 1990 and 1994. The cases of Kenya, Rwanda and Burundi were influenced in part by other reasons: Kenya suspended sales of UAPTA cheques in 1994 following a loss by the Central Bank of Kenya resulting from a misalignment of the exchange rate of the Kenya shillings to the UAPTA; Rwanda and Burundi experienced political unrest in 1994 that did not permit proper conduct of business transactions. Whatever the causes of the reduced sales, it is a serious case of concern that the instrument is losing popularity and faces the risk of being phased out as member countries aim for global convertibility of currencies.

Table 5.7   PTA travellers' cheques, sales and encashment (UAPTA)

	1988	1989	1990	1991	1992	1993	1994	Total	% of total
Zimbabwe	329 710	1 309 710	1 406 550	1 221 220	1 117 670	1 112 560	393 685	6 891 105	12.365
Burundi	121 780	1 284 780	2 532 290	2 356 810	1 737 170	1 641 830	989 835	10 664 495	19.136
Ethiopia	54 390	99 370	161 220	74 210	196 760	239 830	218 490	1 044 270	1.874
Lesotho	44 130	38 820	26 500	15 850	11 800	13 750	1 110	151 960	0.273
Malawi	142 770	692 670	899 180	830 940	501 800	581 090	2 823 900	6 472 350	11.614
Mauritius	130	0	300	640	50	400	3 300	4 820	0.009
Swaziland	34 400	101 480	50 090	92 430	117 030	25 140	2 000	422 480	0.758
Zambia	576 180	3 313 320	3 969 680	6 277 360	2 985 720	1 814 565	526 920	19 462 745	34.923
Uganda	152 890	885 630	1 070 190	260 650	365 510	9 895	445 690	3 190 455	5.725
Tanzania	13 030	72 350	100 040	32 390	81 330	9 750	1 833 435	2 142 235	3.844
Rwanda	31 520	220 700	623 090	396 860	347 130	839 565	43 480	2 608 345	4.680
Somalia	0	10 730	15 220	0	0	0	0	25 950	0.047
Kenya	0	63 010	416 570	474 690	321 870	305 040	8 050	1 589 230	2.852
Comoros	0	0	250	0	1 200	3 200	0	4 650	0.008
Djibouti	0	0	0	0	0	0	0	0	0
Sudan	0	0	0	0	0	0	0	0	0
PTA Bank	0	0	0	0	50 000	114 890	889 740	1 054 630	1.892
Mozambique	0	0	0	0	0	0	0	0	0
Total	1 500 930	8 071 570	11 033 170	12 033 960	7 961 040	6 711 505	8 179 635	55 729 830	100.00

Source: Eastern and Southern African Trade and Development Bank.

Macroeconomic Performance of the PTA Countries, 1970–93

The 1970s were quite difficult years for a number of countries in the region. Apart from the oil crisis, they suffered extensively from the commodity price collapse on the international market since many are exporters of primary commodities. The foreign exchange constraint tightened and currencies became highly over-valued,[7] while inflation accelerated into the double-digit range.

Governments in the region indirectly taxed peasant agriculture by paying farmers predetermined producers prices. This distorted domestic relative prices by reducing the real income of the farmers and artificially made manufactured goods more profitable while agricultural exports were hurt and consumption became biased towards imports. By 1980, most economies had failed to diversify their export base and continued to rely on only one or two primary commoditics. The primary products generated almost 80 per cent of total PTA exports revenue, roughly the same share as in the 1960s. Due to high import demand at wildly over-valued currencies, foreign exchange reserves fell fast and external debt arrears accumulated. Member states could not raise foreign or domestic capital to finance their budgets, yet aid inflows declined drastically. Governments therefore resorted to printing money to finance budgetary operations, as non-banking finance was not developed and tax revenues remained low.

Uncontrolled expenditures on non-productive consumption fueled inflation in the economies. The domestic inflation rate accelerated during the 1980s compared to the 1970s (see Table 5.2) with a few exceptions. Some countries even recorded inflation rates of over 150 per cent per annum. Budget deficits that had been as low as 2 per cent of GDP in the 1960s soared to more than 7 per cent of GDP for most African economies, and subSaharan African had an even higher average of 10 per cent of GDP – high by any standards. Interest rates were administratively determined at levels far below inflation rates as a way of providing cheap credit to selected sectors of the economy. These negative rates in real terms discouraged savings.

The growth performance in the first half of the 1980s reflects on average a deepening economic crisis in almost all PTA member states. The turnaround was experienced in the second half of the 1980s with the exception of countries that suffered from political unrest at the time, namely Rwanda, Burundi and Sudan (see

Table 5.8). Improved macroeconomic performance in countries of the PTA region has followed far-reaching reforms in policy frameworks making them more market-orientated. More generally, almost all countries in subSaharan Africa have embarked on structural adjustment programmes. One clear fact that emerges is that the PTA was launched at the time of an unfavourable economic climate. The region is currently going through a transition and it is not generally the case that the streamlined macroeconomic framework designed to correct distortions in the individuals of the region is in tandem with all the tools designed by the PTA secretariat to promote regional integration.

5.4   MAIN OBSTACLES AND CONSTRAINTS TO THE PERFORMANCE OF THE PTA

Conflict Between the Liberalization of Economies and Illiberal Arrangements in the PTA

Payments Systems

For the majority of PTA member states, currency over-valuation characterized exchange rate management for most of the period 1975–85. The over-valued currencies indirectly taxed exports, resulting in deliberate efforts by exporters to rely on unofficial parallel arrangements in export trade. This caused serious foreign exchange constraints for members states, as discussed in Section 5.4. The PTA clearing and payments arrangements designed during the 1980s suited an administered system centred around the central banks. The UAPTA cheques, for example, were guaranteed by the central banks and could only be converted into local currencies. The intention was to save on the use of foreign currencies in financing services or trade in the region. Holders of cheques could neither use them outside the region nor convert any excess holding of the local currency back into UAPTA cheques or into any major currencies. Furthermore, conversion of the cheques at highly over-valued official rates implied a tax on the holder and parallel market operators who offered better rates did not trade in the instrument. This made the instrument highly unpopular among the travelling public within the region. The cheques also suffered from the lack of wide acceptability within the region. In particular, countries with

Table 5.8 GDP growth rates

	% annual change									Average annual GDP growth rates		
	1982	*1983*	*1984*	*1985*	*1986*	*1987*	*1988*	*1989*	*1990*	*1975–80*	*1980–85*	*1986–90*
Angola	—	—	14.7	3.0	12.1	12.1	14.8	(0.1)	—	—	—	7.1
Burundi	(3.1)	7.0	0.0	11.6	3.8	4.1	3.6	6.5	2.5	3.9	4.5	4.4
Comoros	—	—	4.3	2.8	2.1	2.0	0.7	0.2	2.0	—	—	1.0
Djibouti	—	—	—	(0.4)	(6.9)	(0.6)	0.9	(0.8)	0.7	—	—	0.1
Ethiopia	1.6	5.1	(2.1)	(6.8)	6.7	9.1	3.8	2.3	(2.5)	2.8	0.4	3.1
Kenya	1.9	1.5	1.7	4.3	7.1	5.9	6.0	4.6	4.2	6.6	2.4	5.2
Lesotho	3.7	(5.7)	7.6	3.2	(0.9)	7.3	12.3	4.1	7.8	11.1	1.6	7.9
Madagascar	(1.9)	0.9	1.7	1.2	1.8	1.1	3.8	4.9	4.6	1.8	(1.1)	3.8
Malawi	2.5	3.7	5.7	4.5	(0.5)	1.6	2.9	5.4	3.7	6.1	2.6	3.5
Mauritius	5.8	0.3	4.7	7.4	10.3	10.5	6.5	3.5	6.4	4.5	4.3	6.4
Mozambique	(3.4)	(12.8)	1.5	(8.0)	1.9	5.2	5.6	3.1	3.0	—	(5.0)	4.3
Namibia	(4.7)	(3.1)	(2.0)	5.7	5.9	0.2	5.0	(2.5)	—	—	(1.3)	1.2
Rwanda	1.7	6.3	(4.7)	3.0	5.2	(0.4)	0.1	(6.9)	(2.7)	8.2	2.5	(2.7)
Seychelles	(1.5)	2.2	3.6	9.5	2.4	4.1	6.2	5.6	5.3	8.9	1.3	5.4
Somalia	3.6	(9.2)	3.4	8.1	3.7	6.1	(1.3)	2.7	(1.5)	5.0	1.3	1.3
Sudan	12.7	2.1	(5.0)	(6.3)	9.7	1.1	(1.9)	7.4	5.8	(4.6)	1.5	0.6
Swaziland	1.2	(0.8)	3.8	2.4	8.8	1.2	9.2	4.7	4.6	2.4	2.2	5.3
Tanzania	(0.3)	(0.5)	4.6	1.5	5.4	4.1	5.2	4.3	4.5	2.0	0.9	4.6
Uganda	11.7	9.6	(8.5)	(1.9)	(1.5)	5.7	6.1	6.4	6.3	(3.0)	3.7	6.1
Zambia	(2.7)	(2.1)	(1.1)	1.7	0.2	3.0	5.5	0.1	0.9	(0.3)	(0.3)	2.4
Zimbabwe	2.6	1.6	(2.5)	6.7	2.7	(1.4)	(1.5)	13.4	3.0	(0.1)	3.1	3.7

Source: African Development Indicators, UNDP and IBRD, April 1992.

currencies pegged and/or convertible to hard currencies did not offer full support to the UAPTA cheques – for example, members of the rand area.

Similarly, the clearing process was centred on an administrative system running from central bank through commercial banks to the traders and was also intended to save on the use of foreign exchange in the financing of transactions. It was equivalent to an exporter surrendering export proceeds to the central bank at the official exchange rate and the central bank utilizing the proceeds to finance authorized imports from within the region. Under the administrative allocation of foreign exchange coupled with licensing of potential importers, the central bank could conveniently route import documentation through the clearing house to take advantage of the credit arrangements therein.

In an effort intended to boost growth, many African countries have progressively moved within this continuum of exchange rate arrangements towards more flexible exchange rate regimes. They have moved away from pegging into a single currency toward either pegging to a basket of currencies or adopting a more flexible arrangement under which the domestic currency is frequently adjusted. Available information indicates that in 1983, of the current 22 members of the PTA for eastern and southern African states, eight countries were pegged to a single currency; nine countries were pegged to a currency composite, either the SDR or a basket of currencies; and five had more flexible exchange rate regime in the form of a managed float. By the end of 1992, six countries remained pegged to a single currency and eight countries were pegged to a currency composite, mainly a basket of currencies. Seven countries had adopted some form of flexible exchange rate regime; of the seven, five currencies are independently floating.

A key development in the reform of exchange rate arrangements in the PTA region is that central banks have delegated substantial authority to authorized market participants. In a number of PTA countries, illegal parallel foreign exchange markets had developed over time. As a step towards reform in the exchange rate arrangement, trading in foreign exchange has been liberalized. The authorized dealers in most of the countries include commercial banks and foreign exchange bureaus. Uganda allowed dealing in foreign exchange by foreign exchange bureaux in July 1990, and has since been followed by Tanzania (1992), Angola (1992), Zambia (1993), Ethiopia (1993), and Kenya (1994), and Rwanda is considering setting up bureaux.

In parallel to permitting trading in foreign exchange, central banks have substantially liberalized the surrender requirements. A number of countries initially allowed 100 per cent retention of invisible receipts and private transfers. These have since been extended to some or all export receipts. Kenya, Uganda, Tanzania, Zimbabwe, Ethiopia, Malawi and Angola have substantially liberalized surrender requirements.

The transition in the reform of exchange rate arrangements in most of the countries has involved an official tolerance of a dual exchange system. On the one hand, there is a system based on market determination of the exchange rate under a bureau system and, on the other, official determination of the exchange rate or an auction system involving mainly the sale of donor resources. In most cases, the transitional period involved official effort to eliminate segregation in the market exchange rates. For example, the following countries unified their exchange rates: Tanzania (1993), Angola (1993), Uganda (1993), Kenya (1993) and Zimbabwe (1994). The narrowing/elimination of the gap between the parallel and official exchange rate plus the relaxation of surrender requirements have combined to permit the build-up of foreign exchange reserves in commercial banks and strengthened private sector trading in foreign exchange. In a further development over the past two years, the foreign exchange systems in Malawi (1994), Uganda (1993), Kenya (1993), Zimbabwe (1994) and Angola (1993) have developed into an inter-bank system.

The trade regime in most of the PTA countries was characterized by a combination of restrictive licensing of imports and exports, allocation of foreign exchange to different importers and products (or sectors), imports bans, and high import tariffs. These restrictive trade practices in addition to the over-valued exchange rate were a source of policy distortions that constrained optimal resource allocation in these economies.

As a consequence of structural adjustment policies, a number of measures have been implemented for a competitive, outward-looking regime. Administrative controls on imports have been eliminated or extensively relaxed. For example, in Uganda licensing of imports and exports have been replaced by import/export certificates valid for six months. Similarly, Kenya, Tanzania, Zimbabwe and Malawi have abolished licensing and shortened the negative import list to include goods restricted for health or security reasons. The move towards the active involvement of the private sector in the review and financing of import application without reference to a central bank is sweeping across the developing world. It will not be long before the whole PTA region will have highly liberal outward-looking regime. As of 30 June 1994, Mauritius, Kenya, Swaziland and Uganda had accepted Article VIII status of the IMF, implying full liberalization of current-account transactions.

With the surrender of the responsibility of financing foreign trade and services to commercial banks and bureaux, the guarantee of directing documents through the clearing house was eliminated. Further, the dealers in foreign exchange under liberal systems rely on purchases from the market as opposed to allocations from the central banks. Again, the mechanism for using the clearing house is consistent with market-based allocation of foreign exchange and is bound to suffer as member countries liberalize foreign exchange dealing. The COMESA secretariat should design new instruments and mechanisms to suit a liberal system of managing foreign exchange markets and high import tariffs.

Dependence on Trade Taxes

The tariff reduction programme is likely to lead to significant revenue losses to countries heavily dependent on international trade taxes. These include Uganda, Ethiopia, Somalia, Mauritius, Burundi Rwanda and Lesotho (see Table 5.9). Because of the risk of fiscal revenue loss, there have been delays in implementing the tariff reduction programme. By 1994, only three countries, Kenya, Sudan and Zambia, had reached the highest degree of trade liberalization on PTA products. These were followed by Djibouti, Mauritius, Uganda and Zimbabwe with differing lags in the implementation of programme. Counter-arguments that since intra-PTA trade is small, the losses will be marginal and bearable, have failed to satisfy members. Furthermore, the distribution of benefits from financing of projects by the Eastern and Southern Africa Trade and Development Bank has not yet been managed in a manner that favours countries that are likely to lose most from implementing the tariff reduction programmes.

In parallel to the above, member countries have implemented a new tariff schedule. A minimum tariff has been introduced, the maximum tariff reduced and the number of tariff bands has been narrowed. For example, Ethiopia had by August 1993 reduced the maximum tariff rate from 230 per cent to 80 per cent. Other examples

Table 5.9   Taxation on international trade as a percentage of total central revenue current revenue

Country	1993	1992	1990	1987	1980	1972
Uganda	—	—	75.3	75.3	44.3	36.3
Kenya	10.6	14.2	15.8	19.2	18.5	24.3
Tanzania	—	—	—	8.8	17.3	21.7
Ethiopia	—	—	—	—	28.4	30.4
Somalia	—	—	—	—	—	45.3
Mozambique	—	—	—	—	—	—
Zimbabwe	19.0	19.0	17.5	15.6	4.4	—
Mauritius	41.4	—	46.4	50.5	51.6	40.2
Burundi	—	—	—	—	40.4	40.3
Rwanda	31.1	31.1	—	—	42.4	41.7
Malawi	—	16.3	17.7	16.8	22.0	20.0
Lesotho	51.8	51.8	54.5	67.8	61.3	62.9
Zambia	—	—	15.8	32.9	8.3	14.3

Source: The World Bank, *World Development Reports*, 1989, 1990, 1992, 1994 and 1985.

include Uganda, Tanzania and Malawi, who have also reduced the maximum tariff rate to 40 per cent. Therefore, progress in liberalizing the trade regime in a number of PTA member states has been accompanied by introducing a system of low average tariff rates.

Constraints on Trade

Regional integration has been championed as a means of overcoming limits on industrialization in narrow domestic markets and thus promoting economic growth (see Kiggundu, 1990). The PTA is currently made up of 22 member countries stretching from Southern Africa to Eritrea. These countries have immense diversities in regard to income per capita, macroeconomic framework and culture, and do not possess a well-developed physical infrastructure to facilitate trade. As a result of infrastructural constraints, most of the trade is limited to neighbouring countries.[9]

A number of countries in the region have completely liberalized or are in the process of relaxing restrictive imports licensing and have by and large abolished non-tariff barriers such as quotas. However, there have been cases of policy reversals or reluctance to break any remaining non-tariff barriers. Uganda, for example, maintains import bans on sugar, beers, sodas and milk for health and fiscal revenue reasons. Similarly, Kenya has from time to time imposed import bans on foodstuffs, especially from Uganda, and has at times varied transit requirements to the inconvenience of importers in Uganda.

The lack of a developed physical infrastructure and the existence of residual non-tariff barriers make it difficult for potential investors to take advantage of a wider market. Equally, it makes it difficult for potential exporters to use it as a training ground to break through to markets of third countries.

Sequencing and Speed of Policy Reform

At the time of launching the PTA in December 1981, member states were characterized by a number of serious economic distortions. There was enormous scope for efficiency gains through liberalization in the individual nation states and for the region as a whole. Indeed, countries have implemented far-reaching measures. However, the reform programme had progressed in a very uncoordinated manner, with different member countries at different level in the reform process.

Unilateral trade liberalization increases the feasibility of regional integration; however, if the speed and sequencing are not co-ordinated, the trade potential may not be fully exploited. Secondly, if the reform programme is subject to reversals in one or more of the member states, then again the trade potential will remain constrained. The PTA should have the tools to reinforce commitment by member states to announce unilateral liberalization policies, otherwise the objective of an effective regional group will be weakened.

The Cross-Border Initiative (CBI) for the Eastern and Southern Africa, which is sponsored by the ADB, the World Bank, the IMF and Commission of the European Community, is aimed at addressing some of the weakness in the regional group with a view to strengthening cross-border trade and investment. Under the new approach, emphasis is placed on promoting mobility of factors of production, goods and services across national boundaries in an environment of relatively low tariff against third countries. Participation of countries in the initiative is voluntary. Each participating country is expected to be implementing policies to promote a sustainable macroeconomic framework and, as much as possible, policies should be harmonized. The arrangement is intended to strengthen commitment to the reform process and minimize or eliminate policy reversals.

Political Developments and Evolving Global Environment

The future of regionalism in east and southern Africa is inextricably tied to competing interest among the regional groupings and the consequences of the new political realities emerging in the countries of the region. The evolving global environment, especially the move towards regional trading blocks, also has some bearing on the direction of the development of regional co-operation within the EAC/COMESA.

The biggest challenge facing regionalism in east and southern Africa is the conflict of COMESA and the SADC. A summit of the heads of states held in Lusaka, Zambia, on 31 January 1992 agreed to a merger of COMESA and the SADC. The argument was that the merger would make co-operation within the region effective by reducing duplication of activities. The effort was also seen as a means to a faster movement toward an African Economic Community through a single sub-regional group in eastern and southern Africa. The first reason made sense in that a look at the objectives of the organizations clearly indicates many cases of duplication. It is not evident, however, that having one sub-regional grouping in eastern and southern Africa would necessarily lead to a faster movement toward an African community.

As it turned out, not all of the SADC members were actually in favour of the merger. On 17 August 1992 at a summit meeting in Windhoek, Nambia, the Southern African Development Community was established. The member states argued that there was no conflict between COMESA and the SADC since each organization had clearly defined objectives, mandates and programmes. Moreover, the possibility existed for the two organization to co-ordinate and rationalize their programmes and activities to avoid duplication and overlap in policy and programmes. Another PTA summit in January 1993 called for the problem of the merger to be solved at the political level. The PTA, however, saw the merger of the two institutions as inevitable. This single-mindedness of the PTA/COMESA for the merger of COMESA and the SADC seemed to harden the stance of SADC member states. Since 1993 the SADC has argued for the split of COMESA into north and south and has openly asked its member states to reconsider their position in COMESA. The rhetoric from both institutions makes the break-up of COMESA inevitable. The accession of South Africa to the SADC and its refusal to join COMESA is another pointer to the imminent collapse of COMESA.

The rivalry between PTA/COMESA and the SADC did not start with the issue of the merger. Anglin (1983) has suggested that the manner in which each of the two institutions was established explains the differences between them. The PTA/COMESA was designed by bureaucracy at the ECA as part of a grand plan for an African Economic Community. Its membership is therefore defined more by geography than shared common interest. On the other hand, SADC was established with a political motive, that is, to reduce economic dependence on apartheid South Africa by the Southern African states. It is for this reason that Anglin suggests that the heads of states of the southern African countries are more personally involved in the SADC than COMESA.

The other more compelling reasons for the SADC member states to be reluctant to let the SADC merge with COMESA is that the SADC is project-orientated. The benefits of the projects to member states are direct and therefore more noticeable than the more policy-orientated programmes of the PTA/COMESA. Moreover, the projects are mostly donor-funded and therefore member states do not want to risk the funds being diverted. The countries of southern Africa have also not been convinced that there are any economic benefits to be had by integrating with many – and economically and politically diverse – nations. For example, some have wondered what common interest Eritrea or Djibouti has with Botswana or Angola. In the more recent past, the southern Africa countries have seen the possibility of a few anchoring on the more powerful and prosperous South Africa as a more viable option of regionalism than COMESA.

The new political realities in Africa also shape the aspirations of regionalism. The treaties of both COMESA and the SADC emphasize guarantee of democratic and human rights of the members citizens and the rule of law. Countries have been objecting to some regional economic issues on the basis that they would not be politically acceptable in their countries. A case in point is the initial refusal by Zimbabwe to ratify the COMESA treaty before it was accepted by its parliament. The countries of the SADC have used this point effectively against the merger with COMESA. The evolving economic environment – especially the new world trade order associated with WTO – and the increase in regionalism, exemplified by NAFTA, the European Union, the Pacific Rim and AFTA, also explain the conflict between COMESA and the SADC. The SADC believes that a small grouping with credible commitments and well-articulated policies and programmes is better placed to benefit from the new world trade order by being able to negotiate effectively and obtain favourable access to markets for its members. Those who believe in a large community the COMESA argue that the larger the grouping, the more effective it would be to negotiate on behalf of its members.

5.5 PROSPECTS FOR REGIONAL INTEGRATION UNDER LIBERALIZED ECONOMIC REGIMES

The pessimistic view of regional integration in subSaharan Africa is that there are no economic gains to be had from integration. Fine and Yeo (1994) argue that 'regional integration would appear to be a "dead end" in terms of contributing in any substantive fashion to rapid and sustainable growth of subSaharan African economies.' They further note that:

> [the] fact that African leaders, first in the Lagos Plan of Action of 1980 and then in the Abuja Treaty of 1991, have elected to pursue the quixotic goal of an African Common Market in spite of their continued failure to begin removing even modest impediments to the flow of goods and services within the region, would suggest that their agenda is driven by political rather than economic consideration, and by domestic rather than regional pressures.

History would seem to vindicate these sentiments, although recent political and economic changes provide a cause for optimism. This is especially true for East African countries and those of southern Africa.

Our discussions have shown that the East African community was formed during a period of macroeconomic stability in the member states. The purpose of the union was primarily to promote trade and development. To the contrary, the PTA and the SADC were formed when the member states faced serious macroeconomic problems. The stated aims of trade promotion therefore faced immediate serious constraints. Non-tariff barriers in the member states resulted mainly from poor economic performance. To design a programme to eliminate the barriers without addressing the cause of poor economic performance was setting a goal beset with difficulties in implementation. No wonder, therefore, that some member states resisted the elimination of non-tariff barriers.

We have also seen the SAPs have been designed to eliminate macroeconomic distortions in many of the countries in the region. Studies by Ng'eno (1994) and KEDS (1994) show that countries in the region have implemented far-reaching economic reforms in the last few years. The reforms are set to be continued in the coming years. For all practical purpose these countries have decontrolled prices, interests rates and exchange rates. Quantitative restrictions and subsidies have been abolished and tariffs have been rationalized and are being lowered. Policies to promote exports and to attract foreign investment have been adopted. Restrictive fiscal and monetary policies are being used to fight inflation and in some countries, notably Uganda, inflationary tendencies have been checked. At a more general level, a number of countries are now experiencing a stable economic environment as a result of implementation of SAPs.

Unilateral economic liberalization, by eliminating distortions in individual countries, facilitates the process of intra-regional trade liberalization. The polarization effects of trade reforms will be minimized as the countries move towards macroeconomic stability. This is enhanced by the current move by the East African countries towards macroeconomic policy co-ordination.

More remains to be done before the regional integration grouping in SSA can serve the purpose for which they were established. To start with, there is no mechanism to guarantee the sustainability of the recent economic policy reforms. Some policy changes, such as exchange rate liberalization, have introduced new problems. Recent evidence from Uganda and Kenya indicates that as macroeconomic stability is restored, capital inflows have increased, which in turn has resulted in appreciation of domestic currencies. The authorities have found themselves in the awkward position of being asked to intervene in the foreign exchange market to avoid over-valuation of the domestic currency.

A potentially serious problem is what Collier and Gunning (1994) present as the likelihood that reforms may not be sustainable. They argue that since reforms in SSA are normally supported by the donors, they are open to the problem of time inconsistency. Governments that commit themselves to policy reforms on the basis of aid conditionality are likely to reverse the reforms once the funds are exhausted. The example often cited is Nigeria, which reversed policies it has been carrying out for the last 10 years. It would appear, however, that Nigeria suspended the policies because they had become too costly, both socially and politically. Collier and Gunning (1994) and Fine and Yeo (1994) suggest that subSaharan African countries, through regional integration groups, can improve the credibility of their policy reforms by 'locking into' an external guarantor such as the European Union (EU). Under this arrangement SSA could be guaranteed existing market access as long as it sticks to the policy reforms. It is not evident, however, what benefits the EU would gain from such an arrangement. Fine and Yeo argue that SSA countries could make side payments to EU in the form of adherence to agreed policy reforms or protection of intellectual property rights. SSA regional groupings could enhance their credibility by designing and implementing credible programmes. Individual countries should be willing to stick to timetables for regional integration reforms and should, when desirable, favour regional policies over domestic policies.

In the case of the PTA and the EAC, a set of well-defined rules for membership should be established. In particular, the pursuit of policies geared towards promoting a stable macroeconomic environment must be one of the initial qualifying conditions. Others should include: prudent fiscal management consistent with low inflation; convertible currency; and a liberalized trade regime. It is only with these conditions that harmonization of macroeconomic policies is possible. This, however, does not offer a 'lock in' mechanism for policy reforms, because there are not credible sanctions for default in policy implementation or policy reversal. What is required, in our view, is a mechanism along the lines of the cross-border initiative, with a well-defined policy matrix including an implementation time frame supported by the multilateral agencies. Under the CBI there are financial benefits to be gained from compliance with agreed reforms, which is not the case under the current arrangements of the PTA/COMESA.

Easterly and Levine (1994), in a study of the causes of economic growth in Africa, found that a country's growth rate is significantly affected by a neighbour's growth rate. Furthermore, economic growth is enhanced when neighbouring countries co-ordinate their economic policies. Without doubt this strengthens the argument for regionalism, but, as mentioned above, policy co-ordination is enhanced if there are clearly defined rules for entry and a credible 'lock in' mechanism. In terms of sequencing, one could support elimination of economic distortions before regionalism.

There are a number of problems that continue to plague regional co-operation in eastern and southern Africa. One of them is the multiplicity of groupings. The participation of the countries in more than one of these groupings implies duplication of political will and dissipation of energies and resources in activities that could well be carried out under one organization. The presence of overlapping sub-groups within eastern and southern Africa is a sign of the existence of divergent views and interests within the sub-region. The struggle between the PTA and the SADC secretariat does not augur well for regionalism in the region. This is not helped by the inability of the authority in the sub-region to give clear direction to the two secretariats. On 17 August 1992, the SADC authority signed the protocols establishing the SADC despite the fact that nine of the ten heads of states had earlier called for the merger of the SADC and the PTA. Moreover, the SADC summit of August 1994 adopted the proposal by a joint PTA/SADC study that the PTA be divided into two: one in the north, which would include the Indian Ocean islands, and the other the SADC, which now includes South Africa.

The other problem facing the PTA is the notion that sheer numbers is the source of strength. The region should have borrowed a lesson from the European Union, which – though formed in 1957 – currently has only 12 members. These countries have taken time to evolve institutions, notably the council of ministers, the commission, the parliament and the court of justice. Regional co-operation should arise out of shared interest and common objectives. This condition is not fulfilled by the membership in the PTA. It is therefore less surprising that other sub-groupings exist within the PTA/COMESA area.

Regional integration should also allow for 'variable geometry' and subsidiarity. The application of 'variable geometry' means that the pace of implementation of regional policies will no longer be dictated by the slowest member as in the past. Those countries that are able to work faster than others should be able to do so.

The principal of subsidiarity implies that decisions should be decentralized as much as possible. In this connection it will be important for civil society to be more involved in the debate on decisions that are eventually to be carried out by the sub-regional organizations. At the minimum, the policies should be debated and passed in national parliaments. This will make it difficult for heads of states or the sub-regional secretariats to contradict or reverse regional policies.

The above arguments point to the need to rethink regionalism in eastern and southern Africa. The lack of common interest among COMESA members and the conflict with the SADC are not conducive to stable regional co-operation. This is further complicated by the move by Tanzania, Kenya and Uganda to revive the East African Community. To promote stable economic grouping, countries in the region should belong to one economic group that fully represents their interests. In our assessment, the SADC and the EAC should be formalized as sub-regional entities without dual membership. These sub-groupings should be responsible for sectoral projects and harmonization of macroeconomic policies in their sub-regions.

It would be quite logical for Rwanda and Burundi to join the EAC once they meet the entry requirements. Formation of a sub-group to cover Sudan, Ethiopia, Eritrea, Djibouti and Somalia may be appropriate. The remaining countries may consider joining any of the three sub-groups. The PTA, however, should remain and specialize in areas that cut across all countries in the region. In this regard, the PTA should deal with intra-regional trade liberalization and work towards the unification of the sub-groupings for a future COMESA.

Notes

1. Dr Sullaiman Kiggundu (1990) strongly argued that domestic markets were too small to permit efficient production in the industrial sector. He advocated the formation of regional markets as a way to promote industrialization and economic growth.
2. The existence of fairly high level of intra-regional trade has been identified as one of the key initial conditions necessary for successful integration (Collier and Gunning, 1994 and Langhammer and Hiemenz, 1991). In the case of subSaharan Africa, the share of intra-SSA trade flows are low and are likely to remain low given the trade potential (Foroutan and Pritchett, 1993).

3. According to Langhammer and Hiemenz (1991), the initial conditions conducive to integration include an existing high level of intra-regional trade, congeniality of foreign policy, capability to provide compensation payments and similarities in income. Collier and Gunning (1994), established three steps appropriate for regional integration: (1) collaborative trade policy must be superior to unilateral trade policy; (2) reciprocal discrimination must be superior to reciprocal non-discrimination; and (3) regional reciprocal discrimination must be superior to South–North reciprocal discrimination.

4. The 1994 total annual report of the Eastern and Southern African Trade and Development Bank has a full discussion of the activities of the bank.

5. Measurement of the potential for intra-PTA trade in this manner should be treated with caution, given findings using gravity models. See Elbadawi (1994) which finds no evidence that countries in subSaharan Africa trade less with each other than would be expected given their low trade potential.

6. Elbadawi (op cit) found that the experience of regional integration has been a failure. In particular, he found that in the first half of 1980s, the presence of a regional integration scheme on average enhanced intra-scheme imports by 31 per cent without causing trade diversion. However, in the second half of the 1980s the story changed dramatically. In case of the PTA, import trade was diverted by 90 per cent without leading to increased intra-PTA imports. The regional grouping is estimated to have increased exports to the rest of the world by 79 per cent with minimal effect on intra-bloc trade.

7. Results from a gravity model (Elbadawi, 1994) reveal across-the-board robustness in terms of both sign and significance for four variables: distance; economic size (GDP); the indicators of cultural affinity for some influential languages; and GDP per capita differential.

References

Anglin, D. G. (1983) 'Economics Liberation and Regional Cooperation in South Africa: SADC and PTA', *Industrial Organisation*, **37**(4).

Baldwin, R. (1993) 'A Domino Theory of Regionalism', CEPR Discussion Paper no. 857.

Bingu-wa-Mutharika (1994) 'COMESA: New Trade and Development Opportunities', COMESA Policy Paper no. 1.

Chhibber, Ajay and S. Fischer (eds) (1991) *Economic Reform in Sub-Saharan Africa: A World Bank Symposium* (Washington, DC: World Bank).

Collier, P. and J. W. Gunning (1994) 'Trade Policy and Regional Integration: Implication for the Relations Between Europe and Africa', CEPR Discussion Paper no. 1012.

De la Torre, A. and M. R. Kelly (1992) 'Regional Trade Arrangements', Occasional Paper no. 193 (Washington, DC: IMF).

EAC (1967) *The Treaty of East Africa Economic Co-operation,* (Nairobi: Government Printer, June 1976).

Easterly, W. and R. Levine (1994) 'Africa's Growth Tragedy', A paper presented to an AERC workshop (May).

Elbadawi, I. (1994) 'The Impact of Regional Trade/Monetary Schemes on Intra-subSaharan Africa Trade', AERC Collaboration Research Project.

Fine, J. and S. Yeo (1994), 'Regional Integration in sub-Saharan Africa: Dead End or a Fresh Start?' a paper presented to the AERC Workshop on *Regional Integration* (May).

Foroutan, F. and L. Pritchett (1993) 'Intra Sub-Saharan Trade: Is it too Little', *Journal of African Economies,* **2** (1).

Hazelwood, A. (1975) *Economic Integration: The East African Experience* (London: Heineman).

IMF (1994) 'Initiative for promoting Cross-border trade, investment and payments in eastern and southern Africa', IMF document (8 April).

KEDS (1994) 'Export Competitiveness Study', a Report prepared by Kenya Export Development Scheme Project for USAID/Kenya.

Kiggundu, S. (1990) 'Regional Economic Integration: Africa's Challenge for the 1990's Joseph Mubrin Lecture, Bank of Uganda, Kampala.

Kim, K. (1979) 'Appraisal of the East African Economic Integration Scheme: Critical Issues and Possibilities' in Kim *et al.,* Paper on the Political of Tanzania (Nairobi: Heinemann).

Kim, K. *et al.* (1979) *Paper on the Political Economy of Tanzania* (Nairobi: Heinemann).

Kasekende Louis A. (1994) 'Experiences Under Stabilization and Structural Adjustment Programs: Lessons From Uganda', a paper presented at a East Africa Central Banking Course in Mutono, Uganda (June).

Langhammer, R. J. and U. Heimenz (1991) 'Regional Integration Among Developing Countries: Survey of Past Performance and Agenda for Future Policy Action' (Washington DC: Trade Policy Division, The World Bank).

Lipumba, I. and L. A. Kasekende (1991), 'The record and prospects of the Preferential Trade Area for Eastern and Southern African States' in A. Chibber and S. Fisher (eds) *Economic Reform in Sub-Saharan Africa: A World Bank Symposium* (Washington DC: World Bank).

Lyakurwa, W., A. McKay, N. Ng'eno and W. Kennes (1993) 'Regional Integration in Sub-Saharan Africa: A Review of Experiences and Issues', A paper presented to the AERC Collaborative Research on Regional Integration and Trade Liberalisation in Sub-Saharan Africa; Nairobi (2–4 December).

Ng'eno, N. (1994) 'Comparative Analysis of Economic Reform and Structural Adjustment Programs in East Africa: With Emphasis on Trade Policies', a report prepared for USAID/Kenya.

OECD (1993) *Regional Integration and Developing Countries* (Paris: OECD).

PTA (1994) *Intra-PTA Trade Potential: How to gain access to the market,* PTA/FCC–1/COMESA/1/2B (June).

PTA Secretariat (1989) 'PTA Report of the Study Team on the Equitable Distribution of Costs and Benefits in the PTA' (November).

PTA Bank (1994) Eastern and Southern African Trade and Development Bank *Annual Report 1994*.
UNECA (1994) 'Optimal and Sustainable Exchange Rate Regimes: The Case of PTA Countries' (Addis Ababa, Ethiopia).
World Bank, The (1989) *Sub-Saharan Africa: From Crisis to Sustainable Growth* (Oxford University Press).

6 The Southern African Customs Union (SACU)

Ngila Mwase and Gavin Maasdorp

6.1 INTRODUCTION

This paper examines the theoretical basis of the Southern African Customs Union (SACU), its performance, current status, and the potential for transforming it into a deeper, wider and more effective mechanism for economic integration and development. This is done in the context of the changing political economy of the subregion, particularly the emergence of post-apartheid South Africa, the liberalization of national economies and the future of other regional organizations. Also important are recent global trade, political and technological changes that have created an entirely new climate for the Southern African economies and their prospects for integration. These changes include:

- Namibian independence and the collapse of apartheid, enabling the Republic of South Africa (RSA) to play a pro-active role in a post-apartheid Southern Africa with its economy becoming more effectively integrated into that of the region; the RSA is now available as a market, middleman, transit country or port of exit. Various studies with very comprehensive models and scenarios based on a hostile South Africa have become irrelevant. These include transportation studies by the Maputo-based Southern African Transport and Communication Commission (SATCC, 1988);
- the adoption of IMF/World Bank structural adjustment programmes (SAP), which have involved policies to liberalize national economies, deregulate economic activity, and commercialize or privatize public enterprises, allow market forces to allocate resources, and subject firms to national and international competition;
- various initiatives to establish a regime of trade liberalization and cross-border investment within the COMESA/SACU region;
- the effects of the GATT/WTO Uruguay Round Agreement on the global trading environment;

- the deepening of integration in Europe, the proliferation of regional trading blocs, notably Southeast Asia and the Americas, and moves to establish an Indian Ocean Rim;
- donor 'fatigue', increased aid conditions and changing global priorities, leading to diminishing interest in, and reduced flows of (concessional) development aid;
- rapid technological advance and innovation, with the region, save for the RSA, lagging far behind;
- the marginalization of central planning and planned approaches to economic integration;
- COMESA and SADC rivalry, with the former evolving out of the PTA in December 1994 and the latter moving towards becoming a trade integration organization; South Africa joining SADC but not COMESA; and the SADC countries calling for COMESA to be divided into northern and southern section with SADC taking over COMESA operations in the south;
- the emergence of the post-apartheid RSA, the cessation of war in Mozambique and Angola, and the spread of multi-party democracy.

We discuss not just measures to redress the drawbacks of orthodox customs union theory but to advance, in a Tinbergenian (1965) sense, 'positive integration': that is, measures for the promotion of an effective and functional integrated market coupled with attendant broader joint policy objectives and designs. Robson (1987) has shown that successful integration depends on the extent to which participating countries exhibit significant trade flows among themselves, actual and potential complementarity, low levels of extra-regional trade, and enlarged domestic and sub-regional markets. With the increasing production of competitive primary commodities for the external market, extra-regional trade as a percentage of the GNP of African countries is quite high. Since external tariffs may account for 50–90 per cent of government revenue, the common external tariff is usually high, limiting economic integration benefits.

Despite moves towards trade integration in Eastern and Southern Africa (ESA), the African experience leaves much to be desired. There has been too extended a period of Tinbergen's (1965) 'negative integration' – a preoccupation with the establishment of institutions. Worse still, trade expansion has been slow and intra-group trade increases modest. Save for SACU and its monetary counterpart, the Common Monetary Area (CMA), industrial, monetary, financial and fiscal policy co-ordination has been negligible. Other shortcomings include low levels of investment, negligible scale economies, high administrative and operational costs, and unequal distribution of costs and benefits. However, the situation does fall short of the integration 'crisis' experienced elsewhere (Vaitsos, 1978).

6.2 THEORETICAL ASPECTS

The term 'economic integration' is used in modern literature to denote integration of markets; it differs from 'planning integration' – for example, some co-ordination of development plans, transport projects, and so on, on a regional basis. The aim of economic integration is to promote trade and economic co-operation among member countries. There are four hierarchical types:

(1) *a free trade area*, entailing removal of quantitative trade restrictions (quotas) and customs tariffs among member countries. This may be preceded by a preferential trade area (PTA), entailing gradual reduction of customs tariffs;
(2) *a customs union* in which the free trade area conditions are extended to include the adoption of a common external tariff against outside countries;
(3) *a common market*, in which the customs union arrangements are extended to include the abolition of all restrictions on the movement of factors of production (capital and labour) among member countries;
(4) *an economic union*, involving harmonization of economic policies: for example, monetary and fiscal policies.

The conventional treatment of economic integration stems from Viner's (1950) theory of customs unions, and revolves around whether or not the protected industries in each country prior to integration are competitive. By competitive is meant that these countries (call them A and B) are producing similar types of manufactured products. This competition leads to trade being created within the customs union in these goods, but imports from the rest of the world in other goods continue so that little or no trade diversion occurs. But if the protected industries in A and B prior to integration are complementary – that is, they are producing dissimilar products – and trade in their products is not taking place between A and B, the removal of tariffs within a customs union will cause trade diversion: the previously lower-cost (and hence more efficient) external suppliers will be supplanted by producers within the customs union. Trade creation enhances overall efficiency in the customs union, whereas trade diversion reduces it.

Wonnacott and Lutz (1989) have argued that the trade diversion argument requires some reassessment, for three main reasons:

(1) Economic integration may produce economies of scale. Production costs in A and B could be equal to, or lower than, those in the rest of the world.
(2) If the industries of A and B are protected mainly by quotas rather than tariffs, trade diversion need not reduce efficiency.
(3) If the costs of producing complementary goods in A and B prior to union are higher than those in other countries, this could be the result of over-valued exchange rates. Then, the lower monetary costs of imported goods may not necessarily be conterminous with lower economic costs.

Nevertheless, empirical research shows that countries with similar GDP composition and structure of manufacturing are one another's best customers. Wonnacott and Lutz (1989) have reinforced the conventional view that economic integration has the best prospects if partner states are at similar levels of industrial development, have competitive industrial sectors, and the potential to develop complementary industrial sectors, and already conduct a significant proportion of their foreign trade among themselves. Other conditions for successful economic integration are as follows:

• Governments should cede some sovereign rights to the supranational authority.
• A supranational authority should have real powers to make governments implement agreed REI decisions.
• All member countries should perceive that they are gaining.
• The tendency of manufacturing industries to concentrate in the most industrially advanced country of the grouping should be addressed.
• Member countries should broadly agree on economic systems: integration cannot succeed between market and centrally planned economies.
• Political differences within the grouping should be containable.

Table 6.1 SACU countries – some salient statistics, 1992

Country	Area (km.² m.)	Population (millions)	Total GDP (US$ m.)	GNP per capita (US$)
Botswana	0.58	1.4	3 700	2790
Lesotho	0.03	1.9	536	590
Namibia	0.82	1.5	2 106	1610
Swaziland	0.02	0.86	955	1090
South Africa	1.22	39.8	103 651	2670
Total	*2.67*	*45.46*	*110 948*	
South Africa %	*45.7*	*87.5*	*93.4*	

Source: World Bank, 1994.

Economists are divided as to the desirability of regional trading blocs. It is now generally agreed that economic integration schemes are theoretically inferior to a global non-discriminatory abolition of tariffs and quantitative restrictions. In an imperfect world, however, the creation of regional trading blocs might offer an alternative route to global free trade. These regional blocs therefore appear to be here to stay, and the challenge is to ensure that they facilitate free trade. However, there is no consensus as to whether developing countries should integrate among themselves or with one of the strong industrial economies.

Despite its durability, SACU does not rate well according to the criteria for successful integration set out above. However, SACU does meet significant requirements: its members have a history of significant intra-group trade; all member countries perceive that they are gaining (or at least not losing); there is broad agreement on a market-based economic system; and political differences have always been containable. The dissimilarities among the countries are shown in Table 6.1.

Table 6.1 shows that SACU is a partnership between one relatively large economy and four tiny economies. The RSA accounts for 45.7 per cent of SACU's geographic area but has 87.5 per cent of the population and 93.4 per cent of the GDP. In per capita income terms it has recently been overtaken by Botswana, but this masks a wide gap in the level of economic development between the two countries. In particular, the RSA has a significantly more-developed industrial sector than the rest. For example, in 1989 the RSA had an MVA of US$19 030 m. as against US$17 800m. for

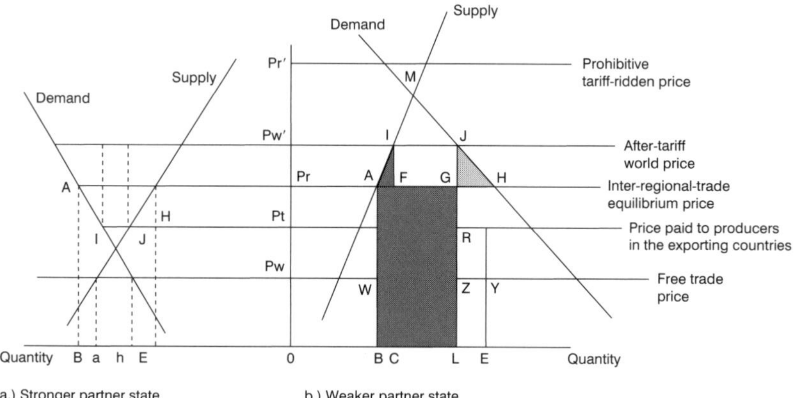

Figure 6.1   Trade diverting and trade creating effects of a customs union

SSA (or only US$2892m. for Nigeria). The RSA's rail network of 23 740km. is larger than the rest of SSA's rail network combined (or Zimbabwe's 3394km.). It handles 170 million tons of cargo per annum as against Zimbabwe's 12 million–13 million tons. Economic integration would on balance benefit the RSA if polarization of industrial growth were to follow conventional theory.

Although the RSA has a high per capita income of US$2460, income distribution is skewed; RSA whites and blacks register per capita GNP of US$6530 and US$670, respectively. Because of similar white-black dichotomy in Namibia, per capita GNP is in the range of US$500–US$1499. Such high income disparities are least favourable to internal and external trade.

The theoretical implications of lopsided trade on the trade-creating and trade-diverting effects of a customs union on partner states are illustrated in Figure 6.1. Assume two integrating countries; an economically stronger, essentially exporting partner (Figure 6.1(a)) and a weaker, essentially importing partner (Figure 6.1(b)). Each partner state is assumed to be small and hence a price-taker rather than a price-setter *vis-à-vis* the world market, in which case the world supply schedule is infinitely elastic at the given price *PW*. It is assumed that the price of intra-customs union traded goods is affected by each other's reciprocal demand. The autarkic price in the weaker partner is greater than that prevailing in the stronger member, which in turn is assumed to exceed the world price *PW*.

Let *PW* be the domestic price prevailing in the importing country after imposition of a tariff on imports from the rest of the world. In Figure 6.1(b) the import tariff on goods from the other partner state, before the formation of a customs union, is prohibitive. With the formation of a customs union, the equilibrium price determined by the market equilibrium condition (that the excess supply *A 'H'* from the exporting country is equal to the excess demand *AH* in the importing country) will be set at *Pr*.

As Johnson (1962) showed, this movement is trade-expanding (the trade-creating effect) and gives rise to a shift of trade from the world's to the union's most efficient producer (trade-diverting effect). The trade-creating welfare gain to the importing country is denoted by triangles *AIF* and *JGH*. The former shows a net saving in real resource use represented by the difference between the domestic resource cost of producing quantity *BC* and the foreign payment for importing the same quantity. The latter depicts the net consumer surplus increase – that is, the difference of the area *JLEH* – which reflects the marginal gain in the surplus as a result of an increased consumption of *LE*, and the area *GLEH* representing the payment for the corresponding consumption of *LE*. The net welfare effect therefore depends on the relative magnitude of the trade-creating and diverting effects. The trade-diverting effect is shown by the area *FTZG* in Figure 6.1(b).

Lowering or eliminating internal trade barriers leads to contraction of import-competing industries in the weaker members, thereby releasing variable factors, such as labour, that may remain idle. Developing countries' resources are relatively immobile between uses, and adjustments through structural shifts to meet changing demands are generally sluggish and costly. The welfare effects of integration could, therefore, include increased unemployment in the economically weaker partner state. Measured in value terms this can be shown to be area *FABC* in Figure 6.1(b).

In the context of static analysis, the relevant comparison for evaluating the integration effects is between the cross-hatched area *JGH* and the shaded area *ABCTZG* in Figure 6.1(b). The net loss incurred by the economically weaker partner is far more than the differences between the trade-creating and the trade-diverting effects of the traditional analysis.

That the weaker partner would be a loser becomes apparent if we take the case of a common price level and compare the alternatives of joining and not joining the customs union. Assume a reduction of the external tariff rate so that the world free-trade price after tariff becomes competitive with the regional free trade equilibrium price indicated at *Pr* in Figure 6.1(b). The weaker partner could, by staying away from the customs union, obtain quantity *AH* of importables at price *PW* rather than at price *Pr*, in which case there would then be a net saving of real resources equivalent to area *AWYH*.

The economically stronger partner state should benefit from the expanded employment and income in Figure 6.1(a). The latter effect is shown by area $A^1B^1E^1H$. The gain is greater if, in the pre-customs union position, the more-developed partner was a net importer from the rest of the world. In Figure 6.1(a) the initial level of imports in a free-trade position is shown by distance *AH*. The income effect of integration overrides other welfare consideration for the exporting partner state.

However, the Vinerian approach to customs union is static, and today it is generally agreed that long-term dynamic effects are more important. These are difficult to quantify, and for this reason there is no entirely satisfactory method of measuring the costs and benefits of economic integration. European Union (EU) economists have attempted to quantity the economic consequences of integration with particular emphasis on the costs and benefits to member states from financial flows to and from the EU budget.

A number of different trade effects pertinent to SACU may be distinguished (Ohly, 1992). These include changes in trade flows and the resulting adjustments in the structure of production; changes in employment and income, terms of trade, rate of growth, and economies of scale; improvements in technical efficiency; learning effects in production; cost savings arising from the elimination of non-tariff barriers; and price reductions ensuing from increased competition. Some of these effects are static (they are once-and-for-all: for example, as a result of a more effective allocation of resources), while others are dynamic (they create additional resources in the long run). The effects will differ among sectors, industries and enterprises.

Because of the complexities arising from static and dynamic effects as well as from microeconomic and macroeconomic processes, the analysis of costs and benefits is imperfect. There is an element of arbitrariness in that integration has to be compared with some benchmark; that is, actual performance has to be weighed against estimates of what would have happened in the absence of integration. The problems surrounding the construction of such a bench-mark are substantial: different hypotheses and assumptions can be used and these yield different results. The use of macroeconomic models in the EU has also not yielded good results, but a more modest approach, that has been used with some success, is the business survey that canvasses the views of entrepreneurs in order to assess the effects of integration (Ohly, 1992).

6.3　SACU IN THE LITERATURE

Although customs unions in the Southern African region date back to 1889, the immediate precursor of the present SACU, established in 1969, is the 1910 agreement between South Africa and the three British High Commission Territories (HCTs) of Basutoland, Bechuanaland and Swaziland. In contrast to the 1910 agreement, which was virtually ignored in the literature, the 1969 Southern African Customs Union (SACU) agreement has been the subject of academic works, mostly a membership cost-benefit analysis for Botswana, Lesotho and Swaziland (BLS) (Landell-Mills, 1971, 1979; Ettinger, 1974; Mosley, 1978, 1979; Robson, 1978; Cobbe, 1980; Hall, 1980; Hudson, 1981; Maasdorp, 1982, 1988, 1990, 1993 a; b; Weimer, 1983; Walters, 1989; Guma, 1990; Kumar, 1990; Lundahl and Petersson, 1991; Leith, 1992, 1993; McCarthy, 1992, 1994). Partly because of apartheid, this analysis has been more vig-orous than would otherwise have been the case. Studies of SACU have focused mainly on extensive appraisal of the 1969 SACU Agree-ment; examination of the revenue-sharing formula (especially the 1976 amendment; SACU and associated bodies, especially the RMA; country-specific impacts of SACU; the broader context of integra-tion in Southern Africa; and questions of economy-wide and sectoral development issues. Landell-Mills and Ettinger each examined in detail the stipulations of the 1969 agreement. Ettinger (1974) hypothesized the kind of tariff structure the BLS would institute if they had the option of doing so independently. He explored the consequences of imposing 'iso-price' tariffs (that is, tariffs that would leave existing prices in the BLS countries unaltered) an as-sumption that subordinates the objective of encouraging growth of infant industry to the objective of preventing a rise in the cost of living.

The literature recognizes the disadvantages for the BLNS countries

(Botswana, Lesotho, Namibia and Swaziland, from 1990) of being in a custom union with a more developed industrial economy like RSA, including in particular the polarization effects of development, the loss of fiscal direction and the trade diversion effects of RSA's protective tariffs (Mosley, 1978, 1979; Robson, 1978; Hudson, 1981). As Landell-Mills (1971) noted, in joining the customs union the BLNS countries forfeited effective control of indirect taxation. A lot of inconclusive research effort (Hall, 1980; Cobbe, 1988; Mwase, 1993, 1994) has examined the compensation arrangements and hypothesized whether the BLNS countries would be better off without the customs union. In particular, they examined whether the junior partners would raise the same level of revenue if they withdrew from SACU and imposed their own tariffs. Mosley (1978) provided quantitative estimates of static gains and losses (*vis-à-vis* industrial development, exports, government revenue and the cost of living) likely to accrue to the BLS countries for 1973 if they had withdrawn. Robson (1978) reworked the figures and discussed other relevant issues including the 'enhancement factor' of 1.42 in the formula. Maasdorp (1993a) noted that the BLNS partners have undoubtedly valued 'the relative certainty of revenue flows from the SACU'. Selwyn (1975) concluded that Botswana and Swaziland might not do too badly (with respect to lost revenues and customs duties) if they left SACU, but felt the question hardly worth exploring in the case of Lesotho. Isaksen (1993) in examining the advantages and disadvantages for all SACU contracting partners concluded that they 'end in a draw'. This is also the conclusion of consultants' reports commissioned by the BLNS in 1994.

6.4   DIFFERING VIEWS OF PARTNERS

There are major differences between the RSA and the BLNS in the interpretation, implementation and renegotiation of the SACU agreement. Under the customs union commission and various technical committees' consultative machinery, several relatively minor amendments have been made. A major amendment was the introduction of a stabilization factor into the revenue-sharing formula in 1976. By the end of the 1970s, all parties had reservations about the agreement; and renegotiation has been the subject of official investigations and discussions since 1982.

Revenue or Development?

Fixed Revenue Shares 1910–69

The 1910 agreement was concerned mainly with revenue allocation based on the proportion of the average customs and excise duty revenue of each territory to total customs and excise revenue of the customs union area for the three completed pre-agreement financial years. On this basis, the total share of the High Commission Territories was calculated as 1.31097 per cent: Basutoland was to receive 0.88575 per cent of all customs and excise revenue, Bechuanaland 0.27622 per cent and Swaziland 0.149 per cent. No provision was made in the agreement for the share to be reviewed, the tacit assumption being that the proportion of total customs revenue earned by the three territories would remain relatively stable until their incorporation into the Union of South Africa.

This fixed allocation of revenue among the contracting parties became increasingly anomalous as time wore on. It was not reviewed and did not take into account economic development in either the RSA or the High Commission Territories. For example, the consumption of goods in any one territory might have increased much faster than in the others for a variety of reasons, such as a higher population growth rate, a more rapid rate of economic growth leading to improved living standards and higher incomes, and so on (Kruger, 1956). By the late 1950s, the revenue-sharing arrangements were coming under increased criticism, especially as it had become clear that the territories would not be incorporated into the union.

The UK, which was giving recurrent budgetary aid to the High Commission Territories, was interested in a revised customs agreement, but it was the RSA that opened the negotiations in 1961 and prepared a draft revised agreement. The British response relied not on a detailed economic study of the position of the territories in the customs union but on a brief report prepared by a statistician, F. M. M. Lewes (Robson, 1967). According to Lewes, the HCTs together deserved 1.23 per cent of the total revenue pool, whereas they were actually receiving 1.31097 per cent. He therefore recommended that, instead of the formula being renegotiated, the share should merely be redistributed among the three territories according to their relative level of imports of dutiable goods. Table 6.2 compares the 1910 distribution and the Lewes formula.

Table 6.2   Percentage distribution of customs union revenue

Country	1910 Agreement	1965 Amendment	% Change
Basutoland	0.88575	0.47093	−46.8
Bechuanaland	0.27622	0.30971	+12.1
Swaziland	0.14900	0.53033	+255.9
Total HCTs	*1.21097*	*1.31097*	*+8.25*
South Africa	98.68903	98.68903	0
Total	*100*	*100*	*0*

The Lewes formula was accepted by Britain and was implemented from the 1965/66 fiscal year. Swaziland, because of its rapid economic growth, gained at the expense of the other territories, particularly Basutoland. But because the Lewes report was based on inadequate statistics and contained no arguments of a wider economic nature – for example, the implications of the RSA's protectionist policies – the British Colonial Office views were not accepted by the BLS countries at independence (Ettinger, 1974); discussions commenced in 1967 to consider terms for a new agreement.

The RSA's introduction of a sales tax in March 1969 had serious implications for the BLS countries. The tax was regressive, having a disproportionate effect on the low-income population of the BLS countries. According to Landell-Mills (1971), it was both the tax structure and its introduction without consultation that impressed on the BLS governments the urgency of concluding a new customs agreement. He argues that the political will to withdraw existed and that the RSA was aware that its unilateral action had placed the customs union in jeopardy.

The 1969 Revenue-sharing Formula

Unlike the 1910 agreement, the 1969 agreement was quite comprehensive. It contained a preamble whose aims were 'to ensure the continued economic development of the customs union area as a whole, and to ensure in particular that these arrangements encourage the development of the less advanced members of the customs union and the diversification of their economies. . .'. Moreover, to compensate the BLS countries for being in a customs union with a more developed country (for example, regarding trade-

Table 6.3   BLS revenue from common customs pool, 1968/69–1969/70
(R000s)

	1968/69	*1969/70 %*	*% Change*
Botswana	1.612	4.847	+200.6
Lesotho	1.950	5.000	+156.4
Swaziland	2.450	7.082	+189.1
Total	*6.012*	*16.929*	*+181.6*

diversion effects, polarization of industrial development between core and peripheral areas, and the loss of fiscal sovereignty), Article 14 inserted a multiplier into the revenue-sharing formula. The preamble and the enhancement factor have been central to the renegotiation.

In the 1980s, the RSA and the BLS countries differed on the emphasis to be placed on revenue versus development. According to Walters (1989), SACU 'was to be a tool of integration designed to promote economic development and it was explicitly recognized that this could only be achieved if there were discriminatory measures in favour of BLS'. One of these measures was the enhancement factor. Since the new agreement led to an immediate and substantial increase in the revenue accruing to BLS (Table 6.3) this aspect rather than development was singled out for emphasis by their spokespersons (Lovell, 1970; McCarthy, 1986).

Until recently BLNS (Namibia formalized membership in 1990) continued to emphasize the revenue aspect, arguing that changes in the RSA's tax structure have negated the concept of a revenue tariff. By contrast, the RSA has been concerned about its declining share of revenue and the priority attached to the revenue aspect by BLNS, which contradicted the preamble. In order to examine these views, it is necessary to consider the operation of the formula. All customs, excise and sales duties (but not general sales tax), as well as import surcharges collected in the four countries, are pooled at the South African Reserve Bank. A formula provides the basis for calculating the amount due to each of the BLNS countries. There are three stages in this calculation. First. the basic amount due to each country, let us say Swaziland, in any financial year is given by the equation:

$$R = \frac{A + B + C}{D + E + F + G} \tag{6.1}$$

where:

R = the amount payable to a junior partner; that is, Swaziland
A = c.i.f. value (including all duties) at border of imports into Swaziland from all sources
B = value of excisable and sales duty goods produced and consumed in Swaziland
C = excise and sales duties paid on B
D = c.i.f. value at border of imports into the common customs area from the rest of the world
E = customs and sales duties paid on D
F = value of excisable and sales duty goods produced and consumed in the customs union
G = excise and sales duties paid on F
H = total revenue pool of customs, excise and sales duties.

The formula thus seeks to divide the common revenue pool among the partners in proportion to their annual imports and their production and consumption of dutiable goods, but, as mentioned above, an enhancement factor was added, so that the formula may be rewritten as:

$$R_c = \frac{A + B + C}{D + E + F + G} \ (H) \ (1.42) \tag{6.2}$$

where 1.42 = enhancement factor.

The enhanced rate of revenue received by Swaziland is then

$$\frac{R_c}{A + B + C}$$

In 1976 the formula was amended in order to provide BLS with a stabilized rate of revenue of about 20 per cent. This may be written as:

$$R_s = \frac{R_c}{A + B + C} \tag{6.3}$$

subject to the constraints

$$0.23 \geq R_s = \frac{R_c}{A + B + C} \geq 0.17$$

Let us clarify this further. First, the amount due to Swaziland is calculated as per Equation 6.2. Then, if the enhanced rate of revenue

$$\frac{R_c}{A + B + C} - 0.20$$

one-half of the difference between the enhanced rate and 20 per cent is either added to or subtracted from 20 per cent subject to the constraints that the stabilized rate may not be less than 17 per cent or greater than 23 per cent.

The reason for the introduction of the stabilization factor was that, in 1969, BLS had wanted a rate of revenue of 20 per cent – the average in Commonwealth African countries. However, the rate fluctuated widely from year to year, making revenue forecasting and economic planning difficult. Thus, they negotiated for an amendment that would guarantee them a rate of revenue of 17–23 per cent, fluctuating around a mean of 20 per cent. In fact, the stabilized rate has tended towards the bottom end of the range and in 1981 BLS proposed that the range be increased to 19–25 per cent.

The BLS countries also proposed an econometric method of calculating the cash flows due to them. The actual payments made from the common pool in one year do not equal the accrued revenue – that is, the revenue calculated by the stabilization factor. The reason for this is that relevant statistics are not available to enable the accrued revenue to be calculated immediately; instead, there is an elaborate formula for making payments in respect of any particular year over a two-year period in three instalments.

As far as revenue-sharing is concerned, a number of issues are pertinent. For one thing, the formula includes BLS imports from the RSA but not vice versa. The inclusion of the RSA's imports from BLNS would increase the denominator, albeit by a relatively small amount, and thus reduce the share payable to BLNS. Walters (1989) points out, however, that the cost of the RSA maintaining customs posts at BLNS borders to record imports might well be more than the revenue it could earn from the inclusion of those imports. Nonetheless, because most BLNS imports are from the RSA and hence are duty-free, they contribute very little to the common revenue pool by way of duties collected. Botswana for instance, once claimed that it received twice what it paid in (*Africa Economic Digest*, 12 July 1986).

By including excise duties and sales tax, the formula takes the agreement beyond a pure customs union and towards fiscal harmonization, a characteristic of economic unions. Excise duties raise government revenue. Since the bulk of excisable goods produced in SACU are South African, and contribute on average over 60 per cent of the common revenue pool, McCarthy argued that 'South Africa's fiscal problems could be eased immensely if excise revenue was excluded from the CUA' (1986). That would certainly have been the case, but he conceded, and both the Margo Commission (South Africa, 1987) and the subsequent White Paper accepted that practical problems of administering such a system, requiring as it would strict border controls, made it essential to retain excise duties in the formula.

Indeed, as Walters (1989) states, excise duties were included in the formula in order to reduce the administrative costs incurred under the 1910 agreement, involving rebates on intra-union trade under removal-in-bond procedures. This underlines the fact that it is necessary to eliminate customs frontiers and documentation in a customs union, a uniform excise tariff. However, this implies a high level of consultation among member countries. More recently, the share of excise duties in the common pool has fallen; in 1991/92 it was 52.3 per cent.

Is the 20 per cent BLS target rate of revenue a justified norm? McCarthy (1986) examined 35 small developing countries and concluded that it is not sufficiently common. Walters (1989), however, excluded the upper-middle income countries from McCarthy's list and found that the mean rate was in fact slightly above 20 per cent. If one accepts 20 per cent as a target, there is a case for increasing the stabilization factor range, given the tendency for the rate to approximate only 17 per cent. But, as Walters points out, if 20 per cent is an acceptable target, why then not simply fix R_s at 20 per cent rather than retain the constraints in Equation 6.3 above? It is noteworthy that the effect of the stabilization factor is that in recent years the nominal multiplier has exceeded 1.42, standing at 1.94 in 1991/92 (Maasdorp, 1994). However, Leith's (1993) calculations show that Botswana could gain slightly (on a static basis only, ignoring transitional and long-term dynamic effects), from having its own independent tariff regime. It may well be that iso-price tariff calculations of what some of the other smaller countries could raise on their own by applying the SACU common external tariff would also show that the effective enhancement was much lower than the nominal figure of 94 per cent.

A common argument in the literature regarding the actual payments to the BLNS is that lags in the cash flow may be regarded as an interest-free loan to the RSA, which uses the funds in the meantime. Walters (1989), however, argues that because estimation errors are corrected each year, cash flow will only lag behind accruals if estimation errors are increasing. He interprets the payments formula as a forecasting formula based on the assumption that the absolute growth in accrued revenue over any two-year period is constant. Cash flow will then lag only if absolute growth of accrued revenue increases, causing the equation to forecast too low a value for accrual. Thus, the alleged two-year lag is a misnomer for a forecasting method believed to underestimate consistently. He quotes evidence from Swaziland to the effect that the formula suggested by BLS and accepted by the Customs Union Commission in 1981 would not have been 'unequivocally preferable' to the existing formula. Walters concludes that the two-year lag might well have been characteristic of the 1970s but not of the 1980s.

The White Paper of 1988 accepted the Margo Commission recommendation that attempts should be made to prevent a time-lag in payments to BLS by making them monthly instead of quarterly, but this was never implemented. However, apart from BLNS not receiving interest on the amounts owed to them, these funds are also eroded by inflation. There are better ways of arriving at the first estimate, and these should be examined more closely. For instance, the graph of BLNS on which their revenue share is based is a curve. It is incorrect to fit a tangent – that is, a straight line – to a curve (as the formula does) for the purposes of estimating the revenue in two-years' time. It will undershoot the curve and the corrections will be bigger than forecast. It would be better to use either a polynomial (such as a parabola) or to fit a straight line after first taking logarithms of the data. The latter method would correct for any tendency for deviations away from the underlying curvilinear trend to get larger as the figures get larger. By fitting a straight line to log data, projecting the result by two years, and then using antilogarithms to get back to the original scale, we obtain a weighted geometric average of past figures. In this way, the problems with the time-lag would be overcome.

Proceeds from SACU contribute a substantial proportion of government current revenue in BLS: for example, 60 per cent in Lesotho. Remittances from the customs revenue pool as a percentage of total government revenue over 1981–4 was 64 per cent, 61.4 per cent and 30.6 per cent for Lesotho, Swaziland and Botswana, respectively. As Table 6.4 shows, remittances to Namibia, hitherto R250 m. per year, increased to R300 m. in 1986/87, R394.2 m. (1988/89), R447.8 m. (1989/90) and R657.6 m. (1990/91). They form about 20 per cent of total Namibian government revenue. In 1990/91 the remittances as a percentage of BLNS government revenue were Botswana 14.5 per cent, Lesotho 57.7 per cent, Swaziland 32 per cent; and Namibia 43.8 per cent. By contrast, South Africa has been concerned about its declining share of customs revenue. Until 1993 this derived mainly from the so-called 'political independence' granted by Pretoria to Transkei (1976), Bophuthatswana (1977), Venda (1979) and Ciskei (1981) – the TBVC states. Since the concept of Bantustans was unacceptable to BLS, the TBVC states could not accede to SACU as formal members. Pretoria concluded bilateral agreements with each of the TBVC states, applying the terms of the SACU agreement to them. In Pretoria's eyes this has meant a greatly diminished share of overall SACU revenue accruing to South Africa (last column, Table 6.4). In fact, as Table 6.4 shows, from 1981/82 onwards, the TBVC states received more from the common revenue pool than did BLNS – their combined greater population meant higher import volumes. McCarthy (1986) calculated that if all the homelands were to accept 'independence', Pretoria might receive nothing, and in fact might make an absolute loss, on SACU. The possibility of this happening was zero, however; more important was the BLS contention that the RSA would in any event have had to transfer an equivalent sum to TBVC in lieu of funds they would have received had they elected not to become 'independent', and that it was no concern of theirs if the customs union were used as the mechanism to transfer these funds.

As far as BLNS were concerned, the RSA received the share shown in column 4, not column 6, in Table 6.4. This argument was incontrovertible. However, even column 4 of Table 6.4 shows a declining share of SACU revenue accruing to the RSA. The main reason for this is that the BLNS economies are highly open with a high propensity to import and, with average rates of economic growth exceeding that of the RSA, the numerator in the formula has grown rapidly. In contrast, the denominator has not increased as rapidly because of the RSA's move away from customs tariffs to quotas as a means of protecting industry, as well as from sales duties to GST (McCarthy, 1986) and later VAT, neither of which are included in the formula. It has been calculated that, had the RSA's economy grown by about 3 per cent per annum since the mid-1970s, its im-

Table 6.4 Payments from Common Revenue Pool, 1969/70–1992/93

Year	Pool (R mill)	To BLS (R mill)	(%)	Transfer to Namibia (R mill)	(%)	SA (%)	To TBVC (R mill)	(%)	SA-TBVC
1969/70	430.7	16.9	3.9			96.1			96.1
1970/71	463.9	16.0	3.4			96.6			96.6
1971/72	640.7	22.7	3.5			96.5			96.5
1972/73	747.3	29.7	4.0			96.0			96.0
1973/74	859.1	48.9	5.7	19.6	2.3	92.0			92.0
1974/75	864.3	66.3	7.7	22.1	2.6	89.7			89.7
1975/76	1010.9	58.1	5.7	30.1	3.0	91.3			91.3
1976/77	1113.6	51.1	4.6	36.0	3.2	92.2			92.2
1977/78	1447.5	104.9	7.2	46.2	3.2	89.6	40.0	2.8	86.8
1978/79	1723.6	162.6	9.4	47.6	2.8	87.8	133.5	7.7	80.1
1979/80	2290.3	228.7	10.0	44.5	1.9	88.1	173.8	7.6	80.5
1980/81	2246.4	260.1	11.6	41.5	1.8	86.6	244.8	10.9	75.7
1981/82	2122.6	243.8	11.5	257.8	12.1	76.4	231.6	10.9	65.5
1982/83	2418.8	314.7	13.0	250.0	10.3	76.7	341.2	14.1	62.6
1983/84	3167.8	390.8	12.3	250.0	7.9	79.8	516.4	16.3	63.5
1984/85	3299.8	462.5	14.0	250.0	7.6	78.4	700.2	21.2	57.2
1985/86	3614.6	472.1	13.1	300.0	8.3	78.6	747.4	20.7	57.9
1986/87	4118.0	496.9	12.1	350.0	8.5	79.4	751.2	18.2	61.2
1987/88	4706.6	577.3	12.3	350.0	7.4	80.3	985.3	20.9	59.4
1988/89	6867.5	719.8	10.5	394.2	5.7	83.8	1241.4	18.1	65.7
1989/90	7675.6	918.0	12.0	447.8	5.8	82.2	1484.4	19.3	62.9
1990/91	7922.2	1353.7	17.1	657.6	8.3	74.6	1566.1	19.8	54.8
1991/92	8017.0	1814.2	22.6	735.5	9.2	68.2	1824.8	22.8	45.4
1992/93	8917.9	2248.7	25.2	751.6	8.4	66.4	2423.2	27.2	39.2

Sources: McCarthy (1986); *Report of the Auditor General for the Financial Year* (annual, 1973/74–1983/84); *Report of the Auditor, General on the Appropriation and Miscellaneous Accounts of General Affairs* (annual, 1984/85–1989/90); Central Economic Advisory Services, Pretoria (for 1990/91).

ports in 1991/92 would have been 50 per cent higher than they were. Had that been the case, South Africa would have received 78.7 per cent, not 68.2 per cent, of the pool. Moreover, it would have been a greatly expanded pool and, because of the stabilization factor the absolute amounts accruing to BLNS would not have been affected (Maasdorp, 1994).

Under the new GATT/WTO liberal trade regime, the share of customs duties as a source of government revenue will decline. It might, therefore, be difficult to argue in favour of the retention of the present stabilization range geared to a 20 per cent average rate of revenue. The SACU offer to the GATT on tariff bindings under the Uruguay Round involved, *inter alia*, the acceptance of the obligation to implement cuts in industrial and agricultural tariffs over a specified period. In addition, all quotas and quantitative import restrictions have to be converted into tariffs. In agriculture in particular, this conversion sometimes results in very high initial rates that serve as the starting point for the process of liberalization. An average reduction of 36 per cent in tariffs for agriculture is required. The offer for industrial products entails a reduction of *ad valorem* duties by an average of one-third over a five-year period. Tariff rates for these products will be standardized at zero, 5 per cent, 10 per cent, 15 per cent and 20 per cent, with a normal maximum of 30 per cent. Some rates will come into effect immediately, while others are phased over five years. The offers for the highly protected sectors of industry, notably motor vehicles, textiles and clothing, differ from the standard pattern. The reduction in their tariffs is generally to be more than the average 33 per cent, and phasing-down period in their case will be longer – as much as 12 years in the case of textiles and clothing.

Detailed proposals have been made by the South African Board on Tariffs and Trade for implementing the proposals, and in many cases the rates proposed are lower than those set out in the initial offer. Tariff changes consequent upon the GATT/WTO negotiations will affect the customs union renegotiations. They will have significant impact on the input costs of the industries affected. Together with increased pressures from external competition on final prices and on industrial efficiency, these should affect export competitiveness and domestic prices, thereby reducing the costs of trade diversion (price-rising effects) in the customs union. These tariff rates changes will affect the size of the revenue pool, subject to the elasticity of substitution between SACU products and imports. On balance, however, in the longer run this effect in itself is unlikely to be positive, although sufficiently significant positive growth effects from trade liberalization on the SACU economies could generate an expanded common revenue pool.

SACU faces the problem of unequal sharing of benefits arising from industrial imbalances between the stronger RSA and the weaker BLNS economies. As in the case of the East African Common Market, it is unlikely that the redistribution of customs and excise revenue will adequately compensate the BLNS. Hence there is a need to emphasize the development of SACU's smaller, poorer, less-developed partner states, especially economically depressed areas.

Development Objectives

Apart from revenue-sharing, there are a number of contentious points relating to the RSA's view that the preamble's development objectives have been downplayed. The White Paper accepted the Margo Commission (1987) recommendation that instead of the compensation and stabilization components of SACU revenue being paid into current government revenue in BLS, they should be paid into a development funds or else replaced by direct, conditional assistance. The BLS countries argued that, while it cannot be shown that SACU revenue is allocated to any specific development project, a substantial proportion is applied to the development and diversification of their economies (Walters, 1989). Clearly, expenditure on road maintenance, education and health is of a developmental nature, and Pretoria's argument appears invalid. McCarthy, indeed, states that BLS would view such moves as 'paternalistic' (1986).

South African officials incorrectly viewed these payments as aid grants. The payments represent (1) revenue BLNS countries would have earned had they had their own independent tariff regimes, and (2) compensation for the disadvantages of being the RSA's captive market. If BLNS were not in SACU they could replace the RSA's quantitative restrictions with customs tariffs. To the extent that imports were still sourced from the RSA rather than from alternative suppliers, there could be price and cost of living increases for their low-income populations. Smuggling across porous borders and the costs of administering and policing full-scale customs department could be problematic, but they would possess an additional revenue-earning instrument. Moreover, because RSA goods enter BLNS duty free, they provide severe competition for, or inhibit the establishment of, domestic industries. McCarthy (1986) calculated that in 1980, 12.8 per cent by value of the RSA's export went to BLS, which represented a more important market than the UK. Clearly, the payments from the revenue pool represent an entitlement on the part of BLS, not largess on the part of Pretoria.

During the 1969 negotiations, the RSA was persuaded not only to withdraw its proposal for protection of its existing industries, but to agree to infant industry protection (Article 6) and a pioneer industries clause (Article 7) for the BLS countries. Economic integration cannot guarantee that all member countries will attract industry. Textbooks advocate a planned regional programme of industrial development, but in practice it has been impossible to reach agreement on the divisions of industries. The Andean Pact and East African Community experiences are cases in point. The reason is that locational decisions are made not by governments but by firms, and firms cannot be coerced into locating in countries to which they do not want to go (Krugman and Venables, 1993). Industrial concentration in the most-developed country meant that the RSA would attract the great bulk of new industrial investment in SACU. This tendency was exacerbated after the 1969 agreement of the RSA's industrial decentralization policy, adopted to further the development of the Bantustans, and later by a more sophisticated regional industrial development programme (RIDP) from 1982 onwards. BLS simply did not have the resources to match the incentives available under these programmes (Maasdorp, 1988). McCarthy (1986) correctly pointed out that the industrial concentration problem in a customs union cannot, in principal, be countered by compensatory revenue transfer, but it was not politically feasible to include BLS in a co-ordinated industrial programme together with the TBVC states. Compensation for industrial polarization via the revenue-sharing formula, then, might not have been merely a second-best solution for BLS as McCarthy (1986) suggested; it might have been both politically and practically the best, but in itself not capable of solving the problem of industrial growth for BLS.

Unfortunately for BLS, neither these articles, nor Article 11 (which allows member countries to prohibit the importation of goods for economic, social, cultural or other reasons), are sufficient to offset the forces of concentration. Furthermore, the BLS countries have not always made the maximum use of these articles, and some differences of interpretation have also occurred (Maasdorp, 1982). For instance, the accusation is often made that South Africa has attempted to crush new industrial ventures in BLS by acting contrary to the agreement. However, these allegations relate to instances in which proposed industries in BLS would have penetrated the RSA market by flouting non-tariff barriers applicable there (Maasdorp, 1982). Article 2(5) allowed BLS to import goods from outside SACU without regard to the RSA's import controls, provided they did not re-export those goods to the RSA and thereby obstruct the attainment of the economic objectives of that import control legislation. The cases in which it was alleged that the RSA had attempted to crush new industrial ventures in BLS related to instances in which new industries there had been freed from non-tariff barriers by their governments. These non-tariff barriers included South Africa's import controls. The two plants usually mentioned were a fertilizer factory in Swaziland and a motor vehicle assembly plant in Lesotho. Both were designed primarily to serve the South African market and represent attempts to penetrate that market by avoiding non-tariff barriers imposed by the RSA on its own industries. In the case of the motor vehicle assembly plant in Lesotho, the Japanese investors (Honda) would have avoided the local content stipulation laid down by the RSA government, and their exports to the RSA would have threatened the viability of existing RSA motor manufacturers. South Africa therefore invoked Article 2(5), but it could also have used Article 1(7), which states that if one member sells a product to a partner in such increasing quantities as to threaten producers in the partner country, the two governments should consult and cooperate in finding a mutually acceptable solution.

Although some relevant articles, especially Article 2, could be made more explicit and obviate misunderstandings (Walters, 1989), the best prospects for BLS industrialization lay in their attracting as much industry as possible while the RSA was subjected to anti-apartheid disinvestment and sanction campaigns, and using the articles in the agreement, especially those relating to infant and pioneer industries, to the maximum.

Moves to Renegotiate, 1981–91

By the end of the 1970s it was clear that neither the RSA nor BLS was entirely satisfied with the 1969 agreement, albeit for different reasons.

The 1981–2 Discussions

Scheepers' (1979) argument that emphasis in the agreement should shift from revenue-sharing to modalities for encouraging economic development in BLS influenced Pretoria's thinking throughout the 1980s. By contrast, BLS raised problems *vis-à-vis* the formula, and these formed the basis of the discussions at the Customs Union Commission meeting in 1981–2.

First, and contrary to their hopes, the stabilized rate of revenue for BLS had tended towards the bottom end of the 17–23 per cent range. They therefore proposed that the range be increased to 19–25 per cent. Second, the BLS countries were concerned at the time-lag in payments to them from the common revenue pool, and they proposed an econometric method for calculating these cash flows. These proposals were favourably considered by a sub-committee of the Customs Union Commission. However, in 1982 the latter's recommendations were rejected by Pretoria, whose wish to rene-gotiate the whole agreement led to commissioning a study by Pro-fessor Colin McCarthy to investigate the matter.

The McCarthy Report and BLS Reactions

The McCarthy report (1986) re-emphasized the RSA's concern about the different emphasis placed on revenue-sharing and development by member states and brought into sharp focus the RSA's primary concern, its declining share of the common pool revenue. As McCarthy pointed out, this meant that the RSA was also empha-sizing the revenue-sharing aspect! McCarthy recommended that emphasis should be placed on three principles: co-ordinated econ-omic development, a fair distribution of revenue and a recognition of the RSA's position as the dominant economic power in the region.

The McCarthy report, accompanied by the RSA government's views, was sent to BLS for comment in 1986. The RSA had viewed the McCarthy recommendations as justifying their SACU stance. It advised BLS that it would press for a revised, 'clean' formula with no enhancement or stabilization factors but including BLS imports from the RSA, a strategy to counter industrial concentra-tion and provide for an equitable development in the customs union; the establishment of a council of ministers and a permanent secre-tariat; and ways of improving BLS relations with the then RSA Board of Trade and Industries.

BLS contested the McCarthy recommendations, criticizing the RSA interpretation of its declining revenue share, the 'clean' for-mula with no enhancement argument, the treatment of compensa-tion as a subsidy from the RSA, the criticism of the 20 per cent rate of revenue norm, the effect of the RSA's decentralization policy on industrial concentration and the adoption of a co-ordinated econ-omic development strategy. BLS reiterated the need for renegotia-tion of the agreement to provide stronger provisions for assisting the less-developed partners.

A study group was established in 1986 with terms of reference to examine the agreement, but no progress was made. Pretoria's position was influenced by the publication of the Margo Commission report on taxation in South Africa (1987) and the government's White Paper (1988) in response thereto. These documents advocated the replacement of GST by VAT in RSA, and Pretoria was obliged to discuss with BLS the implications for the customs union of a destination-based invoice VAT. Furthermore, the RSA was investigating its tariff policy and the future role of the Board of Trade and Industries.

In the event, BLS took the initiative and negotiations recommenced in 1990, coinciding with Namibia's formal SACU membership. The BLNS position revolved around the following points:

- inadequate compensation for payment delays from the common pool, the loss of fiscal discretion, the price-raising;
- the effects of the RSA's protective tariffs and industrial concentration;
- greater protection for BLNS agriculture and infant industries and measures to encourage industrial development;
- arbitrary and unilateral decision-making by the RSA; and
- the conversion of the Board of Trade and Industries into a multilateral institution, and establishment of multilateral dispute arbitration procedures.

South Africa's Response

In 1991, responding to the BLNS position, the RSA argued that the demands arising from a changing economic environment could no longer be fully met by the existing agreement, which had become an 'outmoded instrument for economic co-operation in the region'. The RSA and BLNS had diametrically opposing viewpoints that were a natural result of the differences in the level of industrial development. The RSA was moving away from an inward-looking, import-replacement policy of industrial development behind high tariff barriers towards a more outward-looking, export-orientated approach. This might not necessarily suit BLNS. Any accommodation of the BLNS industrial development objectives would conflict with SACU's free movement of goods. The RSA concluded that SACU was becoming 'financially unaffordable', and that it wished to have greater freedom in designing industrial development policies. The differing objectives of members could no longer be accommodated within the present agreement, and consequently 'serious attention should be given to the creation of a looser type economic co-operation with broader regional participation'. South Africa suggested that the agreement in its present form should continue pending further discussions, but that the terms of reference of the study group should be suspended.

In the following two years the RSA occasionally made public comments suggesting that Pretoria wished to dissolve the customs union. Both the director general of the department of trade and industry (DOTI) and the new minister of finance and of trade and industry stated that the customs union was inappropriate and too costly, and that a new model of regional co-operation should be sought (Naude, 1992). The minister of finance was reportedly on the verge of withdrawing the RSA from SACU, being dissuaded by the department of foreign affairs (*Sunday Business Times*, 7 February 1993). In May 1993 it was reported that Pretoria was about to publish a document recommending the dissolution of SACU and the formation of a wider customs union, including Zimbabwe, Zambia, Mozambique and Angola, as well as steps to rationalize this customs union with SADC and the PTA (Natal *Mercury*, 20 May 1993). Such a document was never released. Instead, South Africa suddenly changed its views on SACU.

6.5 TOWARDS CONVERGENCE

The Joint Technical Group

The RSA's changed views on SACU were manifested in August 1993, when the RSA's minister of finance stated at a special meeting of SACU finance ministers in Mbabane that SACU was an important instrument for regional integration. Given BLNS's positive views, it was agreed to established a joint technical group to examine:

- the RSA's draft tariff offer in the GATT Uruguay Round;
- co-operation options in Southern Africa, including possible relationship between SACU, the European Community, SADC and the PTA;
- improving various mechanisms of the agreement, including contact between the Board on Tariffs and Trade with other SACU members; three RSA task forces for textiles and clothing, motor

vehicle and electronic industries in the RSA; and combating fraud and evasion of obligations under the agreement; and

- the revenue-sharing formula.

The joint technical group dealt first with the GATT offer. Thereafter, the RSA agreed to present its (revised) views to the Customs Union Commission. However, Pretoria commissioned a study on a common vision for future regional economic integration and co-operation and this, plus general inaction in government in Pretoria in the run-up to the April 1994 elections, meant that customs union matters took a back seat.

Political Change in South Africa

In the meantime, the director general of the DOTI underlined the importance of SACU when he stated that 'the SACU was chosen not only for improvement but as the vehicle for addressing the question of wider regional cooperation. It may well turn out to be the core of wider future Southern African economic cooperation' (Maasdorp, 1993a).

The publication of the DOTI visions document (Maasdorp, 1994), set out the views of the DOTI more clearly. Coincidentally, the ANC held a workshop on the SACU in Gaborone (Sisulu *et al.*, 1994). By this time a transitional executive council (TEC) had been established in South Africa and the DOTI vision statement was presented to the TEC and accepted with some minor modifications.

The ANC had stated that the new RSA would not follow a policy of economic hegemony in the region but would promote mutually beneficial relationships, without accentuating existing imbalances. At the Gaborone conference the ANC stated that it wished to see a more open renegotiation of the agreement, that it would not be just governments that would participate in the renegotiations, but the business sectors, organized labour and civil society as well. In other words, it wished the SACU to be 'democratized'.

The salient features of the DOTI report (Maasdorp, 1994) are as follows:

(1) Economic relations between the various countries should foster mutually beneficial links (a positive-sum game for all); promote economic development in all countries; minimize the economic dominance of any country or countries; promote interdependence;

facilitate intra-regional trade and investments flows; and strengthen the competitiveness of individual countries and SACU as a whole in the global economy.

(2) Not all countries benefit equally from membership, but all should be better off inside than outside SACU.

(3) All countries should commit themselves to a policy of good neighbourliness and eschew a position of regional hegemony. South Africa in particular should commit itself to a policy of full co-operation as an equal partner.

(4) A mutually acceptable revision of the revenue-sharing formula holds the key to the renegotiation of the SACU agreement. Since one of the conditions for successful integration is that all members countries should perceive that they will gain, there will have to be a trade-off to keep the BLNS countries contented if the revenue-sharing formula is amended. The RSA and the BLNS countries have different concerns with regard to the agreement, customs and excise revenue being more important to BLNS than to the RSA. It is accepted that BLNS should be compensated in the agreement, but this need not be through the formula. All other aspects of the agreement should be examined in this regard.

(5) In re-examining the formula, account should be taken of the following:

- the changed global economic environment, and in particular the implications of the GATT/WTO agreement for the SACU and for future revenue flows from customs duties;
- the possibility of a differentiated revenue-sharing formula being applied to each country, since the BLNS economies are not homogeneous, and SACU is of varying importance as a source of revenue;
- an improved revenue estimation method to overcome the disadvantages to BLNS of the two-year time-lag in cash flows; and
- a common statistical base for purposes of calculating intra-SACU trade.

(6) In order to assist BLNS countries in their economic development efforts, the following revisions to the remainder of the agreement should be considered:

- to mitigate the problem of loss of fiscal sovereignty, the RSA Board of Tariffs and Trade would become a SACU Board of

Tariffs and Trade with representation from each country, and a multilateral authority (or secretariat) independent of any government should be established to administer the agreement;
- to mitigate the problem of industrial polarization, either RSA subsidies to industries under the regional industrial development programme should be abolished or a common industrial and location policy should be adopted by the entire SACU;
- articles relating to infant industry protection in BLNS, the designation of industries of special importance to BLNS, and the protection of their agricultural producers should be re-examined, as should the secret memorandum of understanding and its contents, competition policy and the operation of non-tariff barriers.

(7) In order to further assist the economic development of BLNS, various ways of increasing co-operation in education, health, and so on, should be investigated, and the role of the Development Bank of Southern Africa as a regional institution should be examined.
(8) The relationship of SACU to the Common Monetary Area (CMA) should be investigated with a view to deepening economic integration to ensure, *inter alia*, free mobility of capital and labour within the SACU area. The concept of 'variable geometry' allows countries to enter into a deeper form of economic integration within the basic customs union arrangement.
(9) Once the agreement has been renegotiated, the relations between SACU and other organizations (for example, SADC and COMESA) should be investigated, given the possibility of widening SACU.

After the April 1994 elections a new government of national unity (dominated by the ANC) was formed in the RSA. The DOTI is handling the renegotiations of the SACU agreement, for which a meeting was held in Pretoria on 11 November 1994. A Customs Union Task Team (CUTT) with terms of reference was established. (See Appendix 6A.)

Issues for the CUTT

The timetable for the completion of the CUTT's work was clearly unrealistic, and the renegotiations may be expected to continue into 1996. There are a number of issues that have not been dealt

Table 6.5   Views of firms on usefulness of regional groupings (%)

	Useful	Not useful	Uncertain
SACU	73.3	13.7	13.0
CMA	85.4	2.9	11.7
SADCC	24.1	36.7	39.2
PTA	46.6	25.0	28.4

Source: Economic Research Unit Survey, University of Natal, 1992.

with at length in this report but which require special attention during this period.

The Attitude of Firms

The private sector is the engine of economic growth, and its views on the costs and benefits of SACU should be seriously considered by the CUTT.

The only published attempt thus far at a business survey was made in 1992 and covered 283 firms engaged in cross-border trade in six SADC countries (Maasdorp, 1993a; b). Four (Botswana, Lesotho, Swaziland and Namibia) were members of the SACU, four (Lesotho, Swaziland, Malawi and Zimbabwe) of the PTA and all six of the then SADCC. Firms were asked whether or not they had found these regional groupings to be useful in the course of their business. Their responses are given in Table 6.5.

The CMA received the highest rate of approval of any of the four groupings. The high degree of uncertainty in the SADCC countries was not surprising, since SADCC has not been directly concerned with trade.

Firms in Lesotho, Swaziland and Namibia were also asked which organization – SACU or PTA – they thought their country should belong to if it had to make a choice. SACU was chosen by 85.3 per cent. The inclusion of Namibia, which was not a member of the PTA at the time, made no difference to this result.

The survey did not include the RSA, but organized business in the RSA has generally been very positive towards the customs union and, indeed, to some vague notion of deeper integration. These views are clearly shared by firms in neighbouring countries, as Table 6.5 indicates.

The question relating to membership in SACU was included in all six country surveys. In the SACU countries 77.9 per cent of the firms felt their country should belong; when the results of the Zimbabwean and Malawian surveys were added, this dropped to 75.5 per cent. This is not a significant difference in the results.

The reasons for firms in the BLNS countries favouring SACU membership were grouped around four points: ease of trade, the lowering of prices, the availability of goods and services, and access to markets. Under ease of trade, answers included: a reduction of import problems (borders/customs problems, documentation, bureaucracy, delays), a simplification of business procedures, ease of contact with suppliers and good information. Some firms felt that commodity prices were kept lower while others referred to the importance of the free movement and hence the availability of goods and services. Access both to the RSA market and to the markets of other partner countries was important to some firms. Another point mentioned was that relations with the strongest economy in Africa would be beneficial, while some firms felt that their historical experience had been purely with SACU, they knew how it worked, and they were happy to see it continue.

Those that did not favour membership mentioned loss of sovereignty for their country (the fact that South Africa set duties and quotas), the lack of protection for local industries and competition from RSA incentive schemes, and the costs arising from having to purchase South African goods at higher prices because of protective tariffs.

Malawian and Zimbabwean firms favoured SACU membership because of ease of trade and price reductions, stimulus to trade and the benefits of integration. The reduction of customs formalities and the absence of import licences, together with easy access to spare parts, were important points. A number of firms felt that SACU would help to reduce the price of imports (especially of raw materials), facilitate the movement of their goods through the RSA, allow them to enjoy economies of scale and encourage the development of trade by breaking down regional barriers and facilitating the exchange of technology. Access to the RSA and general SACU markets was held to be important, as was the availability of an advanced infrastructure. Some felt that integration was strengthened by the monetary arrangement, which benefited everyone in the regional bloc, while others felt that they benefited from high tariff barriers.

Malawian and Zimbabwean firms opposed to SACU gave answers relating to RSA dominance, the loss of economic sovereignty, the

Table 6.6   South Africa's top 20 trading partners, 1992 (Rm.)

	Country	Imports (M)	Exports (X)	Total	Ratio X/M
	SACU	*2 188*	*12 933*	*15 121*	*5.91*
(1)	USA	7 625	4 773	12 398	0.63
(2)	German	8 944	2 892	11 836	0.32
(3)	UK	5 829	4 492	10 321	0.77
(4)	Japan	6 016	3 742	9 758	0.62
(5)	Switzerland	1 317	5 375	6 692	4.08
(6)	*Botswana*	*496*	*4 285*	*4 781*	*8.64*
(7)	*Namibia*	*735*	*3 873*	*4 608*	*5.27*
(8)	Taiwan	1 957	2 148	4 105	1.10
(9)	Italy	1 995	1 620	3 615	0.81
(10)	Netherlands	1 372	1 930	3 302	1.41
(11)	Belgium	1 226	1 979	3 205	1.61
(12)	France	2 193	974	3 167	0.44
(13)	*Swaziland*	*804**	*2 234*	*3 038*	*2.78*
(14)	*Lesotho*	*153*	*2 541*	*2 694*	*16.61*
(15)	Hong Kong	1 001	1 509	2 510	1.51
(16)	Zimbabwe	763	1 553	2 316	2.04
(17)	South Korea	806	978	1 784	1.21
(18)	Spain	398	1 090	1 468	2.74
(19)	Israel	317	969	1 286	3.06
(20)	China	709	489	1 198	0.69

Note:
* 1991 figure.

Source: Department of Trade and Industry, Pretoria; South African Reserve Bank, Pretoria (for African countries).

fact that their markets were not inside SACU, the fact that RSA goods would become more expensive as exporters would lose the GEIS benefits, and economic and political differences.

These views of SACU were corroborated in another survey undertaken in Swaziland in 1994, the details of which cannot be revealed at this stage for reasons of confidentiality.

South Africa's Benefits from SACU

South Africa has tended to underestimate its benefits from SACU, and these should be stressed by BLNS.

Table 6.6 illustrates that the RSA has a very favourable balance of trade with its customs union partners. Moreover, BLNS imports approximately 25 per cent by value of the RSA's manufactured exports and 10 per cent of total RSA exports. Partly because of cheap (migrant) labour, industrial and technological advances, and export subsidies, RSA unit production costs have been low, ensuring competitive prices for RSA exports. However, the RSA is not necessarily the cheapest source for a number of BLNS imports. The UNDP (1989) reached the same conclusion with respect to some Namibian imports. In the absence of a customs union, some of the RSA's exports to BLNS would face severe competition and be lost to suppliers from abroad. The proportion is difficult to estimate because many retail and wholesale firms in BLNS are branches of RSA companies and are linked into the buying patterns of their head offices. However, there is no doubt that there are trade-diverting effects in the RSA's favour.

Moreover, apart from being a market for goods, there is a substantial flows of services from the RSA to BLNS. Furthermore, the RSA's trade with BLNS accounts for 30 per cent of new value-added and about 70 000 new jobs in the RSA's manufacturing sector. Clearly, BLNS purchases contribute substantially to RSA company profits and employment attributable to the trade-diverting effects of SACU tariffs, which have been set, as noted earlier, in order to protect South African industry. McFarland (1983) estimated that 3 000 000 jobs in South Africa were attributable to SACU, but his methodology might be questioned. BLNS provides an accessible, lucrative and dependent market to the RSA, especially for capital goods and processed foodstuffs. BLNS producers face unequal competition and possibly 'dumping'. Indeed the Administrator General of Namibia in his 1981/82 budget contemplated taking counter-measures against the possibility of a form of dumping by South African concerns.

Trade between typical African countries is hampered by production of similar agricultural products. However, the RSA produces both primary commodities and manufactured goods. There is, as PTA (1990) and ADB (1993) studies have shown, considerable latitude for production complementarity between the RSA and the SACU/SADC/COMESA countries. SACU accounts for about 75 per cent of the RSA's tradewith the sub-region. Most SACU imports are sourced from or through the RSA. The import dependence on the RSA is as follows: Lesotho 94 per cent, Swaziland 91 per cent, Namibia 90 per cent, Botswana 81 per cent, Malawi 32 per cent, Zimbabwe 25.2 per cent and Zambia 20 per cent. Exports to RSA are less, accounting for 46 per cent, 42 per cent and

Table 6.7   GDP and sectoral growth rates 1970–80 and 1980–92, Botswana, Lesotho and South Africa (% per annum)

	GDP		*Agriculture*		*Manufacturing*		*Services*	
	1970–80	*1980–92*	*1970–80*	*1980–92*	*1970–80*	*1980–92*	*1970–80*	*1980–92*
Botswana	14.5	10.1	8.3	3.4	22.9	8.9	14.8	11.7
Lesotho	8.6	5.4	0.2	0.5	18.0	12.3	13.6	5.3
South Africa	3.0	1.1	3.2	1.7	4.7	–0.2	3.8	2.1

Note: World Bank comparative data for Namibia and Swaziland not available.

Source: World Bank, *World Development Report* (1978, 1994).

25 per cent for Swaziland, Lesotho and Namibia, respectively. Of the RSA's top 14 trading partners, four are SACU members (Table 6.6). Although the balance of merchandise trade is in favour of the RSA, this imbalance can be offset if the RSA's imports of hydroelectric power (for example, from Namibia's Ruacana HEP) and water (from the Lesotho Highland Water Project) are taken into account. Furthermore, the RSA's Northern Transvaal and PWV regions have cost advantages in using the port of Maputo and the trans-Kalahari highway, respectively.

Economic Growth

It is important that all the SACU member countries share in the benefits of economic growth and development. It is therefore worth reviewing comparative performances of member countries since the signing of the 1969 agreement. Table 6.7 shows growth rates of GDP, agriculture, mining and services in South Africa, Botswana and Lesotho over the period 1970–92.

From Table 6.7 it can be seen that BLS countries have enjoyed far higher average annual growth rates than the RSA. It is clearly impossible to disentangle and quantify the effects of the various forces at work, but the RSA's virtual stagnation is attributable very largely to domestic political volatility from 1976 onwards and the effect this had on investment. For BLNS it is clear that SACU membership did not prevent these countries from achieving satisfactory rates of economic growth or from transforming the sectoral composition of their GDP. For example, in Lesotho agriculture's share of GDP fell from 35 per cent in 1970 to 11 per cent in 1992, while that of industry (broadly defined to include manufacturing

Table 6.8   GNP per capita, 1976 and 1992 – BLS and South Africa

	$		% SA	
	1976	*1992*	*1976*	*1992*
Botswana	410	2790	30.6	104.5
Lesotho	170	590	12.7	22.1
Swaziland	470	1090	35.1	40.8
South Africa	1340	2670	100.0	100.0

Source: World Bank, *World Development Report* (1978, 1994).

and non-manufacturing) increased from 9 per cent to 45 per cent. In Botswana, the share of agriculture declined from 33 per cent to only 5 per cent, while that of industry rose from 28 per cent to 52 per cent over this period (World Bank, 1994). Both these economies, therefore, reduced their dependence on agriculture very significantly.

In terms of per capita income growth, the BLS economies have improved their position relative to South Africa over the past 20 years (Table 6.8).

As Table 6.8 illustrates, the per capita income of Botswana now exceeds that of the RSA, while the per capita income of both Lesotho and Swaziland increased as a proportion of the RSA's figure in 1976 and 1992.

Membership in SACU, and the duty-free access to the larger RSA market that this guarantees, has always been a major promotional point of BLS in attempting to attract foreign investment in manufacturing. The second half of the 1980s was the high period of the sanctions and disinvestment campaigns against the RSA. After the political events of February 1990 in the RSA, these campaigns subsided, trade links were normalized, resumed or opened (as the particular case might be for individual countries), and transnational corporations no longer felt under pressure to disinvest. There is no doubt that BLS gained industry during this period, although it is doubtful whether they made the most of their opportunities. Namibia, of course, was tarred with the same disinvestment and sanctions brush as South Africa until it became independent in 1990 – just after the political changes had been set in motion in South Africa!

The extent to which SACU membership *per se* helped BLS in gaining industry cannot be quantified, but it was certainly a factor.

For example, the decision by Coca-Cola in 1986 to disinvest from South Africa and relocate its concentrate plant to Swaziland was based on the continued ability to service the South African market duty free. This is but one example; there is plenty of anecdotal evidence to suggest that this was a factor in the case of other disinvesting companies. However, a number of other factors contributed to speeding up the growth of the manufacturing sector in BLS during the late 1980s. In particular, all three countries revised their incentives for foreign investment in manufacturing. This attracted a number of investments from the newly-industrialized Asian countries; for example, Swaziland's revised incentives of 1985 attracted four Taiwanese textile-related manufacturing plants. Investment in non-agro-processing manufacturing in Swaziland was growing at 10 per cent per annum in the late 1980s, but fell to 3–4 per cent in the early 1990s (EIU, 1995). In Botswana, manufacturing output expanded at 15 per cent per annum between 1985 and 1991, and non-traditional exports of manufactured goods (mainly textiles) more than doubled between 1986 and 1989 (EIU, 1995), albeit from an extremely small base. In Lesotho the growth rate in terms of real value-added in manufacturing was 10 per cent per annum between 1986 and 1991, principally as a result of foreign direct investment in textiles and clothing from the Far East (EIU, 1995).

One example of a resource-based project developed specifically for SACU – that is, for the RSA market, as well as to supply Zimbabwe – is the Sua Pan soda ash plant in Botswana. Sua Pan was held up as an example of co-operation within SACU. It was opened in 1991 with the Botswana government having a 52 per cent shareholding, the balance being held by South Africa's Anglo American Corporation and De Beers conglomerate. The project was to replace imported soda ash from the USA, and a 10 per cent SACU tariff was imposed for this purpose. In mid-1995 the operation was placed under liquidation because of consistent losses; these were caused by a fall in demand as recession conditions took hold in the RSA, rising operating costs, and a fierce international price war that led to accusations of US dumping. It now appears, however, that the company will in fact be rescued as demand in South Africa is again increasing.

Motor vehicle assembly recently became an issue again within SACU. Mention was made above of attempts in the 1970s to establish a plant in Lesotho. In recent years a French manufacturer

(Peugeot) planned to set up a plant in Namibia to serve the South African market, but South Africa objected. Surprisingly, however, a Swedish truck manufacturer (Volvo) and a Korean car manufacturer (Hyundai) went ahead with assembly plants in Botswana. The difference between the Hyundai venture and those of Honda and Peugeot are:

(1) the local content programme of the South African government in respect of the motor vehicle industry has progressed significantly since the 1970s, and is no longer regarded as an import control measure as it was at the time the Honda plant in Lesotho was being planned – thus Article II(5) was not a valid mechanism for South Africa to use to stop the Botswana project; and
(2) the Namibian government requested that excise-duty relief be given for the proposed Peugeot plant, but this was not acceptable to the RSA; By contrast, Botswana saw a loophole in the form of imports under rebate of customs duty in respect of semi-knocked-down (SKD) units – in fact, a number of enterprises were making use of the same loophole to assemble vehicles that were not being manufactured in South Africa.

The South African motor industry and trade unions were upset at these developments, and requested the government to intervene. The Board of Tariffs and Trade agreed to abolish the rebate, and there were also proposals to raise excise duty on imported vehicles and components not conforming to the definition of completely-knocked-down (CKD) units, which had been revised in 1993. The South African industry wanted Botswana's imported SKD kits reclassified as completely-built-up (CBU) units, that would carry a much higher duty. Botswana complained that this would adversely affect its vehicle assembly. The Board of Tariffs and Trade did not implement its new policy pending resolution at the SACU level. The matter was resolved in July 1995 when the RSA and BLNS agreed that the motor industry should be based on CKD units. A new definition of CKD came into effect on 1 April 1995 and allowed SKD assemblers two years (until 31 March 1997) to convert their facilities; Hyundai had asked for an extension and, in July, it was agreed that a further two years, until 1999, should be allowed. Each SKD assembler is now required to submit a plan with a specified timetable within which investment will have to be made and new plant installed. In terms of the GATT/WTO offer, SACU is moving away from excise duties to customs duties, and will allow rebates to manufacturers and assemblers on the basis of their export-import ratios; a favourable ratio will allow an individual manufacturer to import even CBUs.

The experience of the Botswana plant indicates that it is now easier, in one particular industry, for BLNS to establish industries predominantly serving the RSA market. This has in fact been a trend in the production of secondary products – for example, the range of Swaziland's manufactured exports to the RSA has grown rapidly since the mid-1970s, when the industrial diversification of the country started to show in the statistics. This continued in the 1980s, the large increase in export to the RSA in the second half of that decade being accounted for largely by increasing in textiles, miscellaneous manufactured goods and miscellaneous edible products. Soft-drink concentrate's and paper were dominant in these new products ranges. The net result of these developments is that the RSA has become far more important as a destination for Swaziland's exports over the years; whereas in the early 1970s it took only about 16 per cent on average of Swaziland's exports, the figure today is approximately 50 per cent. In the case of Lesotho, while absolute volume of exports to South Africa has grown, the proportion has remained at about 40 per cent, Lesotho's growing exports of clothing and textiles being aimed mainly at preferential markets abroad. The exports of Botswana and Namibia are dominated by minerals (especially diamonds) are sold mainly abroad; nevertheless, South Africa takes 25 per cent of Namibia's exports and the major share of Botswana's manufactured exports.

As far as BLNS imports are concerned, the RSA traditionally has been by far the major supplier. These statistics refer to goods 'from or through' South Africa; that is, they include goods that were imported through South African commercial channels but which might have had their origin elsewhere. In other words, the figures for the RSA reflect the role of South African producers as well as distributors in supplying the BLNS market. Since 1969, Swaziland has imported at least 90 per cent of its requirements from South Africa in all but five years. Lesotho obtains over 90 per cent of its imports from South Africa. For Namibia the figure is about 90 per cent and for Botswana 80 per cent.

The new world trading order under the WTO will lead to a reduction of SACU tariffs over the period 1995–99. This will open up the SACU market to competition from overseas suppliers, and it is possible that the RSA might lose some of its hold on BLNS markets. The liberalization of tariffs, therefore, might have the effect not only on reducing the degree of trade diversion in SACU for BLNS but also of leading to a slightly less-skewed balance in their trade with South Africa.

If SACU is to promote higher rates of economic growth in all member countries, this will also imply higher rates of investment. South African firms have been major investors in the smaller countries, and the flow of funds to Lesotho, Namibia and Swaziland has been facilitated by their membership in the Common Monetary Area (CMA). The relationship of the CMA to SACU will be discussed in greater detail below. In the meantime, suffice it to note that BLNS have not been left out in South Africa's growing cross-border investments since the political changes of 1990. Indeed, South African firms in banking and finance, retailing and wholesaling, and manufacturing have continued to expand in BLNS, although unfortunately no data are available in respect of these flows.

Competitive Advantages

It is important for BLNS that the revised agreement afford them every opportunity for exploiting their competitive advantages. They are concerned that there will be increased industrial concentration, with the RSA attracting the bulk of new industrial investment. The BNLS countries need scope for developing their manufacturing as well as non-manufacturing sectors.

Industrial growth and the spread of manufacturing industry throughout SACU are important issues. BLNS should seek not protection (which often simply means propping up inefficient industries), but rather a common industrial incentives policy, since the SACU market represents a single-space economy. The RSA subsidies for manufactured exports have to be eliminated under the GATT/WTO offer, but it is essential that the RSA is not permitted to replace these subsidies with other measures such as subsidized water and electricity which will place BLNS industries at a disadvantage. Moreover, the existing RSA regional industrial development programme, which has been in limbo for the last few years but which may be resuscitated given the formation of nine new provincial governments, should not be allowed to undermine any provisions of the revised agreement. BLNS cannot afford a repeat of the experiences of the 1970s and 1980s when industrial incentives and export subsidies attracted industries to the RSA, not BLNS, as the DBSA (1992) has argued. Selwyn (1975) quotes the somewhat extreme case of a Lesotho carpet manufacturer who continued to import his mohair through Port Elizabeth, protesting the inadequate standard of preparation of local product. Or we would mention the closure of a local fish-processing factory in Walvis Bay following establishment of a new RSA company subsidized under the RSA's industrial decentralization policy.

RSA non-tariff barriers, for example in the form of agricultural marketing control boards, should be eliminated, and subsidies to farmers should be withdrawn. However, the BLNS countries will want to develop their small-scale agricultural sectors in the face of competition from large-scale RSA commercial enterprises, and this will be a negotiating point, particularly since the RSA will itself be implementing land reform measures aimed at developing a commercially viable small-scale farming sector.

Wages for unskilled labour in BLNS are lower than in the RSA, which should give them an advantage over the RSA in labour-intensive industry. South African labour has been far more unionized than that in BLNS. A recent development is the decision of the South African trade union movement to extend its activities to neighbouring countries is an attempt to reach a position of wage parity. Of course, it is wage costs rather than wage rates which are taken into account by industrialists, wage cost representing the full cost of employing an individual. It is possible for a country to have low wage rates but high wage costs. A study by Selwyn (1975) of industrialization in the BLS found that wage costs were not always lower than in the RSA. Nonetheless, to the extent that lower wages do offer some competitive advantage to BLNS, the regionalization of wages through trade union activity is problematic. A competitive economy implies competition not only at the level of the firm but also at the level of labour; in other words, the market should be allowed to operate. If there are wage differentials, it might be possible for industries in BLNS to enter into joint venture operations with RSA firms on a sub-contracting basis; if wages are uniform, those types of opportunities become doubtful.

The question of more-industrialized countries attempting to influence labour policies in less-industrialized countries was a hot issue in the signing of the Uruguay Round at Marrakech Agreement. The USA, France and a number of other industrialized countries requested that workers' right be placed on the GATT/WTO agenda; they were concerned at the impact of cheap imports from low-wage countries such as Singapore, Malaysia, India and Brazil on their employment, and argued that cheap labour amounts to unfair trade. Third World countries argued that the USA was using workers' right both to cloak its protectionism and to undermine their comparative advantage in labour costs. Significantly, RSA unions are concerned about labour-intensive industries moving to neighbouring countries. This is bound to be an issue in the SACU renegotiation, especially since a 'democratization' of the process would involve the unions. Given the imbalances between supply of, and demand for, unskilled labour in the region, as well as the extent of unemployment and underemployment, the BLNS governments should resist any attempts at imposing non-market-determined wage structures on their economies.

6.6 SACU AND OTHER REGIONAL BODIES

This last section of the chapter discusses future institutional arrangements for economic integration and co-operation in Southern Africa.

The Widening and Deepening of SACU

Within SACU itself, consultative machinery needs to be placed on a formal footing with the establishment of a multilateral authority (or secretariat) and a SACU Board of Tariffs and Trade. The board should oversee issues such as implementation of the SACU tariffication offer to the GATT/WTO, competition and fair trade. These are important instruments in determining the success of economic integration schemes.

A number of neighbouring countries, particularly Zimbabwe, are known to be interested in joining SACU. However, it is debatable whether SACU can be extended in the near future. A number of factors determine a country's capacity to integrate – it is better suited to integration if it is already trading substantially with its neighbours, if its main prices (interest, inflation and exchange rates) are compatible with those prevailing in neighbouring countries, if it has convertible currency, if it is liberalizing its economy, and if it is able to protect its borders. At present Zimbabwe would indeed appear the only country that might be a candidate, but its main prices are still out of line with those prevailing in SACU.

Zimbabwe's preferential trade agreement with the RSA has lapsed and apparently will not be re-examined by the RSA government until the SACU renegotiations have been completed. The agreement had provided Zimbabwean exporters (especially of textiles and clothing) with preferential access to the RSA market, but when it lapsed these exports were subject to normal tariffs. A number of Zimbabwean textile and clothing manufacturers have closed as a results of losing their main market, and this has led to a deterioration in relations between the countries, especially since South African firms have been gaining increasingly easier access to the Zimbabwean market as a result of Zimbabwe's trade liberalization. Improved access to the RSA market is crucial for Zimbabwean manufacturers. Zimbabwe's bilateral trade agreement with Botswana has also occasionally given rise to difficult relationships between these two countries. In the University of Natal survey mentioned earlier, a majority of Zimbabwe firms favoured SACU membership. However, it is clear that a compensatory revenue-sharing formula could not be applied to as large an economy as Zimbabwe's.

The existence of the CMA and its relationship with SACU and the Rand Monetary Area (RMA) has deepened. There are strong parallels in its history, although formalization of monetary integration did not occur before 1974, when South Africa, Lesotho and Swaziland signed the Rand Monetary Area (RMA) agreement. Botswana opted out of the negotiations leading to the 1974 agreement and introduced its own currency (the pula) in 1976. In 1986 the RMA became the CMA as a result of the Trilateral Monetary Agreement, which has subsequently been replaced by the Multilateral Monetary Agreement of 1992 in order to accommodate independent Namibia as a formal member.

In addition to the Multilateral Monetary Agreement, there are bilateral agreements between the RSA and each of its partners, varying the precise terms of monetary integration. The three smaller partners each have their own currencies, which are at par with the rand (which is also legal tender in those countries), although Swaziland and Namibia are entitled to delink their currencies. Other provisions are that common exchange controls apply; there is free movement of funds between member countries (although Swaziland and Lesotho may impose restrictions if there is detrimental outflow of funds to the RSA); and Swaziland, Lesotho and Namibia have access to the South African capital markets.

The Botswana pula in fact is stronger than the rand and is convertible. The SACU area, therefore, is the only part of Southern Africa with convertible currencies, and SACU and the CMA taken together provide Southern Africa with a degree of economic integration hardly matched anywhere else in the world. In our business survey (Table 6.5), the CMA was regarded as the most useful of the Southern African economic groupings.

The question relating to the CMA was put to firms in Botswana as well as in the three countries (Lesotho, Swaziland and Namibia) that are members of the CMA. In Botswana only 33.3 per cent were in favour to their country joining the CMA (another 18.8 per cent were uncertain). All in all, 87.5 per cent of firms in the other three member countries favoured membership.

The main reasons for the favourable response revolved around issues of mobility, the exchange rate and convertible currency. Many firms benefited from the free flows of capital and currency; the reduction of exchange control problems (because of the ability to pay in local currency); the reduction of bureaucratic and administrative problems; the absence of delays in payments; and the facilitating of inter-company business activities and transfer of funds. Rand parity was regarded as useful, the exchange rate was favourable for exporters and foreign exchange fluctuations with neighbouring countries were eliminated. The rand was a fully convertible currency and accepted world wide, and any independent currency would not have sufficient backing to be stable. The CMA was also good for tourism, and most trade was with the CMA.

Save for Stuart (1992), little has been published on the CMA. Stuart was critical of the optimal currency area approach, considering it to be too vague and quantitative, and instead used the Allen–Kenen model to analyse various degrees of monetary integration under different market conditions. He examined the cases of Swaziland and Lesotho, and concluded that there were important advantages to them of remaining in the CMA. By contrast, Botswana faced certain disadvantages of non-membership, and had not been able to follow a significantly different path of financial development to that of Swaziland and Lesotho. He recommended that the CMA be developed further to become more like a true co-operative monetary union with all member countries represented in a union central bank. Stuart's views have basically been corroborated in a recent study undertaken for the Swaziland Central Bank, as well as country-specific case studies with the end of apartheid. These studies show that the advantages of membership far outweigh the disadvantages, and that membership of both SACU and the CMA provides the smaller countries with real benefits in terms of direct trade and investment between themselves and the RSA. Moreover, CMA membership had a constraining effect on monetary expansion in Swaziland and Lesotho; it thus placed limits on their spending and inflation, thereby promoting macroeconomic stability. As Oliver (1991) pointed out, critics who regard the CMA as an obstacle to Swaziland's monetary policy may in fact want to see the removal of an obstacle to 'undue monetary expansion'. So far as exchange rate stability is concerned, a PTA report (1990) found that 'only two Member States have managed to escape from the costs of protracted overvaluation. These are Lesotho and Swaziland, whose continued membership of the CMA appears not to have permitted those macroeconomic policies that induce exchange rate instability.'

The CMA ensures capital mobility, and together with SACU approximates common market conditions. Given the high degree of *de facto* labour mobility, an agreement on this issue would be required to convert SACU/the CMA into a common market. Whether or not a labour mobility agreement would benefit all SACU members is questionable in view of the discussion above on competitive advantages stemming from lower wage rates. Lesotho would probably benefit most from the establishment of a common market or indeed an economic union with the RSA, implying also a harmonization of economic and monetary policies. The Development Bank of Southern Africa finances development projects, which lays a foundation for trade and development in the SACU countries.

Variable Geometry

The final questions relate to trade relations between SACU and the rest of the region. It is not the purpose of this chapter to enter into the debate on the rationalization of the SADC and the PTA/COMESA. Clearly, SACU/ the CMA is the most advanced form of economic integration in the region. A suggested model of co-operation between this core group and the rest of the region is the 1994 EC/EFTA agreement on the European Economic Area. This model would need considerable adaptation, and could specify phased tariff reduction between the core and the rest, monetary agreements such as an exchanged-rate union, and sectoral and technical co-operation. The COMESA treaty makes provision for countries to proceed together on the basis of 'variable geometry', and this would appear to be the logical way of gradually moving towards greater economic integration in the region. This would allow a core group of countries to hasten the integration process without awaiting non-core group countries.

In this connection, an important development is the second phase of the Cross-Border Initiative (CBI), funded by the EU, the World Bank, the IMF and the African Development Bank. The CBI covers the entire COMESA/SADC area, with 14 out of 25 eligible countries participating. The co-operating countries are Burundi, Comoros, Kenya, Madagascar, Malawi, Mauritius, Namibia, Rwanda, Seychelles, Swaziland, Tanzania, Uganda, Zambia and Zimbabwe.

The CBI aims at implementing the trade liberalization and policy measures identified in a 1992 CBI report in order to reduce obstacles to cross-border trade and investment. It is attempting to build on the progress towards liberalization achieved both by national SAPs and the various regional groupings. Under the CBI, progress in reducing tariff and non-tariff barriers was more rapid than had been anticipated. By the time of the 1992 CBI report, tariffs on intra-COMESA trade had already been reduced on average by 60–70 per cent. The second CBI ministerial meeting held in Mauritius in early 1995 endorsed plans to eliminate tariffs on intra-regional trade by October 1998, and to adopt a harmonized external tariff by 1998 with two to three – non-zero rates, a 15 per cent trade-weighted average tariff and a maximum rate of 20–25 per cent. Thus, the CBI countries hope to form a free-trade area in 1998. The harmonized external tariff is not a common external tariff – there is scope for some flexibility – but it could be part of the process of achieving a common external tariff under the COMESA programme. The CBI countries wish to move more rapidly than the rest, but the meeting recognized that within the CBI countries some groups might wish to move even faster. The East African Co-operation countries have apparently discussed the possibility of accelerating the establishment of a common external tariff, as have the countries of the Indian Ocean Commission. These would be examples of variable geometry.

COMESA, the SADC and the Indian Ocean Commission have all been involved in the deliberations of the CBI. The CBI has injected a new momentum into regional integration by strengthening its 'constituency' in favour of a realistic path to integration.

The South African government's main trade concerns are the

renegotiation of SACU (the only example of successful trade integration in Africa) and the conclusion of an agreement with the EU, which is the country's main regional trading partner. The government also wishes to fulfil its obligations as a member of SADC, but some independent observers argue that SADC will not become effective until it revises its operational structure. The RSA business sector feels that Southern Africa is too small as a regional market for the RSA and that the country should maintain sufficient flexibility to be able to interact with countries beyond SADC: for example, non-SADC countries of COMESA, the Indian Ocean Rim, and Australia. The last, hitherto concentrating on the Pacific Rim, is increasingly turning its attention to the RSA, a factor not unconnected with its large migrant population from the RSA and Zimbabwe. The more expansive view is also shared by government and business circles in Mauritius.

The RSA's thrust under de Klerk was the development and consolidation of trade links with key African countries ('growth poles') and through them the zones: Kenya (East Africa), Egypt (North Africa), Nigeria (anglophone West Africa) and Côte d'Ivoire (francophone West Africa). This 'growth centres' strategy was a pointer to Pretoria's determination to go beyond the SACU/SADC/COMESA sub-region in pursuit of wider African markets, replacing in some cases European and North American suppliers. The latter, eager to re-enter the RSA market after many years of disinvestment, may see such a loss as a cost worth paying. More specifically, the RSA should be able to do business with Kenya and Ethiopia (identified by the ADB study as countries with potential for RSA exports), Mauritius (an important trading partner), and Asian countries of the Indian Ocean Rim. 'Variable geometry' does not have to be confined to Southern Africa, and there would appear to be considerable merit in dropping its proposed trade protocol so that COMESA's specialization in trade can be utilized and its existing protocol can remain the instrument under which countries may engage in fast-tracking trade integration in a wider geographic area. Within the SADC region, however, it would appear that Zimbabwe is the country best able to enter into a closer trade relationship with the SACU bloc, but this – and in fact the RSA's ability to sign a SADC trade protocol – depends on the terms of the renegotiated SACU agreement. The 1969 agreement (albeit with some modifications) is still in operation, and it is because of this that Lesotho, Namibia and Swaziland have been precluded by other obligations from effective participation in the reciprocal tariff reductions under the PTA/COMESA. Article 30, Annex xii, of the PTA Treaty granted the BLNS countries 'temporary exemptions from the full application of certain provisions of this Treaty' (UN/ECA, 1981). The same constraint must obtain with regard to the adoption by SACU member countries of a SADC protocol on free trade. The RSA's proposed bilateral trade agreement with the EU should also be subjected to the assent of its SACU partners. Another recent development that holds some potential for a wider trade relationship for SACU is the Indian Ocean Rim (IOR) initiative.

The new world trade regime that came into being in 1995 is based on universal, multilateral liberalization. If regional blocs are to promote such globalism, they must be open, not discriminatory: that is, the regional agreement on trade liberalization should be extended to third countries on a most-favoured-nation basis. This is the approach in APEC to which some IOR countries also belong. Although the establishment of an IOR trading bloc is still on the drawing board, an open regionalism model between ESA regional groupings and other parts of the IOR could forge close links between ESA economies and other 'Southern' economies such as new industrializing ASEAN countries such as Singapore; those adopting successful structural reforms, as India; or with Australia, which is an OECD member. This would impose an economic policy discipline on Africa beyond that offered by participation in sub-regional groupings of poor and relatively unsuccessful countries.

6.7 CONCLUSION

Despite the shortcomings, SACU members even in apartheid days showed willingness to maintain and strengthen SACU. Indeed in a recent study, the African Development Bank (1993) recommended that members negotiate a new agreement with a transitional five-year period for adjustment to a wider Southern African free-trade area or common market. This is understandable given the new political dispensation in South Africa. The new South Africa is already a member of the SADC and may possibly join COMESA and should support reforms in SACU to enhance democracy and equity. As the ANC (1994, p. 60) noted in its *Reconstruction and Development Programme*, 'the current trade pattern between South Africa and the sub-continent is unbalanced, as regional imports from South

Africa exceed exports to South Africa by five to one. A democratic government must develop policies in consultation with our neighbours to ensure more balanced trade.' Thus the new ANC-led South African government is entering SACU negotiations devoid of the one-sided, self-interested and hegemonic approach of past apartheid and neo-apartheid administrations. This may allow intra-(sub)-regional links, as Mwase (1978) has argued, on 'independent' and 'equal' interaction in Southern Africa. This could be enhanced by macroeconomic policy co-ordination and programming that would ensure that major policy reforms in one member state do not result in substantial market distortions in contiguous states.

Finally, it is essential for the future of economic integration in Africa that the SACU Agreement be renegotiated successfully. Failure to do so would send a negative message to the rest of the Africa, and especially to the SADC and the PTA/COMESA. If South Africa and the BLNS countries are unable to improve the SACU agreement, they are hardly likely to work together more harmoniously under any other institution aiming to become an authentic economic integration arrangement. Given the new Southern Africa, an improved SACU can provide the (sub) region with an opportunity for greater interaction and realization of its full potential.

APPENDIX 6A

Terms of Reference – Customs Union Task Team (CUTT), 11 November 1994

In view thereof that

1. The contracting parties to the Southern African Customs Union Agreement of 1969 are desirous of remaining in a customs union which is mutually beneficial; and
2. Recognising that the 1969 Agreement due to the changed economic circumstances in the common customs area, does not adequately provide for sustainable and mutual beneficial economic relations between the contracting parties, the Ministers of the respective Governments of the members states of the Customs Union have agreed to appoint an *ad hoc* Customs Union Team (CUTT), representing all the members of the Customs Union, to review the 1969 Agreement in its entirety with a view to drafting an amended agreement for consideration by the respective Governments of the member countries of the Customs Union.

The CUTT shall, *inter alia*, specifically, but not exclusively, consider the following aspects and make recommendations in this regard:

(i) Provisions to enhance the economic development of the Customs Union area as a whole with specific reference to, *inter alia:*

    (a) Closer co-operation regarding industrial development policies;
    (b) The uniform implementation of specific programmes to develop certain industries;
    (c) The development of agriculture and agro-industries and the marketing of agricultural products in the common customs areas;
    (d) The protection of infant industries;
    (e) The development of industries which are of major importance to the respective members of the Customs Union with due regard to the contracting parties' rights and obligations in the context of the General Agreement on Tariffs and Trade;

(ii) The possibility of creating a Custom Union Authority and an advisory body to serve the Customs Union Authority regarding the customs tariff and other development issues;

(iii) Competition policies with special reference to unfair and/or disruptive trading practices and effective measures to counteract such practices;

(iv) The clarification and definition of all terms used, and/or Procedures provided for in the Agreement, avoiding the creation of additional memorandums of understanding and ensuring transparency;

(v) The strengthening of institutions in the Customs Union including the desirability of creating a permanent Secretariat;

(vi) Consultation mechanism which are adequate and effective, with special reference to the customs (and excise) tariff;

(vii) Dispute settlement mechanisms;

(viii) The possible inclusion of additional fields of cooperation and/or integration not provided for in the present Agreement, such as labour, environmental matters, etc;

(ix) The equitable and sustainable sharing of customs (and excise revenue collected in the common customs area;

(x) The retention or exclusion of excise duties as part of the common revenue pool which is shared amongst the member states;

(xi) Bilateral trade agreements between members of the Customs Union and countries outside the common customs area, the possibility of the Customs Union concluding agreements with third parties and accession of additional contracting parties to the Customs Union Agreement;

(xii) The harmonisation of the objectives of the Customs Union with the economic objectives of the SADC with a view to striving towards the convergence and, ultimately, possible integration of the two organizations; and

(xiii) The relationships with other economic groupings in Africa and elsewhere.

The contracting parties shall be free to appoint nominees of their choice to serve on the CUTT from time to time. The CUTT may appoint working groups to address specific matters.

Meeting of the CUTT and/or its working groups shall rotate among the member countries of the Customs Union. The host country will provide adequate facilities and a competent secretariat for meetings of the CUTT and/or its working groups.

The CUTT shall report to the Governments of the member countries of the Customs Union by the end of March 1995.

Ministers prevail on the CUTT to finalise its task at the earliest possible opportunity.

References

ADB (African Development Bank) (1993) *Economic Integration in Southern Africa*, vols. I, II, and III (Abidjan).

ANC (African National Congress) (1994) *Reconstruction and Development Programme* (Johannesburg).

Cobbe, J. H. (1980) 'Integration among Unequals: The Southern African Customs Union and Development', *World Development*, **8**(4).

Cobbe, J. H. (1988) 'Economic Aspects of Lesotho's Relations with South Africa', *Journal of Modern African Studies*, **26**(1).

DBSA (Development Bank of Southern Africa) (1992) *Annual Report: Framework for Development, 1991/92* (Pretoria).

EIU (1995) *Economist Intelligence Unit Report on Botswana, Lesotho and Swaziland* (London).

Ettinger, S. J. (1974) 'The Economics the Customs Union between Botswana, Lesotho, Swaziland and South Africa,' Unpublished PhD thesis, University of Michigan, Ann Arbor, Michigan.

Guma, X. P. (1990) 'The Revised Southern African Customs Union Agreement: an Appraisal', *South African Journal of Economics*, **58**(1).

Hall, P. H. (1980) 'The Revenue Distribution Formula of the Southern African Customs Union', *South African Journal of Economics*, **48**(3).

Hudson, D. J. (1981) 'Botswana's Memberships of the Southern African Customs Union', in C. Harvey (ed.), *Papers on the Economy of Botswana* (London: Heinemann).

IMF (1994) 'Initiative for Promoting Cross-border Trade Investment and Payments in Eastern and Southern Africa', IMF Document (8 April).

Isaksen, J. (1993) 'Prospects for SACU After Apartheid', in B. Oden (ed.), *Southern Africa After Apartheid: Regional Integration and External Resources* (Uppsala: Scandinavian Institute of African Studies).

Johnson, H. G. (1992) 'The Economic Theory of Customs Union', in *Money, Trade and Economic Growth* (Harvard University Press).

Kruger, H. J. P. L. (1956) 'Customs Union in South Africa', unpublished M. Bus. Econ. thesis, University of South Africa, Pretoria.

Krugman, P. (1991) 'The Move Toward Free Trade Zones', in *Policy Implications of Trade and Currency Zones*, a Symposium sponsored by the Federal Reserve Bank of Kansas City, Jackson Hole, Wyoming (August) pp. 7–42.

Krugman, P. and A. J. Venables (1993) 'Integration, Specialization and

Adjustment', London Centre for Economic Policy Research, Discussion Paper no. 886 (December).

Kumar, U. (1990) 'Southern African Customs Union and BLS Countries (Botswana, Lesotho and Swaziland', *Journal of World Trade*, **24**(3).

Landell-Mills, P. M. (1971) 'The 1969 Southern African Customs Union Agreement', *Journal of Modern African Studies* (Cambridge).

Landell-Mills, P. M. (1979) 'The Southern African Customs Union: A Comment on Mosley's Reappraisal', *World Development*, **9**(1).

Leith, J. C. (1992) 'The Static Welfare Effects of a Small Developing Country's Membership in a Customs Union: Botswana in the Southern African Customs Union', *World Development*, **20**(7).

Leith, J. C. (1993) 'A Simple Measure for the Evaluation of Trade Policy Options with Application for Botswana', Development Discussion Paper no. 452. (Cambridge, Mass.: Harvard Institute for International Development).

Lovell, L. (1970) 'The New Customs Agreement', mimeo (Mbabane: Ministry of Finance).

Lundahl, M. and L. Peterson (1991) *The Development Economy: Lesotho and the Southern African Customs Union* (Boulder, Colo.: Westview).

Maasdorp, G. G. (1982) 'The Southern African Customs Union – An Assessment', *Journal of Contemporary African Studies*, **2**(1).

Maasdorp, G. G. (1988) 'The Southern African Customs Union', in E. Leistner and P. Esterhuysen (eds), *South Africa in Southern Africa: Economic Interaction* (Pretoria: Africa Institute).

Maasdorp, G. G. (1990) 'The Role of the South African Economy, SACU, CMA and other Regional Groupings', Paper presented at Conference on *Rethinking Development Strategy for Mozambique and Southern Africa*, Maputo.

Maasdorp, G. G. (1992), *Economic Cooperation in Southern Africa: Prospects for Regional Integration*, Conflict Studies no. 253 (London: Research Institute for the Study of Conflict and Terrorism).

Maasdorp, G. G. (1993a) 'Trade', in G. G. Maasdorp and A. W. Whiteside, *Rethinking Economic Cooperation in Southern Africa: Trade and Investment* (Johannesburg: Konrad Adenaeur).

Maasdorp, G. G. (1993b) 'The Advantages and Disadvantages of Current Rational Institutions for Integration', in P. H. Baker *et al.* (eds), *South Africa and the World Economy in the 1990s* (Cape Town: David Philip).

Maasdorp, G. G. (1994) *A Vision for Economic Integration and Cooperation in Southern Africa* (Pretoria: Department of Trade and Industry).

Maasdorp, G. G. and A. W. Whiteside (1992) *Towards a Post-apartheid Future: Political and Economic Relations in Southern Africa* (London: Macmillan).

Mayer, M. and H. Zarenda (1994) *The Southern African Customs Union*, report prepared for the Central Economic Advisory Services, Pretoria.

McCarthy, C. L. (1986) *The Southern African Customs Union*, report prepared for the Central Economic Advisory Services, Pretoria.

McCarthy, C. L. (1992) 'The Southern African Customs Union in a changing Economic and Political Environment', *Journal of World Trade*, **26**(4).

McCarthy, C. L. (1994) 'Revenue Distribution and Economic Development in the Southern African Customs Union', *South African Journal of Economics*, **63**(3).

McFarland, E. L. (1983) 'Benefits to the RSA of her Exports to the BLS Countries', in M. A. Oommen, F. K. Inganju and L. D. Ngcongco (eds), *Botswana's Economy Since Independence* (New Delhi: Tata McGraw-Hill).

Mosley, P. (1978) 'The Southern African Customs Union: A Reappraisal', *World Development*, (6).

Mosley, P. (1979) 'Reply to Robson and Landell-Mills', *World Development*, **7**(1).

Mwase, N. (1985) 'The African Preferential Trade: Towards a sub-regional Economic Community in Eastern and Southern Africa', *Journal of World Trade*, **5**(2): 662–76.

Mwase, N. (1991) 'Regional Economic Integration in Southern Africa: Options for Independent Namibia', *Eastern African Economic Review*, **7**(1).

Mwase, N. (1993) 'Economic Integration for Development in Eastern and Southern Africa', *World Competition*, **16**(3).

Mwase, N. (1994) 'Economic Integration for Development in Eastern and Southern Africa Assessment and Prospects', *IDS Bulletin*, **25**(3): 31–9.

Natal *Mercury* (1993) 20 May.

Naude, S. (1992) 'Economic Restructuring and Growth', Paper presented at conference on *Blueprint for Prosperity*, Johannesburg, (October).

Oden, S. (ed.) (1993) *Southern Africa After Apartheid: Regional Integration and External Resources* (Uppsala: Scandinavian Institute of African Studies).

Ohly, C. (1992) 'Measuring the Effects of Economic and Financial Integration', unpublished paper (Commission of the European Communities, Brussels).

Oliver, H. B. B. (1991) 'Scope of a Small Central Bank in a Common Monetary Area: The Case of Swaziland', Paper prepared for University of the Witwatersrand conference on *Economic Policy and Development in sub-Saharan Africa*, Somerset West (March).

PTA (Preferential Trade Area) (1990) 'The Monetary Harmonisation Programme of the Preferential Trade Area for Eastern and Southern African States', report of a Technical Study Group, Lusaka.

Robson, P. (1967) 'Economic Integration in Southern Africa', *Journal of Modern African Studies*, **5**(4).

Robson, P. (1968) *Economic Integration in Africa* (London: Allen & Unwin).

Robson, P. (1978) 'Reappraising the Southern African Customs Union, A Comment', *World Development*, **6**(4).

Robson, P. (1987) *The Economics of International Integration* (London: Allen & Unwin).

SATCC (1988) *A Scenario Model for Goods Transport Demand in the SADCC Region, The Main Results* (Maputo, September).

Scheepers, C. F. (1979) 'The Possible Role of a Customs Union – Type Model in Promoting Closer Economic Ties in Southern Africa', *Finance and Trade Review*, **13**(4).

Selwyn, P. (1975) *Industries in the Southern African Periphery* (London: Croom Helm).

Sisulu, M. *et al.* (1994) *Reconstituting and Democratising the Southern African*

Customs Union (Johannesburg: National Institute of Economic Policy).
South Africa, Republic of (1985) *Report of the Auditor General for the Financial Year (annual 1973/74–1983/84)* (Pretoria Central Economic Advisory Services).
South Africa, Republic of (1987). *Report of the Commission of Inquiry into the Tax Structure of the Republic of South Africa* (the 'Margo Commission) RP 34/1987 (Pretoria: Government Printer).
Stuart, J. (1992) *The Economics of the Common Monetary Area in Southern Africa* (Durban: Economic Research Unit, University of Natal).
Sunday Business Times (1993) 7 February.
Swaziland Central Bank (1995) *Annual Report* (Mbabane).
Tinbergen J. (1965) *International Economic Integration* (Amsterdam: Elsevier).
UNDP (1989) 'Namibia: Fiscal and Financial Policies: Issues, Options and Assistance Requirements' (New York: Office of Project Services, September).
UN/ECA (1981) *Treaty for the Establishment of the Preferential Trade Area for Eastern and Southern African States* (Addis Ababa, December).
University of Natal (1992) Economic Research Unit Survey.
Vaitsos, C. V. (1978) 'Crisis in Regional Economic Cooperation (Integration) among Developing Countries: A Survey', *World Development*, **6**(6).
Venables A. J. (1993) 'Equilibrium Location of Vertical Linked Industries', (London: Centre for Economic Policy Research, May).
Viner, J. (1950) *The Customs Union Issue* (London: Steven & Sons).
Walters, J. (1989) 'Renegotiating Dependency: The Case of the Southern African Customs Union', *Journal of Common Market Studies*, **28**(1).
Weimer, B. (1983) *Die Zollunion im Sudlichen Afrika – ein Stabilitatsfaktor in einer Instabilen Region?* (Ebenhausen: Stiftung Wissenschaft und Politik).
Wonnacott, P. and M. Lutz (1989) 'Is There a Case for Free Trade Areas?', *Economic Impact*, 69.
World Bank, The (1994) *World Development Report 1994* (New York: Oxford University Press).

7 A Regional Case Study of the SADC

William Lyakurwa*

7.1 BACKGROUND

Over the last few years, economic integration in subSaharan Africa (SSA) has aroused growing interest both in Africa and outside, especially within the donor community. The reasons for this interest vary, but all concerned seem to agree on one major point: attempts by African countries to develop within their national boundaries have generally failed, and economic integration with neighbouring countries may be a viable alternative to isolated efforts (Fine and Yeo, 1994). The SSA countries are very small in economic terms, are among the poorest in the world, and are very poorly endowed with human and physical capital. For countries with such characteristics it is economically justified to integrate their markets.

The Southern Africa Development Co-ordination Conference (SADCC), which changed its name to the Southern Africa Development Community (SADC) in 1992 folowing member states' resolution to shift emphasis from project co-ordination to a development community, was established in 1980 with nine members: Angola, Botswana, Lesotho, Malawi, Mozambique, Swaziland, Tanzania, Zambia and Zimbabwe. Namibia became the tenth member following its independence in 1990, South Africa joined in 1994 and Mauritius in 1995. In this chapter we use the term 'SADC' to describe this area both before and after 1992.

The SADC's principal objective originally was to promote co-operation among its member states in order to lessen their dependence on the Republic of South Africa; members decided to concentrate their efforts on the more modest goal of economic co-operation rather than on a customs union. In order to attain this

---

* The author would like to acknowledge research assistance from Ms Sheila Nyanjui and Mr Bruno Ocaya. The views expressed in this paper are those of the author and any errors or omissions are entirely his responsibility.

objective, the SADC established a small secretariat with limited co-ordination duties while leaving the responsibility for various sectors to the member states. The sectors include: energy, food, agriculture and natural resources, industry and trade, mining, tourism, transport and communication, and human resource development. Most of these portfolios are handled by the relevant ministry in the host country, but two separate commissions have been established, namely, for transport and communications and for energy, and these are staffed largely by expatriates (Maasdorp, 1992). The argument has often been raised that some of the reasons for poor performance in the SADC can be attributed to the lack of a central authority with powers to direct and supervise the activities of the units the relevant ministries co-ordinate.

The initial emphasis was on transport and communications and the Southern African Transport and Communications Commission (SATCC) was established in Maputo. Because of the civil war in Angola, the Benguela line (carrying copper from Zambia and the Democratic Republic of the Congo) to the port of Lobito had been inoperative from 1975. Then, growing guerrilla activities in Mozambique (financed and encouraged to a large measure by Pretoria) were threatening – and in fact by 1984 had cut – the lines from Malawi, Zambia, Zimbabwe and periodically Swaziland to the Mozambique ports of Nacala, Beira and Maputo. The result was that, deprived of the use of their natural ports, the landlocked countries north of the Limpopo were obliged to make greater use of South African ports. Not only was this considered politically undesirable but it was much more costly; for instance, it was costing Malawi exporters four times more to use Durban rather than Nacala (Maasdorp, *op. cit.*) Transport and communication, therefore, was the sector in which dependence on South Africa was felt most acutely.

The next preoccupation was food security. The organization has often reacted fairly quick to avert serious food shortages. In 1991/92, for example, the region experienced the worst drought in history. In order to avert imminent famine, the SADC launched an intensive programme for mobilizing necessary resources for acquisition of food. An appeal was made to the international community for contributions and the response was overwhelming, the SADC was able to mobilize 5.67 million tonnes in cereal imports out of a total of requirement of 7 million tonnes. Mechanisms established in 1991/92 have been reinforced and the development of the regional food resource project is pursued vigorously to combat such disasters in future. The regional drought preparedness measures that have been put in place include:

(1) establishment of a regional drought task force;
(2) integration of the transport corridors into the food security programme of action and linked to the early warnings system; and
(3) development of a regional food reserve project.

In 1991, however, the SADC had to face up to the implications of political change in South Africa. With apartheid being discarded, the very bases of the SADC's existence began to be questioned, and the organization was fighting for survival. It accordingly took two steps at its 1992 annual consultations with donors.

First, at its mid-1992 meeting it agreed to establish a treaty that would confer upon it a legal status similar to that enjoyed by the Common Market for Eastern and Southern Africa (COMESA). Second, it considered a theme document spelling out proposals for moving from project co-operation to close political co-operation in order to establish the conditions for suitable trade integration. This would involve implementing measures such as the reduction of tariff and non-tariff barriers between member states and greater co-ordination of external tariffs, promoting freer movement of capital and people, and creating regional infrastructural authorities and a development bank. The SADC also urged that efforts to promote integration in Southern Africa be rationalized. In this regard, a joint COMESA/SADC study on harmonization of the two organizations, completed in July 1994, recommended the need to examine the possibility of overlapping activities, and the effective co-ordination. The study affirmed that in the spirit of African unity there should be co-existence of the common market for Eastern and Southern Africa (COMESA) and the SADC as sub-regional communities.

It is important to emphasize that the SADC was established to react to a specific situation, to reduce dependence on the RSA, in particular on trade including food imports, transport, freight forwarding, insurance and banking. More explicitly, the four objectives of the organization are to:

• reduce economic dependence, particularly, but not only on South Africa;
• forge links to create a genuine and equitable regional integration;

- mobilize resources to promote the implementation of national, interstate and regional policies; and
- take concerted action to secure international cooperation within the framework of the SADC's strategy for economic liberation. Transport and communications, which were seen as critical to the objective of reducing dependence on South Africa, were singled out as economic sectors requiring particular emphasis. The first objective is no longer valid given that South Africa is now a member of the SADC.

Reducing dependence on the RSA, which is the major producer and exporter of manufactured goods and food in the region, meant securing alternative sources either from within the SADC or from outside, particularly during periods of food shortfalls. Two questions immediately follow: (1) was this necessary? and (2) did it constitute the most appropriate strategy of addressing the issue? The answer to the first question is yes. As a way to speed up the process of political liberation, as well as for putting pressure on South Africa to dismantle the apartheid system, the measures taken by the SADC appear justifiable. In response to the second question, it should be noted that initially the strategy was not well articulated. Subsequently, however, the issue of intra-SADC trade gained importance, hence the establishment of the trade sector co-ordinating unit in 1986 with a view to enhancing the flow of goods and services within the region.

An important issue to raise at this point would be the effectiveness of the SADC in addressing the issues of increased intra-SADC trade, given the peculiar situation where all its members also belong to other regional groupings, for example SACU and COMESA. What changes in the SADC would be required both in terms of design and orientation in order to meet emerging global, sub-regional and national challenges?

The objective of this chapter is to address these issues with emphasis on intra-SADC trade as the *sine qua non* for regional integration without losing sight of the fact that this was not one of the initial SADC objectives. Following this brief history of the SADC, section 7.2 is a description of its objectives and achievements; section 7.3 evaluates the experience of the SADC with a focus on co-ordination integration, which has placed great emphasis on transport and infrastructure development, food security, industry and trade flows. On trade flows, the aim is to identify and assess the potential for intra-SADC trade flows, bearing in mind the existence of non-tariff barriers which may be critical. Several studies have found that tariffs do not constitute the major barriers intra-SADC trade (SADC; 1986; TISCO, 1991). Five of the 12 SADC members are also members of the Southern African Customs Union (SACU), eight are members of COMESA, and three belong to all three organizations (COMESA, SADC and SACU). While SACU involves complete duty-free access to the domestic market, COMESA involves gradual reduction and eventual elimination of tariff and non-tariff barriers. Non-tariff barriers include foreign exchange allocations, import controls, customs procedures at border points, permit and visa requirements, government procurement policies, protected monopolies, low level of administrative efficiency, and corruption. The potential for increased intra-SADC trade, given the current wave of unilateral trade liberations among the member states, a domestic South Africa and the changing role of COMESA from a preferential trade area to a common market, will also be explored. The exploration will involve an attempt to answer the question of whether the SADC is a viable trade bloc or not. Section 7.4 discusses the implications of changing conditions for regional integration and section 7.5 explores the impact of the global environment on SADC. Section 7.6 covers some special peculiar to the SADC and Section 7.7 contains concluding remarks.

7.2 ASSESSMENT OF SADC EXPERIENCE

General Characteristics

The present member countries of the SADC are comparatively poor and, hence, despite a large population, the size of their individual markets is limited. The average per capita GNP of the SADC sub-region was US$774 in 1991. Only three of the member states (Botswana, Namibia and Swaziland) had per capita incomes above this average (Table 7.1). They are classified by the World Bank as lower–middle income, while the rest are classified as low income.

The level of per capita income is closely, but not perfectly, correlated with health and education indicators. Relatively high levels of per capita income in Botswana, Namibia and Zimbabwe are associated with relatively low infant mortality rates. Swaziland, for some reason, has a relatively high infant mortality rate. In war-

Table 7.1   Some economic and social indicators for SADC member states

Country	GDP		Per capita GNP		Population		Life expectancy (constant at birth rate) 1992	Infant mortality rate 1992	Adult literacy rate 1990
	US$m	Annual growth rate 1988–91 (%)	US$	Annual growth rate 1980–91 (%)	000s	Annual growth rate 1988–91 (%)			
Angola	7 720	–	620	–	10 000	2.5	46.5	125	42
Botswana	3 644	1.3	2 530	5.6	300	3.5	67.8	35	74
Lesotho	578	3.7	580	–0.5	1 700	2.8	56.8	79	74**
Malawi	1 986	2.7	280	0.1	9 000	3.3	44.2	143	41**
Mozambique	1 219	1.4	80	–1.1	16 000	2.6	46.8	147	33
Namibia	1 961	–	1 460	1.2	1 500	3.1	58.3	70	n.a.
Swaziland	683	4.1	1 050	3.1	828	3.4	57.2	108	68**
Tanzania	2 223	2.6	100	–0.8	25 000	3.0	50.8	115	n.a.
Zambia	3 831	0.8	390	–3.8	8 000	3.6	47.7	108	73
Zimbabwe	5 543	2.7	650	–0.2	10 000	3.4	59.9	47	67
S. Africa	–	–	–	–	–	–	62.9	53	–

Source: World Bank, *World Development Report, 1993*; The Global Coalition for Africa, *1993 Report*.

torn Angola, relatively high per capita income has not led to a marked reduction in infant mortality or any improvement in adult literacy. In the rest of the countries in the region, low levels of per capita income correspond with low values of the social indicators of development, indicating an overall low standard of living.

Average per capita national incomes are highly uneven throughout the region, ranging from US$80 for Mozambique to over 30 times this figure for Botswana in 1991. The dispersion of per capita national incomes has increased over time. Moreover, within each country, the distribution of income is also uneven, with most rural people (at least half the total) estimated to live on around US$100 each, while a minority, comprising 5–10 per cent of the population, earn about 100 times as much. The percentage of the population living below the absolute poverty level in 1985 was as high as 85 per cent in some countries, according to the World Bank. This uneven distribution of income is a major factor in the low purchasing power for goods and services produced in the region.

Long-term changes in GNP per capita point to a decline in many countries in rates of economic growth in the 1980s, which became negative in the cases of Lesotho, Mozambique, Tanzania, Zambia and Zimbabwe, as well as in Angola, for which no figures were available. In the remaining member countries, rates of economic growth were positive, but below population growth in all cases, except Botswana. All countries experienced a decline in the real growth of GDP between 1991 and 1992 (Table 7.2) with Malawi and Zimbabwe experiencing the greatest decline, from 6.5 per cent to -8.0 per cent and from 3.6 per cent to -8.3 per cent respectively. All countries except Namibia and Zambia experienced declines in real industrial growth between 1991 and 1992. In Namibia, real industrial growth increased from 4.1 per cent in 1991 to 13.2 per cent in 1992 while in Mozambique, which experienced the greatest decline, real industrial growth fell from –0.5 per cent in 1991 to –8.1 per cent in 1992, For SADC as a whole real industrial growth increased from 2.3 per cent in 1991 to 2.7 per cent in 1992 with the greatest influence coming from Namibia, which incidentally is a minor player in the region in terms of industrial development. Countries that experienced high growth rates of industry also had high real export and import growth rates. In contrast, China, a reforming country, experienced real industrial growth rate of 9.4 per cent in 1992 with real export growth and import growth rates of 14.6 per cent and 23.6 per cent, respectively (Table 7.2).

Table 7.2 Economic indicators for SADC member states as compared to the RSA and South East Asia

	Real GDP growth (%)		Real industrial growth		Real export growth (%)		Real import growth (%)		Debt service ratio % of exports	
	1991	1992	1991	1992	1991	1992	1988–92	1992	1991	1992
Angola	–	–	–	–	–	–	–	–	6.7	7.2
Botswana	8.9	6.5	3.8	2.8	–	–	–	–	3.4	3.3
Lesotho	1.3	1.3	8.9	3.7	1.6	3.0	1.6	4.0	4.6	5.6
Malawi	6.5	–8.0	3.9	2.7	3.9	–5.5	7.8	–12.6	25.0	24.3
Mozambique	3.1	0.5	–0.5	–8.1	12.8	–1.0	3.6	–0.3	10.6	9.4
Namibia	5.0	1.4	4.1	13.2	5.0	14.2	–5.2	7.3	–	–
Swaziland	4.7	–1.9	–	–	–	–	–	–	3.5	3.1
Tanzania	7.7	3.7	4.4	2.7	–	–	–	–	24.6	32.5
Zambia	–1.7	–2.8	–9.1	2.1	–2.2	–	–17.7	–	51.4	29.3
Zimbabwe	3.6	–8.3	3.1	–	–	–	–	–	30.1	14.2
RSA	16.3	–	–	–	2.8	–3.6	1.6	1.8	–	–
China	8.5	6.3	12.3	9.4	10.9	14.7	6.7	23.6	12.1	9.6
India	3.7	3.7	3.9	5.2	10.0	5.2	–1.2	13.9	29.0	25.6
Indonesia	6.6	7.3	15.2	7.4	9.9	7.9	11.4	–5.2	32.8	32.2
South Asia	3.3	4.8	2.0	6.2	11.0	16.9	3.8	8.8	19.3	19.4

Source: The Global Coalition for Africa, *1993 Annual Report.*

Trade

All countries in southern Africa share a similar pattern of trade. The bulk of exports, about 90 per cent, are mineral and agricultural commodities, marketed in industrial countries with little or no value-added. The bulk of imports – about two-thirds – are intermediate and capital goods, mostly obtained from industrialized countries. Only Mauritius, South Africa and Zimbabwe have any significant capacity to produce such goods. The level of intra-regional trade is consequently low, accounting for less than 5 per cent of total recorded trade. Even when the estimated volume of unrecorded and parallel market trade is taken into account, this would add perhaps no more than 2–3 per cent to the total. The largest proportion of SADC trade is with the rest of the world (Table 7.3), and the European Union, Japan and the USA are the main SADC trading partners. For the BNLS countries (Botswana, Namibia, Lesotho and Swaziland), South Africa is their main trading partner.

An African Development Bank report (1992) argues that outside the SACU area, most countries have experienced a virtual collapse in the availability of finance for intra-regional trade through the domestic and international banking systems. This crucial constraint has throttled both the development of intra-regional trade and diversification into non-traditional exports – a necessary prerequisite for intra-regional trade. The principal constraint to trade finance has been the lack of currency convertibility. With the current liberalization process in the majority of the countries in the region, particularly the elimination of exchange controls, this constraint is currently less binding.

Industrial growth in all countries, including South Africa, has been largely dependent on production for the domestic market, carried on behind high tariff barriers and in most cases a range of significant non-tariff barriers, and subject both to the pace of change in domestic demand and the extent to which import substitution has progressed. However, as indicated in Table 7.2, all SADC countries except Namibia and Zambia experienced declines in real industrial growth between 1991 and 1992. A similar pattern is shown for South and South East Asian countries, except India, whose real industrial growth increased from 3.9 percent to 5.3 percent between 1991 and 1992.

Manufacturing is dominated by South Africa, whose manufacturing sector is more than five times larger than the total for the

Table 7.3   The SADC's main trading partners and main exports and imports, 1980–90

Country	Trading partners		Main exports	Main imports
	for exports	*for imports*		
Angola	USA, Brazil, EEC (Portugal, Spain, UK)	EEC, USA, USSR, Brazil, Japan	Petroleum, fish products	
Botswana	EEC, SACU	SACU, EEC	Diamonds, copper-nickel, matte, meat products	Food, beverages, tobacco, machinery, vehicles & transport equipment, metal products
Lesotho	RSA, EEC, America, other European countries	RSA, EEC, Other European Countries, Americas	Manufacturer, wool, mohair, diamonds	Food, consumer goods, intermediate & capital goods
Malawi	EEC, RSA, USA, PTA	EEC, Japan, RSA, USA, PTA	Tobacco, tea, sugar, coffee, pulses, ground nuts, cotton	Industrial inputs, plant & equipment, commodities, consumer goods, transport means, building materials, spare parts & tools
Mozambique	EEC, Japan, USA, East Germany	EEC, USA, RSA, USSR	Prawns, cotton, cashew nuts, tea, timber	Food, raw materials, spare parts, equipment
Namibia	Switzerland, RSA, W. Germany, Japan, USA	RSA, W. Germany, USA, Switzerland	Uranium and other minerals, cattle, diamonds, fish products, manufactures	Food & beverages, petroleum products & fuel, machinery & equipment, vehicles & other transport equipment
Swaziland	RSA, EEC, Canada, South Korea	RSA, Japan, Belgium, UK	Sugar, soft drinks, cone, wood pulp, canned fruit	Manufactures, machinery & transport equipment, mineral fuel & lubricants, food & live animals, chemicals
Tanzania	China, CMEA, EEC, Hong Kong, India, Japan, USA	Canada, China, Kenya, CMEA, EEC, India, Japan, Uganda, USA	Coffee, cotton, tea, tobacco, cashew nuts, pyrethrum, gold, diamonds	Consumer goods, intermediate goods & capital goods, fuel
Zambia	China, W. Germany, Japan, PTA, RSA, UK, USA	China, Japan, W. Germany, PTA, RSA, UK, USA	Copper, zinc, lead, cobalt, tobacco	Food, beverages & tobacco, crude materials, mineral fuel, lubricants, animal & vegetable oils, chemicals, machinery & transport manufactures
Zimbabwe	EEC, RSA, USA, Japan, Zambia, Botswana	RSA, EEC, USA, Japan, Zambia, Botswana	*Agricultural*: Tobacco, cotton, tea, sugar, coffee, meat *Minerals*: Gold, Asbestos, Nickel, Copper *Manufactures*: Ferro-alloys (iron & steel), textiles, clothing	Foods, petroleum products, chemicals, electricity, transport equipment & other equipment

Source: Economic Intelligence Unit, *Country Profile*, various issues (London: EIU).

SADC region, and nearly 15 times greater than that of Zimbabwe. Zimbabwe's manufacturing sector is far more diversified and sophisticated than those of its SADC partners; it accounts for nearly half of all the SADC's manufactured exports outside Mauritius and South Africa. But of the combined regional total it provides no more than 5 per cent. A comparison of MVA to GDP, however, indicates that manufacturing is as important to the economies of Swaziland, Zambia, Zimbabwe and Mauritius as it is to South Africa. For non-SACU countries – Angola, Malawi, Mozambique, Tanzania, Zambia and Zimbabwe – the result of promoting import-substituting industrialization behind tight restrictions on competitive imports over a period of 30 years or more has been to create similar industrial structures, with a concentration on consumer-goods industries, notably food-stuffs, clothing and textiles. These structural similarities, together with prevailing low levels of capacity utilization, mean that there is considerable excess production capacity for a range of consumer goods. This excess capacity has been further highlighted by the effects of structural adjustment programme designed to raise capacity levels and to expose industries to regional as well as international competition.

It should be noted that while intra-SADC trade increased from US$218.5 m. in 1983 to US$248.8 m. in 1984, an increase of about 14 per cent, intra-SADC trade declined from US$324.7 m. in 1987 to US$318.1 m. in 1988, representing a drop of about 2 per cent. SADC trade with South Africa also declined from US$2792.2 m. in 1987 to US$2182 m. in 1988 or about 22 per cent, a reflection of competition from cheaper sources abroad. On the other hand, SADC trade with the rest of the world increased from US$4760 m. in 1987 to US$5023.5 m. in 1988, an increase of about 5.5 per cent; excluding the BNLS countries, this level of trade was maintained at US$5059 m. in 1991 (TISCO, 1991; World Bank, 1995).

Though the period 1983–4 was only three years after the organization had been formed, this was also the period when most of the SADC member states were faced with serious economic crisis and a critical shortage of foreign exchange. As a result, most SADC members entered into bilateral trading arrangements involving the exchanges of goods that did not require payments in foreign exchange. Botswana, Mozambique, Namibia, Tanzania, Zambia and Zimbabwe all had bilateral trade agreements with one or more SADC members. These arrangements may have contributed to the increased trade flows over the period. Trade flows between Mozambique and

Tanzania, for example, increased by over 100 per cent between 1981 and 1983 but today there is hardly any trade between them.

By 1987/88 most SADC members had embarked on structural adjustment programmes (SAPs) involved substantial trade liberalization and dismantling of foreign exchange controls. The SAPs also led to substantial inflows of foreign exchange from bilateral and multilateral agencies as well as private remittances. In the case of Tanzania, for example, own-funds imports have accounted for between 30 per cent and 40 per cent of total imports over the past 10 years. Although the SADC experimented with a variety of measures aimed at increasing intra-regional trade for example, the regional export credit facility and export pre-financing revolving funds – these measures did not produce the intended results. Unilateral trade liberalization, a result of the SAPs most SADC members have undertaken, seems to explain in part the decline in intra-SADC trade flows and the increase in trade with the rest of the world.

From Table 7.3 it can be observed that, with the exception of Zimbabwe – which counts Botswana and Zambia among its main trading partners – none of the other SADC members have any significant trade between them. On the other hand, most SADC members except Angola and Tanzania have South Africa as one of their major trading partners between 1980 and 1990.

7.3 EMPIRICAL ASSESSMENT

Methodology

A gravity model approach, akin to that of Frankel and Wei (1993), is employed in order to address important trade issues within the SADC. These issues include:

- investigating the extent to which trade patterns have been influenced by natural economic factors and the respective regional policy initiatives thus far undertaken within SADC; and
- establishing whether the SADC has thus far been a viable trade bloc and determining the possible forces promoting or constraining viability.

The gravity model is so called because it assumes that trade between two countries is proportional to the distance between them.

Recent applications can be found in Wang and Winters (1991), as well as Frankel and Wei (1993). Dummy variables can be added to indicate, for example, when countries belong to the same regional grouping. The three most important factors in explaining bilateral trade flows are, according to the gravity model, the geographical distance between countries, economic size and state of development. A large part of the apparent bias towards intra-regional trade is often attributed to simple geographical proximity; Krugman (1991), for example, suggests that most of the bias may be due to proximity. In this context distance may reflect transportation costs in addition to consumer preferences. The economic size of a country is usually approximated by its GDP. In multilateral studies GDP in product form is empirically well established and can be justified by the modern theory of trade under imperfect competition (Smeet, 1994). A country's state of development is represented by the corresponding GDP per capita. It is not excluded, however, that this variable also captures to some extent the overlap of consumption structures between countries.

The main model is:

$$T_t = \beta_0 + \beta_1(GDP)_{ijt} + \beta_2(PCI)_{ijt} + \beta_3(Distance)T$$
$$+ \beta_4(Adjacent) + \beta_5(COMESA)_t + \beta_6(SACU)_t + U_t \quad (7.1)$$

where:

- T_t is trade (dependent variable at t. It is determined as a non-repetitive sum of exports and imports between pairs of countries in a particular year. If a_{ij} represents the exports of country i and imports of country j in a trade matrix in a given year, then

$$T_t = a_{ij} + a_{ij} \; i, j = 1, 2, \ldots, n, i = j. \quad (7.2)$$

As trade flows reported by two countries are seldom the same, the reported flows in the same direction were averaged and added to the average reported flows in the opposite direction to obtain a non-repetitive intra-trade figure.

- The $(GDP)_{ijt}$ variable is a non-repetitive multiple of gross domestic product of country i and j at period t:

$$(GDP)_{ijt} = (GDP)_{it} \times (GDP)_{jt}, \text{ for } i = j \quad (7.3)$$

It is a measure of a country's economic size, and postulates that trade between two countries is proportional to the product of their sizes. This conforms with the modern theory of trade under perfect competition, which asserts that trade between equal-sized countries is greater than trade between a large country and a small country.

- The variable $(PCI)_{ijt}$ is a non-repetitive product of per capita income between pairs of countries i and j at time t. That is,

$$(PCI)_{ijt} = (PCD)_{it} \times (PCI)_{jt}, \, i = j \tag{7.4}$$

The assumption is that the richer the countries become as exemplified by higher per capita incomes, the more they tend to specialize and trade between themselves.

- The $(Distance)_t$ variable stems from the hypothesis that bilateral trade is inversely proportional to the distance between two countries. Distance is taken to be a straight line measure between the capital cities of respective countries.
- The $(Adjacent)_t$ variable is a dummy variable to indicate whether two countries share a common land border.
- The dummy variables $(COMESA)$ and $(SACU)$ represent membership in the two regional groupings. A dummy of 1 indicates that the two countries belong to a common regional grouping, while a 0 means that either one or none belong to the regional group.

Analysis

The gravity model was estimated for three discrete time periods, 1981, 1985 and 1990. The three periods represent the pre-SADC (1981) period, the formative stage (1985), and the period when South Africa was being considered as a potential member state (1990). Least-squares regressions were carried out for each year. For economic robustness, the models were estimated in levels as well as logs. Heteroskedasticity was corrected to allow for different sizes of countries.

The results of the (OLS) estimates are shown in Appendix 6A.3, Tables 6A.3.1–6A.3.3. In all the three time-periods, all the parameters have the right sign (positive for GDP, GDP per capita and border, and negative for distance and membership in COMESA and SACU) except membership in COMESA for the periods 1981 and 1990.

For 1981 and 1985 the variables *(Distance)* and *(SACU)* are significant at 10 per cent. The variable *(Distance)* is significant at 5 per cent for the 1985 model. This conforms with the proposition that trade between any two countries is inversely proportional to the distance between them and that SACU members trade more among themselves than with the rest of SADC.

For the period 1990, when we considered South Africa as a potential SADC member, the results of the regression estimates show that both *(Distance)* and *(GDP)* (indicating economic size) are significant at 5 per cent while *(SACU)* becomes insignificant. This indicates that while the BNLS countries' trade flows are highly in the direction of South Africa as members of SACU, there is higher trade potential between South Africa and the rest of the SADC members than within the customs union. These results are consistent with Elbadawis' (1995) findings for SSA and other low income countries, where almost all the traditional variable of the gravity model were found to be significant and have plausible signs.

In the three time-periods the variables selected for the model are important in explaining the existing of trade potential within the SADC ($R^2 = 0.59$ for 1981, $R^2 = 0.40$ for 1985 and $R^2 = 0.55$ for 1990). These results indicate clearly that the potential for intra-SADC trade is high, based on the economic factors at play with or without a trade protocol. The proposed SADC trade protocol may therefore be superfluous if, in addition, consideration is taken of the fact that most SADC member states have already implemented significant trade liberalization measures as embedded in the SAPs these countries have pursued since the mid-1980s.

Another issue analysed in this chapter is the assessment as to whether the SADC has been a viable trade bloc. Since its inception in 1980, one of the issues that has been raised is whether the formation of the SADC has enhanced trade flows between member countries which would in effect corroborate the theory of economic integration. For an analysis of the issue, the data were divided into pre-SADC (1981), mid-SADC (1985) and post-SADC (1990) periods and a pooled time-series/cross-sectional model that captures the dynamic effects of the SADC's decade existence was estimated. The model used for testing structural change for both intercept and slope with a view to establishing the viability of the SADC as a trade bloc is shown in Appendix 6A.2.

The regression results for the test for the SADC as a trade bloc are shown in Appendix Table 6A.3.4. As demonstrated through the results of the gravity model for trade potential, the variable *(COMESA)* membership has the wrong sign and is significant. All other variables including the constant, except the variable *GDP per capita*, have the right sign and are significant at 5 per cent with $R^2 = 0.5$. Some qualitative forces, as demonstrated by the significance of the constant, have contributed towards the SADC becoming a viable trade bloc. This represents the major investment particularly in transport and communications, over a period of 10 years, as well as the sector co-ordination efforts since the organization was established. The most notable of these are creating an enabling environment for increased production of goods and services, cultivating political will for greater co-operation, and carrying out various studies to identify obstacles to intra-regional trade flows. The studies include trade facilitation, export-processing zones and middle management training for export production.

7.4 IMPLICATIONS OF CHANGING CONDITIONS FOR REGIONAL INTEGRATION

Much of the emphasis for regional integration in SSA should be weighed against the background of changing total conditions including the creation of regional trading blocs as well as changing domestic conditions as a result of the introduction of SAPS.

On the international scene, recent developments in the creation of trading blocs centred around the EU, the North American Free Trade Area (NAFTA) in North America and ASEAN pivoted around Japan, have rekindled interest in regional trading arrangements in SSA. Changing perceptions of the conditions required for effective integration have also influenced the renewed interest. Our main emphasis here will focus on the implications of the rapid changes in the domestic policy front for regional integration.

On the domestic front, a number of countries in SSA, and in fact the majority of countries in the SADC, have embraced SAPs with a view to correcting for macroeconomic imbalances, trade liberalization and greater participation of the private sector in the production of goods and services. De Melo, Panagariya and Rodrick (1993), have demonstrated that unilateral trade liberalization is superior to regional integration arrangements, and concluded that only if one of the countries is willing to accept a sub-optimal position for some exogenous reasons, can the other country benefit more from regional integration arrangement (Free Trade Area – FTA) than from unilateral trade liberalization (UTL). However, they were quick to argue that if the world gets divided into inward-looking blocs, UTL will become a less-attractive option for the countries outside the bloc. The countries will then be better off either seeking access to one of the blocs and adopting its trade policy or engaging in regional integration (RI) so as to promote freer trade among themselves.

In the early development literature, industrialization via import substitution was considered a respectable objective, mainly on grounds of infant industry, on-the-job training or other reasons. Outward-orientated economic policies were considered to be a zero-sum game (Nomvete, 1993). Today, the import-substitution policy has fallen out of favour with policy-makers and an FTA as an alternative to unilateral trade liberalization is harder to defend on grounds of import substitution.

While most of the SADC countries have embraced SAPs, there is also movement towards multi-party democracy in the region, and the elimination of apartheid in South Africa, now the eleventh SADC member, has completely changed the basic premise upon which the SADC was established. Though the participation of South Africa in the SADC reinforces the organization as a strong trading bloc, the movement of COMESA towards a common market and the present efforts towards the revival of the defunct East African Community may detract efforts towards a stronger SADC. However, if the fast-track, variable geometry approach to regional integration is employed, discussions aimed at dividing COMESA into north and south and the revival of the East African Community might strengthen rather than weaken the organization. An important question that should preoccupy the minds of most of the SADC member states would be: Given these developments, which direction should the organization take? Will SACU extend the same preferences to the rest of the SADC member states now that South Africa is a member of the SADC? This can only be judged with the test of time, given that the SACU agreement is currently being renegotiated and discussions aimed at involving other SADC members will only be entertained at the completion of this exercise.

Credibility is central to the twin pillars of regional integration, regional convertibility and the maintenance of regional trade liberalization. It is one of the important ingredients for ensuring an equitable distribution of the benefits of co-operation and integration. It is also a crucial determinant in the ability of any initiative to bring about a restructuring of production on which significant gains ultimately depend. Various studies have contended that the principal disincentive to investment from domestic as well as external sources is the fear of policy reversals.

It has been argued that whatever the underlying arguments for integration, a necessary condition for the realization of the theoretical gains from integration is that either the partners be similar (that is, each has something to gain from integration), or that an efficient and equitable compensation mechanism from gainers to losers be formulated (de Melo, Panagariya and Rodrik, 1993; Foroutan, 1993). This has been a bone of contention in almost all previous regional integration attempts in SSA. Present attempts, such as the attempts to revive the East African Community, which involve more visibly the participation of the private sector, might help to alleviate this problem.

Though integration is now increasingly widely seen as having a potentially important contribution to make to growth and development, a reality that has to be taken into account is that the earlier generation of integration schemes, particularly in SSA, were conspicuous failures. Two main lessons should be learned: (1) integration should be perceived to produce tangible benefits to all participating countries; and (2) these benefits should be seen to be evenly distributed among members. A major reason for earlier failures was that weaker members saw benefits flowing disproportionately to larger members.

An integration strategy more adapted to African realities should include:

- the development of an integrated sub-regional transport and communications network aimed at easing barriers to the movement of people and goods;
- the development of production to generate surpluses for intra-regional trade;
- trade liberalization schemes, including payment facilities, based on the expanded market;
- the gradual convergence of macroeconomic policies (SADC, 1993).

Huge imbalances in trade and the degree of industrialization have two important implications for trade integration: (1) integration benefits disproportionately those countries that happen to have the greatest share of industrial output and intra-regional trade; and (2) it justifiably raises concerns among the poor countries that the removal of barriers to trade may cause the migration of the few industries they possess to the industrially more advanced countries, thereby polarizing, further the existing uneven pattern of industrial development (Foroutan, 1993). The solution, it has been argued, is to compensate the disadvantaged countries (Foroutan, 1993; Nomvete, 1993). In Africa, no satisfactory compensation mechanism has yet been found.

That there are significant potential gains from economic integration in southern Africa is not in dispute. But economic integration is not a development strategy in its own right, merely one piece – albeit a significant one. The OECD's data on ASEAN performance are a striking reminder of the relative peripheral contribution of intra-regional trade to Asian economic growth. Between 1970 and 1988 ASEAN's extra-regional trade grew 40 per cent, while intra-regional trade expanded by only 5 per cent. SSA countries are not going to achieve growth rates of 5 per cent or more on the basis of regional integration alone, though successful integration will make it easier to attain and sustain such growth rates.

The Southern African state are more competitive than complementary in their production structures in that they produce much the same range of products with a very limited degree of product differentiation even at the level of manufacturing. According to customs union theory, there is little basis for regional integration in SSA. On the other hand, there are a number of reasons why the conventional wisdom might not apply in the region.

In a conventional analysis of a regional integration arrangement comprising three countries, A, B and C and two goods, 1 and 2, A and B are potential partners and C represents the outside world. In this setting, there are two possible trade patterns: A and B import the same goods or they import different goods. In the case when A and B import the same good, they will import it from C and there will be no trade between them in the initial equilibrium. If the formation of an RI arrangement leaves the tariff on C unchanged, the initial equilibrium will continue to obtain: the FTA will be vacuous. This situation describes the reality of most RI schemes in subSaharan Africa. In many of these schemes, the partner countries had very similar patterns of trade and integration attempts had a very limited impact on trade flows.

It has been argued further that regional integration under conditions of competitive production structures is likely to lead to trade diversion, which reduces overall efficiency. This theory has recently been re-examined in the light of present world trading conditions, with the conclusion that the trade diversion argument requires some reassessment, for three main reasons.

(1) Economic integration may produce economies of scale. Production costs in the free trade area would then be roughly equal to, or perhaps even lower than, those in the rest of the world.
(2) If the industries in the FTA are protected mainly by quotas rather than tariffs, trade diversion need not reduce efficiency.
(3) If the cost of producing complementary goods in the area prior to union is higher than in the rest of the world, this could be the result of over-valued exchange rates. Then, the lower monetary costs of imported goods, from the rest of the world may not necessarily be conterminous with lower economic costs. Nevertheless, empirical research shows that countries that have a similar composition of GDP and structure of manufacturing tend to be one another's best customers (Maasdorp, 1992).

Project co-ordination of the type the SADC has pursued over the past decade cannot, however, be the major basis for SADC strategy, as it has been found to have limited impact in promoting deeper and wider co-operation and integration. Three weaknesses have been noted:

- lack of strong linkage between national policies and plans and regional integration efforts;
- the potential for conflict arising from differences in national and regional sectoral policies and plans; and
- inability of project-based co-ordination to respond to changes in national sectoral policies and in the economy generally.

The development integration approach has been suggested as appropriate for SADC. It has been argued that a *laissez-faire* approach would exercebate existing inequalities and relations of dependency. However, member states should address themselves to the following: the various bureaucratic, regulatory and administrative non-tariff barriers to the movement of goods; service and production factors in the region; the non-convertibility of currencies and other payment-related problems; the inadequate physical and economic infrastructure in a number of areas; and the low production base.

It has been argued that however weakly or strongly co-ordination activities and regulations are integrated, the fact remains that such an integrative effort will greatly assist the cause of market unification at relatively little or no economic cost to the participating countries. Market unification will ease the circulation of information and create an environment more attractive to domestic and foreign investment as well as the realization of joint projects. Regional co-operation arrangements that have been successful in other parts of the world are those that combine intra-regional preferential arrangements in respect of trade and factor inputs, with global trade liberalization and export-led industrialization policies. The successful economies of South Korea, Taiwan, Hong Kong and Singapore – which maintain a loose economic co-operation programme – and now China, trade substantially among themselves but more so with the rest of the world, based on a highly competitive export-orientated sector with emphasis on manufacturing.

Emphasis on the strengthening of national economies as a condition for promotion of regionalism makes the current waves of SAPs of crucial importance. However, except for the few reasons discussed in this chapter, unilateral trade liberalization leaves little reason for regional trading arrangements. On the other hand, national economies in SSA are much too small to form a strong basis for long-term growth and development.

Another important factor that would enhance the process of regionalism is skills development. Countries that have high levels of literacy and high quality of indigenous skills have achieved high rates of productivity and economic growth. It has been pointed out, for example, that the South East Asian countries achieved universal primary education before they began to industrialize, and simultaneously with the industrialization process invested heavily in technical and managerial skills (Nomvete, 1993). It should also be pointed out that poor macroeconomic management, where inflation as well as inefficient market organization have been allowed to prevail, has interfered with economic development and progress. The impressive performance of the South East Asian countries was supported by an excellent record with respect to inflation (Klein, 1993).

In the SADC region, which for the moment includes South Africa and Mauritius, only in Zimbabwe, Mauritius and South Africa has industry developed to any significant extent, but many of their manufactures are uncompetitive outside the region. In addition, a major obstacle to regionally integrated industrial development is the domination of manufacturing industry by foreign-owned enterprises, in particular large manufacturing companies and transnational corporations (TNCs) which prefer to deal with sister and parent companies which, to a very large extent, are situated outside the region. A number of these enterprises source raw materials from outside the region, even if they are available locally. Some create barriers against the entry of new local firms.

Compounding all of these problems, in the cases of Angola and Mozambique, in particular, the impact of decades of war will continue to be felt for some time to come, notwithstanding the signature of peace agreement. Both countries suffered major damage and disruption as a result of external aggression and the activities of armed bandits. The insecurity created in the rural areas had a profound impact on both agricultural and mineral production (with the exception of oil production in Angola). The disruption of transport and distribution systems both reduced revenue and foreign exchange earnings, particularly in the case of Mozambique, and adversely affected the delivery of agricultural produce to markets. Other problems created by war, were the diversion of foreign exchange and budgetary resources to defence and the case of displaced persons (SADC, 1993).

7.5 IMPACT OF THE GLOBAL ENVIRONMENT ON THE SADC

Results of the gravity model indicate that the SADC is a viable trade bloc with potential for increased intra-regional trade flows. Given that in most parts of the world, countries are moving towards the creation of trade blocs, the SADC should consolidate its efforts to form a strong bargaining position. Individually, the countries will have no voice to be heard.

SADC has benefited enormously from donor funds; but with the end of the cold war and continuing economic recession in the West, the flow of funds from donors is likely to be reduced. If alternative sources are not handy, the longer-term sustainability of the organization may be put in jeopardy. However, with South Africa on board, it may act as a conduit through which external resources may be channelled to the rest of the region if political stability prevails.

Substantial infrastructural development in the form of transport and communication, power distribution and an enhanced production base, all of which are long-term in nature, has been created. These represent the necessary but by no means sufficient conditions for SADC regional integration efforts. Co-ordination of macroeconomic policies among the member states would contribute immensely towards the realization of those efforts. The SADC's long-term sustainability lies in the further development of infrastructure, hence creating an enabling environment for the production of goods and services, and the co-ordination of macroeconomic policies rather than integration based on customs union theory that requires the drawing up of a trade protocol for its implementation. Provisions for trade integration within SACU and COMESA treaties may suffice. Moreover, the SACU agreement is currently being renegotiated and who knows whether provisions will be made for SADC member states outside SACU to join. In addition, most SADC member states have implemented significant trade liberalization measures, to the extent that provisions for tariff reductions and the elimination of non-tariff barriers in the treaties have been overtaken by events and are no longer binding.

7.6   SPECIAL ISSUES

The intra-SADC trade study of 1986, which formed the basis for introducing trade as one of the coordinating sectors (to be handled by Tanzania, which was already co-ordinating the industry sector) found that intra-SADC trade was very low, 4–5 per cent. In the same study, it was found that trade between the SADC and the Nordic countries, the largest contributors in terms of financial flows to support the SADC, was also low. This revelation led to discussions between the two groups of countries aimed at exploring ways and means of increasing trade flows between them.

In 1988/89, a Nordic/SADC initiative was created. This initiative was to cover, among other issues, the development of measures to increase trade flows not only among SADC member states but also between the SADC and the Nordic countries.

On trade, some of the measures taken include the establishment of the Nordic/SADC Trade Advisory Group which has initiated a number of studies including trade facilitation, export development and promotion strategy for the SADC, trading houses, export-processing zones in the SADC and middle management training for export development in general and intra-regional trade in particular. Some of the trade advisory group's recommendations led to the establishment of a NORSAD fund with headquarters in Lusaka, Zambia, whose main objective was to act as an export pre-financing facility and revolving fund to support SADC manufacturing industries with a view to enhancing intra-regional trade flows arising from increased output.

To date, a sum of DKr187.4 m. has been committed for this purpose, with DKr30.0 m. having been disbursed. However, the present economic liberalization efforts, particularly on the foreign exchange front, have rendered these facilities less attractive. On the other hand, the studies carried out under the initiative have addressed very crucial areas, which if implemented would lead to enhanced intra-regional trade in future.

Another special SADC issue is that the co-ordinating units are placed within government ministries and have to operate within the government bureaucracy with little influence from the secretariat in Gaborone. This arrangement at times makes implementation of decisions of a regional nature rather slow. If the units were to operate with greater autonomy, independent of government machinery and in closer co-operation with the secretariat, this might help speed up implementation of decisions of a regional nature.

Earlier attempts to establish an SADC business council with greater participation of the private sector seem to have failed. Although a political consensus is necessary for the success of regional integration arrangements, there seems to be 'too much government' in the SADC, which may stifle the success of the organization.

7.7 CONCLUDING REMARKS

To date, progress on intra-SADC trade flows has been limited. Most SADC members are preoccupied with national policies, with little attention to regional concerns. What seems to be evident is that regional co-operation, if it is to succeed, requires that the national economies be strengthened. Therefore, in the current state of the national economies, integration via trade and import substitution or via sectoral integration *à la* SADC may not constitute the most cost-effective method of allocating scarce resources. The present debate on splitting COMESA into north and south wherein the south will constitute all the SADC members, and the prospects for the revival of the defunct East African Community seem to be gaining ground. If this should constitute a fast-track, variable geometry approach to regional integration, it may facilitate faster achievement of the SADC objective of regional co-operation. Given the political obstacles to a broad regional agreement, an alternative would be to negotiate liberal arrangements among smaller groups of countries, then offer conditional 'most-favoured nation' status to other countries that will be required to abide by the rules and obligations under the small regional arrangement. In this regard, membership in SACU may be a natural starting point. Experience has shown that considerable advantages exist in limiting the number of participant countries in any regional agreement to those truly committed to the process. The EU started with six members, with others added later.

Transport and communication absorbed the lion's share of all SADC projects, which has seen the development of the Beira corridor, a 300 km. strip running from Beira on the coast of Mozambique to the border with Zimbabwe; if contains Beira port, a railway, a road and oil pipeline, an electricity line, and a number of development projects. The Beira project has brought about greater co-operation between Zimbabwe and Mozambique, the repopulation of the port and return of private businesses. On food security, regional drought preparedness measures have been put in place, the success of which is yet to be determined. Another area where success has been registered is in the mobilization of donor support for its sectoral programmes. By 1985, for example, net ODA support to all SADC members was about US$1775 m.

With hindsight, it can be argued that SADC activities over the past 14 years have laid a firm foundation on which to build closer co-operation and integration in Southern Africa. The infrastructural development projects undertaken under the organization's auspices have contributed to overcome a number of significant bottlenecks to regional development. While many of the projects undertaken under SADC remain of great importance for regional development, co-operation on projects has served as a catalyst for deeper or wider regional co-operation and integration, to only a limited extent. Regionally co-ordinated investment in physical, social and institutional infrastructure could lead to large cost-savings due to scale.

The regression results of the gravity model indicate that the SADC is a viable trade bloc with great potential for the intra-regional flow of goods and services. Emphasis should now be placed on removing obstacles that affect the production of goods and services. Given the existence of trade protocols for SACU and COMESA, a trade protocol for the SADC may be superfluous, since all its members belong to one or the other of those groups.

The issue of the distribution of the benefits of regional integration is crucial for the success of integration efforts and government commitment to regional schemes. Members of a regional group are not likely to gain equally from economic integration. While the region as a whole may gain from integration, single members could be worse off. Integration schemes must, therefore, observe the principles of equity, mutual benefit and interdependence for any successes to be registered. For the SADC this is particularly important given the disparities in incomes between the member states. The daunting task is to work out an acceptable formula.

APPENDIX 7A.1: DATA SOURCES

Trade Data

These were obtained from the following sources:

United Nations, *Yearbook of International Trade Statistics* (various issues)
International Monetary Fund, *Directory of Trade Statistics Yearbook* (various issues)
Trade Statistics Supplement (Republic of Botswana: Central Statistics Office, 1994)
Annuario Estatistico (Republic of Mozambique, date unknown)
External Trade Bulletin (Republic of Zambia: Central Statistical Office, 1994)
Quarterly Digest of Statistics (Harare, Zimbabwe: Central Statistical Office, June 1994)

GDP and Population Data

These were obtained from World Bank, *African Development Indicators* (various issues).

Other Data

The distance was obtained by measuring the physical distance between capital cities, and adjacency was determined on a map.

APPENDIX 7A.2: THE DYNAMIC EFFECTS MODEL OF STRUCTURAL CHANGE FOR SADC

$$\begin{bmatrix} T_{1981,i} \\ T_{1985,i} \\ T_{1990,i} \end{bmatrix} = \begin{bmatrix} X_{1981,i} & 0 & 0 \\ 0 & X_{1985,i} & 0 \\ 0 & 0 & X_{1990,i} \end{bmatrix} \begin{bmatrix} \beta_{0,1981} \\ \beta_{0,1985} \\ \beta_{0,1990} \\ \beta_{1981} \\ \beta_{1985} \\ \beta_{1990} \end{bmatrix} + u$$

where, $T_{1981,i}$, $T_{1985,i}$ and $T_{1990,i}$ represent vectors of bilateral trade flows in the years, and $i = 1 .. n*(n - 1)/2$, $X_{1981,i}$ $X_{1985,i}$ and $X_{1990,i}$ are matrixes of regressors [*GDP, PCI ... SACU*] including a column vector of units for the two periods, $i = 1 .. n*(n - 1)/2$ and u is the disturbance term.

The null hypothesis of no structural change within the SADC is:

$$H_0: \begin{bmatrix} \beta_{0,1981} \\ \beta_{1981} \end{bmatrix} = \begin{bmatrix} \beta_{0,1985} \\ \beta_{1985} \end{bmatrix} = \begin{bmatrix} \beta_{0,1990} \\ \beta_{1990} \end{bmatrix}$$

The restricted model is a pooled regression given by:

$$\begin{bmatrix} T_{1981,i} \\ T_{1985,i} \\ T_{1990,i} \end{bmatrix} + \begin{bmatrix} X_{1981,i} \\ X_{1985,i} \\ X_{1990,i} \end{bmatrix} [\beta] + u$$

where, β is a common vector of parameters including the constant for both sets of data.

The test statistic is:

$$F = \frac{(e'_* e_* - e'e)/J}{e'e/(n - K)} \sim F(J, (n - K))$$

where $e'_* e_*$ and ee denote the restricted and the unrestricted residual sum of squares from the respective OLS regression models. J represents the number of restrictions, n is the total number of observations in either model, and K is the total number of parameters including a constant.

APPENDIX 7A.3

Table 7A.3.1   Regression estimate results (model for 1981)

Variable	Coefficient	Standard error	t-statistic	2-tail significance
C	6.4223626	10.582939	0.6068600	0.5525
GDP81	0.8399562	0.5150203	1.6309188	0.1224
PCI81	0.5476871	0.4405247	1.2432608	0.2317
Distance	-1.6599992	0.9409094	-1.7642498	0.0968
Adjacent	1.5896494	0.9936301	1.5998403	0.1292
PTA/COMESA	0.2704318	1.0559711	0.2560977	0.8011
SACU	-2.6975381	1.5378060	-1.7541472	0.0985

R^2	0.596976	Mean of dependent variable		14.53877
Adjusted R^2	0.445843	Standard deviation of dependent variable		2.342063
Standard error of regression	1.743473	Sum of squared residual		18.63516
Log likelihood	-41.24739	F-statistic		3.949984
Durbin–Watson statistic	1.753077	Probability (F-statistic)		0.012950

Notes:
Observations excluded because of missing data
No. of observations: 23

Table 7A.3.2   Regression estimate results (model for 1985)

Variable	Coefficient	Standard error	t-statistic	2-tail significance
C	20.091165	10.673495	1.8823417	0.0710
GDP85	0.5702210	0.5792812	0.9843611	0.3340
PCI85	0.0401297	0.4532968	0.0885284	0.9301
Distance	-2.2426760	0.8339920	-2.6890856	0.0123
Adjacent	1.6221716	1.0326366	1.5709027	0.1283
PTA/COMESA	-0.0611368	1.0960655	-0.0557785	0.9559
SACU	-2.8286916	1.5437668	-1.8323309	0.0784

R^2	0.400270	Mean of dependent variable		13.41906
Adjusted R^2	0.261870	Standard deviation of dependent variable		2.696132
Standard error of regression	2.316367	Sum of squared residual		139.5045
Log likelihood	-70.61120	F-statistic		2.892138
Durbin–Watson statistic	1.243248	Probability (F-statistic)		0.026986

Notes:
Observations excluded because of missing data
No. of observations: 33

Table 7A.3.3   Regression estimate results (model for 1990, which includes South Africa)

Variable	Coefficient	Standard error	t-statistic	2-tail significance
C	15.977415	8.2105718	1.9459565	0.0614
GDP90	0.6785392	0.2987525	2.2712422	0.0307
PCI90	0.3306391	0.5187984	0.6373172	0.5289
Distance	−2.2494589	0.8742355	−2.5730581	0.0155
Adjacent	0.5967411	1.7971795	0.7485656	0.4601
PTA/COMESA	0.3889860	0.9090832	0.4278883	0.6719
SACU	−1.2827168	1.1770731	−1.0897511	0.2848

R^2	0.554838	Mean of dependent variable		15.36397
Adjusted R^2	0.462735	Standard deviation of dependent variable		2.636277
Standard error of regression	1.932348	Sum of squared residual		108.2850
Log likelihood	−70.90425	F-statistic		6.024133
Durbin–Watson statistic	1.570858	Probability (F-statistic)		0.000349

Notes:
Observations excluded because of missing data
No. of observations: 36

Table 7A.3.4   Regression estimate results (model for the period 1981–90)

Variable	Coefficient	Standard error	t-statistic	2-tail significance
C	14.827818	5.0778596	2.9200921	0.0045
GDP	0.7404562	0.2223185	3.3306093	0.0013
PCI	0.2802629	0.2626222	1.0671714	0.2889
Distance	−2.2025175	0.5386025	−4.0893194	0.0001
Adjacent	1.2664513	0.5084602	2.4907581	0.0147
PTA/COMESA	0.1955820	0.5645792	0.3463610	0.7299
SACU	−2.1526229	0.8277369	−2.6006125	0.0110

R^2	0.501176	Mean of dependent variable		14.46004
Adjusted R^2	0.465965	Standard deviation of dependent variable		2.696873
Standard error of regression	1.970813	Sum of squared residual		330.1487
Log likelihood	−189.3191	F-statistic		14.23347
Durbin–Watson statistic	0.884737	Probability (F-statistic)		0.000000

Notes:
Observations excluded because of missing data
No. of observations: 92

References

African Development Bank (1992) 'Economic Integration in South Africa', a report.

de Melo, J., A. Panagariya and D. Rodrik (1993) 'The New Regionalism; a country perspective', in J. de Melo and A. Panagariya (eds), *New Dimensions in Regional Integration* (Cambridge University Press for Centre for Economic Policy Research).

Elbadawi, I. (1995) 'The Impact of Regional Trade/Monetary Schemes on Intra-sub-saharan Africa Trade', paper presented at the AERC Collaborative Research Workshop, Harare (18–20 March 1995).

Fine, J. and S. Yeo (1994) 'Regional Integration in Sub-Saharan Africa: Dead End or a Fresh Start', mimeo (May).

Foroutan, F. (1993) Regional Integration in Sub-Saharan Africa', in J. De Melo and A. Panagariya (eds), *New Dimensions in Regional Integration* (Cambridge University Press for Centre for Economic Policy Research).

Frankel, J. A. and S.-J. Wei (1993) 'Trade Blocs and Currency Blocs', in G. de la Dehesa, A. Giovannin, M. Guitian and Richard Portes (eds), *The Monetary Future of Europe* (CEPR).

Global Coalition for Africa (1993) *Annual Report.*

Kiggundu, S. (1983) *A Planned Approach to a Common Market in Developing Countries* (Nairobi: Coign).

Klein, L. (1993) 'African Economic Development: Situations and Prospects', *The South African Journal of Economics.*

Krugman, P. (1991) *Geography and Trade* (Leuven University Press and the MIT Press).

Maasdorp, G. (1992) 'Economic Cooperation in Southern Africa: Prospects for Regional Integration', *Conflict Studies*, no. 253 (Research Institute for the Study of Conflict and Terrorism, UK).

Nomvete, B. (1993) 'Regional Development and Economic Cooperation in Africa', *The South African Journal of Economics* (December).

OECD (1993), *Regional Integration and Development Countries* (Paris: OECD).

SADC (1986) *Intra Regional Trade Study* (Prepared by the Chr. Michelsen Institute, Bergen, Norway).

SADC (1992a), *Declaration Treaty and Protocol of Southern African Development Community* (Namibia: Windhoek).

SADC (1992b), *Towards Economic Integration*, The Proceedings of the 1992 Annual Consultative Conference, Maputo, Mozambique.

SADC (1993), *Regional Relations and Cooperation Post Apartheid*, A Macro Framework Study report (Gaborone, Botswana).

Smeet, H.-D. (1994) 'The EC as a Trading Bloc – The German Experience', CREDIT Research Paper no. 94/14.

TISCO (1991) 'SADC Export Development and Promotion Strategy' (Dar-es-Salaam).

Wang, Z. K. and L. A Winters (1991) 'The Trading Potential of Eastern Europe', CEPR, Disc. Paper 610 (November). London: Centre for Economic Policy Research.

World Bank (1994) *World Tables 1994* (Baltimore and London: The Johns Hopkins University Press for the World Bank).
World Bank (1995) *African Development Indicators 1994–95* (Washington, DC).

8 Cross-Border Trade and Regional Integration: A Welfare Analysis

Jean-Paul Azam

8.1 INTRODUCTION

This chapter analyses the welfare effect of smuggling as it relates to trade liberalization. When it occurs because of a tariff or an export tax, smuggling is detrimental if it entails some real resource cost over and above the cost of official trade, and if it does not drive out official trade. If it does, then the trade creation effect of smuggling may offset its cost. With Pitt's specification, where official trade provides a cover for unofficial trade, the consumer surplus goes up, thanks to smuggling. In all cases, the presence of smuggling enhances the case for trade liberalization. In particular, it is shown that smuggling may be a useful complement to official trade in the case of the creation of a free-trade area, since by increasing the tradeability of imperfectly tradeable goods, it strengthens the case for joining a monetary union.

Most developing countries do not have the administrative capacity for raising tax revenues in an efficient way. Foreign trade turns out to be one of the easiest tax handles to use, insofar as traded goods have to pass through some easily monitored points, like harbours, train stations and airports. Customs officers thus play a major role in collecting fiscal revenues for the government. This is especially true in Africa, where taxes on foreign trade often amount to about half the total tax revenues. Table 8.1 illustrates this point by showing the ratio of trade-related tax to total tax revenues in some subSaharan countries.

All these levies, which generally bear more heavily on imports than on exports, create a lot of distortion. They provide some protection to the firms that produce import substitutes, and thus in many cases create an anti-export bias. Moreover, these figures

Table 8.1   The share of trade taxes in tax revenues (%)

Country	For 1988	For previous dates
Cameroon	18.4	29.0 (1981–3)
Congo	32.3	17.0 (1978–80)
Côte d'Ivoire	42.3	46.3 (1980–2)
Gambia	77.9	78.8 (1976–8)
Ghana	37.9	37.1 (1981–3)
Kenya	3.1	22.3 (1979–81)
Niger	n.a.	40.0 (1978–80)
Nigeria	17.5	19.4 (1976–8)
Senegal	37.7	38.5 (1980–2)
Uganda	46.7	55.8 (1981–3)
Zaire	46.9	35.8 (1980–2)

Sources: Tanzi (1987, 1992).

underestimate the situation in some countries. For example, oil-rich Nigeria levies about 60 per cent of oil exports as royalties, which appear under the corporate tax heading and not as a trade-related tax. A similar effect occurs in uranium-exporting Niger. In the case of Cameroon, the royalties on oil exports have been kept hidden for a long time, so that they too are not included in the figures given in Table 8.1.

Exports are often taxed in Africa in another way, by a marketing board or a stabilization fund. This type of levy is not included in Table 8.1, although it sometimes amounts to a very large percentage of the border price. This was for a long time the case in Côte d'Ivoire, where a stabilization fund in fact captured a large share of the export proceeds, until the fall in international prices for its export goods – coffee and cocoa – in the late 1980s (Azam and Morrisson, 1994). Then, it turned out that most of the money levied on producers through the fund had not been invested in liquid assets that could easily be sold in order to raise funds to compensate farmers for the price fall, as a proper stabilization fund should do. The stabilization fund was thus only able to stabilize prices when they were going up on the world market, not when they went down. Hence, it is reasonable to regard these levies as taxes, although they do not appear explicitly in the government budget.

In addition to these explicit taxes, one may add the effect of exchange rate over-valuation, especially in countries where a parallel foreign exchange market is active. The premium on foreign currencies can be interpreted as a tax on the export proceeds that are surrendered at the official exchange rate, and as subsidy on official imports. Some countries, like Nigeria, are not sellers of foreign exchange to their private sector. There, the government sells the foreign currencies from oil exports and international aid through the central bank at a discount, which enables it to transfer some money to privileged agents, who have access to these sales (Azam, 1994; Odubogun, 1994).

But traders usually find various ways of sidestepping, at least to some extent, the problems raised by these trade taxes. Smuggling and misinvoicing are extremely common in Africa, and the list of countries represented in Table 8.1 contains many well-known cross-border trade partners. Smuggling between the Gambia and Senegal is a very active business, to the extent that official imports of sugar in the Gambia, on a per capita basis, probably hit the world record. This is a way of avoiding the heavy protection granted to this sector in Senegal. Many other goods are involved in the Gambia–Senegal cross-border trade, which has been studied by Daubrée (1995). Côte d'Ivoire and Ghana similarly have a very active smuggling activity, involving cocoa and manufactured goods, crossing the border one way or the other, depending on the changing pattern of trade taxation (May, 1985; Azam and Besley, 1989a). In the late 1970s and the early 1980s, it was estimated that about 50 000 tons of cocoa were smuggled out of Ghana (May, 1985). Azam and Besley (1989b), in a regression analysis, found that the difference in cocoa producer prices between Côte d'Ivoire and Ghana, evaluated at the parallel market exchange rate, had a significant impact on official sales of cocoa by the Cocoa Marketing Board (Cocobod). During the worst days of the Idi Amin and Obote regimes in Uganda, a lot of coffee was smuggled out across the Kenyan border. Similarly, in the days of the Mengistu regime, a lot of coffee was illegally exported from Ethiopia into Kenya (Kidane, 1994). The proceeds from these illegal exports were partly used for financing imports of manufactured goods, and partly for capital flight.

Nigeria and its neighbours, including Cameroon and Niger, as presented in Table 8.1, trade many goods across their common borders. These include cowpeas, cigarettes, Nigeria-made Peugeot cars, and so on (Azam, 1991(a), 1991(b); Daubrée, 1995). In the last case of the cars, the parallel market for foreign exchange plays a crucial role, as the parts for making the cars are paid at the official exchange rate, while the cars are then sold at the parallel market rate. As the premium on foreign exchange on the naira market can be quite substantial, about 80 per cent on average in the early 1980s, this amounts to a large input subsidy, which makes Nigerian-made Peugeot cars more competitive than those made in France. In the case of Nigeria, the over-valuation of the local currency has also triggered some fake exports from neighbouring countries, with massive over-invoicing. For example, Niger had an agreement with Nigeria allowing some cattle to be exported to Nigeria, the proceeds of which were allowed to be purchased by the Central Bank in Niger at the official exchange rate. Traders would export a couple of sick cows into Nigeria, in order to get a receipt for a large sum of nairas, which they in fact bought on the parallel market, for selling eventually at the official exchange rate at the Central Bank. This simple way of pocketing the parallel market premium was widely used in Niger.

However, trade taxes and exchange rate over-valuation are not the only reason for cross-border trade and smuggling, as African governments often use quantitative restrictions instead of tariffs.

The reason non-tariff barriers have been so popular in Africa has to do with the political economy of resource redistribution. A quota imposed on the import of a particular good creates two types of rents (McKinnon, 1979): (1) it creates a wedge between the border price and the consumer price, which is pocketed by the importer; and (2) quotas create some monopoly power for import-substituting firms, as they prevent external competition. Hence, by selective quota policy, the government is able to redistribute some resources in favour of some privileged groups, in an unobtrusive way. From the government's point of view, this way of diverting resources from the budget has the definite advantage of reducing the possibility of the parliament or the Bretton Woods institutions controlling their use. It is a method of redistributing income to some privileged groups that is akin to what was described above, regarding the sale of foreign exchange at a discount through the central bank. But it may be socially costly, if real resources are invested by rent-seekers to capture the benefits of these distortions. Krueger (1974) has illustrated the social cost of competitive rent-seeking in her classic paper.

The present chapter aims first to analyse whether cross-border trade and misinvoicing are an efficient way of getting around these distortions. As shown below, the answer to this question depends on whether the smuggling is triggered by tariffs or quotas, and whether it involves resource costs, or just transfers like bribes and fines. As suggested in particular by Johnson (1987), the welfare analysis of cross-border trade bears close resemblance to the classical Vinerian analysis of the free-trade area (Robson, 1987). We systematically develop this insight in what follows. Our analysis sheds some light on the case for trade liberalization in Africa. Is there any room left for liberalizing, or can it be said that smugglers have done all the job? This question has been raised recently by Roemer (1987) and Azam (1990). Moreover, trade policy in Africa is more and more discussed within the frame work of regional integration and policy co-ordination (Foroutan, 1993). We discuss how the existence of cross-border trade changes the analysis of a free-trade area, within the traditional Vinerian framework. Then, establishing a free-trade area may be regarded as a way to create official trading activity that competes with the smugglers. Lastly, we raise the issue of the effect of smuggling on the efficacy of exchange rate policy.

The first ingredient for these analyses is the discussion of the nature of the cost of smuggling, to which we now turn.

8.2 ALTERNATIVE MODELS OF SMUGGLING OR MISINVOICING COSTS

In their seminal paper, Bhagwati and Hansen (1973) assume that smuggling involves a cost difference compared with official trade. Neglecting any cost of official trade, they model the (extra) cost of smuggling as a real resource cost, captured by assuming that a constant fraction of the goods being smuggled is lost. This results in a constant returns to scale supply curve of smuggled goods, so that official and parallel trade cannot co-exist in general in their model. We either observe official trade, if the unit smuggling cost is too high, given the distortion imposed on trade, or official trade is driven out by smuggling, in the opposite case. However, in the real world, it is often the case that official and non-official trade occur simultaneously.

In order to model the simultaneous activity of official and parallel trade, two main routes have been followed.

The Increasing Marginal Cost of Smuggling

The first approach is based on the assumption of the increasing marginal cost of smuggling. This assumption is discussed, among others, by Azam and Besley (1989a), Daubrée (1994, 1995), Devarajan, Jones and Roemer (1989), Kamin (1993), and O'Connell (1992). In this framework, a typical parallel trader seeks to maximize trading profit:

$$\pi \ (p - p^*) = \max \ (0) \ (p - p^*) \ Q - c(Q) \tag{8.1}$$

In this problem, we simplify the analysis by assuming that the smuggler being studied is only an importer. The volume traded is denoted as Q, while p and p^* denote, respectively, the local price of the good and its international price. The extra cost of smuggling is denoted as $c(Q)$, assumed increasing and convex, while the unit cost of official trade is set to zero.

The first order condition for this problem can be written:

$$p = p^* + c' \ (Q) \tag{8.2}$$

The right-hand side of Equation (8.2) is the marginal cost of smuggling, being the sum of the price of the good across the border, plus the marginal cost of transporting it and selling it inside the country. In the competitive equilibrium, it must be equal to the price of the good sold on the local market. If official and unofficial trade are simultaneously active, and have access to the good on the international market at the same price, then we must also have the following arbitrage condition:

$$p = (1 + t) \ p^* \tag{8.3}$$

where t is the tax rate on officially imported goods, or the tariff-equivalent of the quantitative restriction on imports. Combining equations (8.2) and (8.3) shows the crucial role of this tax rate in determining the level of smuggling activity:

$$c'(Q) = tp^* \tag{8.4}$$

It is obvious that equation (8.4) cannot hold if the smuggling technology has constant returns to scale so that $c'(Q) = 0$, unless there is a cover effect, discussed below.

Equation (8.2) makes it clear that the quantity smuggled is an increasing function of the price difference $p - p^*$. By differentiating one gets:

$$d\ Q = (1/c'')\ d\ (p - p^*) \qquad (8.5)$$

The case of an exporter can be analysed in a similar way, as seeking to maximize:

$$\pi^X(Q^* - Q) = \max_x (q^* - q)\ X - C\ (X) \qquad (8.6)$$

Here, q represents the local price of the good being smuggled out, q^* its price on the international market, and X the quantity exported. Then, the first order condition can be written as:

$$q^* - c'(X) = q \qquad (8.7)$$

The left-hand side can be interpreted as the inverse derived demand for the good,[1] which in a competitive equilibrium must be equal to its price. Then differentiating equation (8.7) would give X as an increasing function of $q^* - q$, in a way close to equation (8.5).

These two examples assume, for the sake of simplicity, that the marginal costs of exporting and importing are independent of each other. Azam and Besley (1989a) discuss the case of economies of scope in smuggling, whereby the marginal cost is a decreasing function of the quantities of goods smuggled out. This is a simple way of modelling the fact that the transportation technology usually implies that some vehicle must be driven back, after being used for exporting some goods. Therefore, the marginal cost of transporting something on the return trip is lower, as the vehicle would need to be driven back anyway, even if empty. The same reasoning can be applied when the main trip is the importing one, ensuring symmetry of the argument.

O'Connell (1992) emphasizes that assuming decreasing returns to scale at the level of the individual smuggler is not enough to explain the simultaneous activity of official and unofficial trade, as we might have a perfectly elastic supply curve of smuggled goods, with free entry, each smuggler trading a very small amount. He solves the problem by assuming some externality; for example, that the congestion of discrete smuggling routes increases the probability of being caught by the customs officers when too many smugglers take it. He also discusses the alternative assumption of barriers to entry, resulting in a fixed number of smugglers. Then, the upward sloping supply curve results as well.

Because of indivisibilities and credit market imperfections, the latter assumption may be quite realistic in some cases, at least in the short run. For example, a very juicy smuggling activity in the late 1980s was the illegal import of a famous English brand of cigarettes across the Niger–Nigeria border, when Nigeria was trying to protect its cigarette-makers by a ban on imports (Azam, 1991a, 1991b). According to some very reliable sources, there were exactly 14 traders involved in this trade, which suggests that some barriers to entry in this type of smuggling were operating at the time. One must assume some kind of Bertrand competition, or that the number of incumbent smugglers is rather large, for equation (8.2) or (8.7) to hold.

The Cover Effect

The other route for explaining the simultaneous existence of official and parallel trade has been presented by Pitt (1981, 1984), who assumes that official trade provides a cover to the smuggler, so that some goods are traded in the open in order to cloak the undeclared part of the trade. Then, even with constant returns to scale, the two types of trade can co-exist. To see this, we use Q^F and Q^S to denote the quantities that are declared and undeclared, respectively; we use t to denote the tax rate on official imports, including any effect of the parallel market premium on foreign exchange. Then, the trader's profit function becomes:

$$\pi(p, p^*, t) = \max_Q (p - p) Q^s +$$

$$(p - (1 + t)p^*)Q^F - C(Q^S, Q^F) \qquad (8.8)$$
$$(+)\ (-)$$

With C_S and C_F as the partial derivatives of $C(-)$ with respect to Q^S and Q^F, respectively, the first order conditions can be written as:

$$p - p^* = C_S > 0 \qquad (8.9)$$

and

$$p - (1 + t)p^* = C_F < 0 \qquad (8.10)$$

These two equations can be combined to yield:

$$p^* < p < (1 + t)p^* \qquad (8.11)$$

This implies that the declared units of the imported good are sold at a loss on the local market, which is compensated by the profit made on the sale of the undeclared units of the good. This result also implies that the consumer surplus under this assumption, is higher with smuggling than without it, as we show below.

For determining the quantities imported Q^S and Q^F we can jointly solve equations (8.9) and (8.10) if there are decreasing returns to scale. Otherwise, in the case of constant returns to scale, with the function $C(-)$ being homogeneous of degree one, C_S and C_F are homogenous of degree zero in their two arguments, so that equations (8.9) and (8.10) can only determine the ratio Q^S/Q^F as a function of $(p, p^*, 1)$. Then, one must bring into the analysis the demand function, say $D(p)$, as done below, for determining the values of Q^S and Q^F.

Under the assumption of constant returns to scale in the smuggling business, one can solve simultaneous equations (8.9) and (8.10) and get the following reduced form price equation:

$$dp = (1/(C_{SS} - C_{FS})) ((1 + t)C_{SS} - C_{FS}) dp^* + C_{SS}p^* dt). \quad (8.12)$$

In this equation, the various subscripts denote the corresponding second derivatives, taking into account the homogeneity property of the $C(-)$ function. It is natural to assume $C_{SS} > 0$ and $C_{SS} > C_{FS}$. Then equation (8.12) states that any increase in p^* or t is passed on to the consumer, but not necessarily one-for-one. In particular, the impact of an increase in p^* is larger than 1.

In the discussion of the welfare effect of smuggling that follows in the next section, it is important to specify whether the costs involved are only a kind of transfer (bribes, fines, and so on), or whether they involve some real resource costs. We now discuss this issue.

The Nature of the Cost of Smuggling

Devarajan, Jones and Roemer (1989) assume that the cost difference between official and unofficial trade only involves transfers like bribes or fines. Denoting $0 \leq q \leq 1$, the probability of being caught smuggling, and F the fine (or the bribe) per unit of smuggled good, their assumption may be written:

$$C(Q^S, Q^F) = q\,(Q^S, Q^F)\,fQ^s \qquad\qquad (8.13)$$
$$(+)\ (-)\qquad (+)\ (-)$$

Then, the direct cost of smuggling is only a transfer from the smuggler to the government or to the customs officer.

However, Daubrée (1994), Kamin (1993) and O'Connell (1992), following the classic paper by Bhagwati and Hansen (1973), assume that the smuggling cost difference involves some real resource cost, namely the use of some quantity of labour. This is a bit surprising in Kamin's model, which only aims at describing misinvoicing. Daubrée (1994, 1995) combines the two approaches, assuming both transfers and resource costs.

Deardoff and Stolper (1990) challenge this view, arguing that unofficial trade involves less resource cost than official trade. They argue that transaction costs on the official market are extremely important in African countries. Because of bureaucratic behaviour, getting goods cleared through customs may be a very costly activity, involving both labour time and bribes aimed at accelerating the process. Bureaucratic delays at customs can as well be very damaging when the goods involved are perishable. Smuggling would then be an efficient way of reducing real resource costs, by taking a faster route that avoids customs. This is an important point affecting the impact of smuggling on welfare. However, their assumption does not answer the question of what explains the simultaneous activity of official and unofficial trade.

8.3 THE WELFARE EFFECT OF SMUGGLING AND TRADE LIBERALIZATION

For the sake of simplicity, we only discuss here the case of imports without a local substitute. It would be straightforward to add a sector producing import substitutes. Then, we extend the analysis for discussing the case of exports. Besides the nature of the smuggling cost, discussed above, the welfare effect of smuggling depends on the type of distortion that triggers it. As is customary in the international trade literature, we only discuss welfare in terms of consumer, producer and government surplus, taken together. As we all know, many distributional issues would have to be added in order to provide a fully convincing welfare analysis. We first analyse the case where official trade does not provide any cover effect, before we turn to the case corresponding to Pitt's specification.

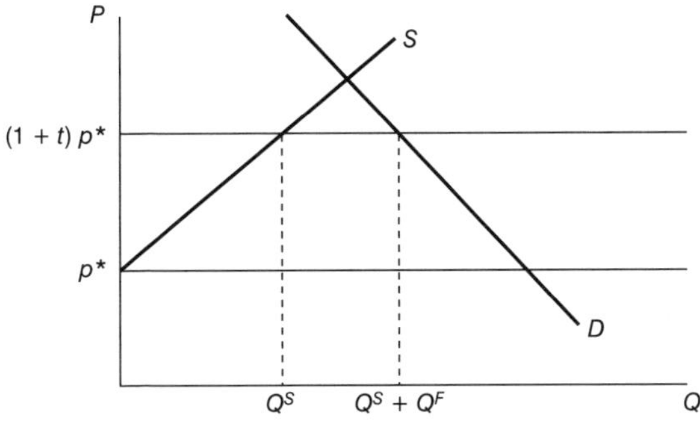

Figure 8.1

The Import Side

Figure 8.1 illustrates the case where the trade distortion is created by a tariff, and when both official and unofficial imports are non zero. The demand curve for the imported good is labelled D, while the upward-sloping curve describes the supply of the smuggled good, corresponding to equation (8.2). In this case, smuggling only diverts trade from the official market to the parallel market, using the classic Vinerian terminology. At best, this trade-diversion effect leaves welfare unaffected only if the real resource-cost difference between official and unofficial trade is zero. If any real resource cost is involved, then welfare goes down. If the smuggling costs are only made of resource cost, then the welfare loss entailed by smuggling costs are only made of resource cost, and the welfare loss entailed by smuggling is measured by the triangle below the S curve, to the left of Q^S, and between p^* and $(1 + t)\,p^*$. This welfare loss must be added to the usual deadweight loss of the tariff, measured by the area of the triangle below D, to the right of $Q^S + Q^F$, and between p^* and $(1 + t)p^*$, in order to measure accurately the welfare loss entailed by the tariff. Insofar as smuggling is the automatic response of the private sector to the imposition of a tariff, the welfare loss implied by smuggling must also be blamed on the tariff protection.

Notice that smuggling entails a fall in the tax revenues of the government equal to tp^*Q^S. In this case, smuggling may both reduce social welfare, as seen above, and the welfare of the government, as measured by its tax revenues. Therefore, it drastically reduces the appeal of the tariff, from both a welfare point of view and a

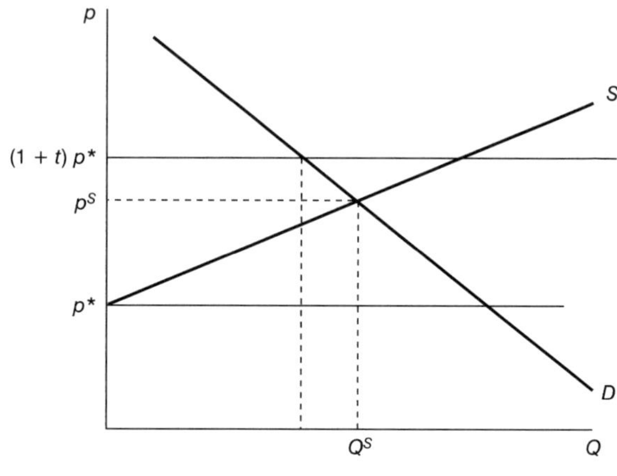

Figure 8.2

public finance point of view. Taking due account of smuggling should thus reduce the attractiveness of tariff protection for African governments and make the case for trade liberalization more appealing.

It is straightforward to show that trade liberalization increases welfare. This can be seen graphically using Figure 8.1, by shifting the $(1 + t)p^*$ line downwards. Then, the areas of the two relevant triangles shrink, showing a positive welfare effect. Notice that a part of this welfare improvement comes from the diversion of a trade flow from the parallel to the official segment of the market, if smuggling entails any real resource cost. Hence, in the case where the smuggling activity is triggered by a tariff, and where both official and unofficial trade are active simultaneously, the existence of smuggling strengthens the case for trade liberalization. However, it is not certain that the tax revenues of the government increase, as the tax rate goes down while the tax base goes up. The outcome depends on the elasticities of $D(-)$ and of S.

Figure 8.2 illustrates the case where the trade-creation effect is dominant. Official trade has been driven out, and welfare may have increased if the real resource cost of smuggling is low enough not to offset the benefit of the trade-creation effect. The domestic price of the imported good is now $p^S < (1 + t)p^*$. As official trade has vanished in this case due to smuggling, the government loses the tax revenue that the tariff would provide in the absence of smuggling.

Trade liberalization understood as a cut in the tariff rate, could be beneficial to both the consumer and the government. If t is cut by a large enough percentage, so that $(1 + t)p^*$ now falls strictly below p^S, then consumption of the good goes up, with the consumer surplus moving in the same direction, while the tax collected by the government goes up as well. In this move, only the smugglers lose something, as some trade is diverted from the parallel to the official market, as in the previous case. This may entail an additional welfare improvement if there is any real resource cost in smuggling. However, from a political economy point of view, this suggests that one should expect smugglers to be the most active lobby against trade liberalization.

We would basically get the same diagram with Pitt's specification discussed above, except that the S curve would be replaced by a horizontal line located between p^* and $(1 + t)p^*$. The main differences are that, with Pitt's assumption, the case of Figure 8.1 is not relevant, whereas the case of Figure 8.2 prevails while official trade is not driven to zero. As shown above at equation (8.12), the market price p is an increasing function of the tariff rate t, so that the case for trade liberalization is unambiguously favourable here.

These examples show that the welfare impact of smuggling is ambiguous when it is triggered by a tariff. The impact is probably negative when there is no cover effect, if the two types of trade are simultaneously active, and if there is some resource cost difference in favour of official trade. At best, there is no impact, unless official trade is driven out. In the latter case, the outcome is ambiguous, and depends crucially on the nature of smuggling cost. If the latter mainly involves expected transfers, as in Devarajan, Jones and Roemer (1989), then smuggling makes a positive contribution to social welfare. Otherwise, the trade-creation effect might be offset by the real resource cost of smuggling. But the assumption that smuggling completely drives out official trade from the market seems a bit unrealistic, or to say the least, not very common in the real world.

Pitt's assumption makes a positive diagnosis more likely, as a positive outcome may result even when official trade is not driven out by smuggling, as it provides a cover for the latter. In other words, cheating at customs, which is the most common interpretation of Pitt's model, is probably more beneficial for the society as a whole than smuggling narrowly defined as importing goods without going through customs at all.

There is no ambiguity when the smuggling activity is triggered

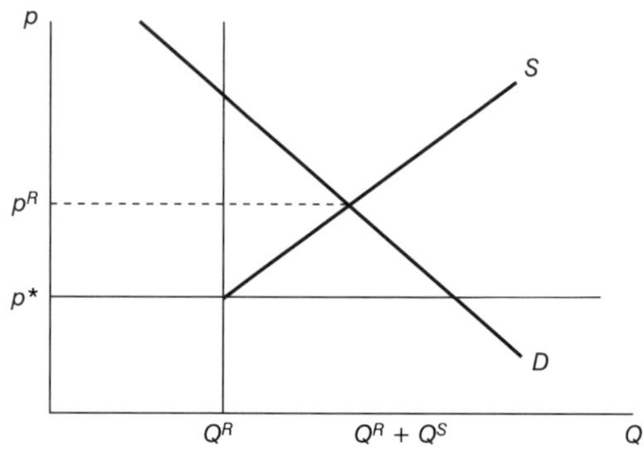

Figure 8.3

by a quota, as shown in Figure 8.3, where Q^R represents the quota. If the latter is binding, in the absence of smuggling, then smuggling necessarily improves welfare by expanding the quantity sold and reducing its price.

Let p^R denote the resulting price. In this case, any partial trade liberalization, defined as an increase in Q^R is bound to improve welfare, without necessarily reducing the value of the rent. It all depends on the elasticity of demand and the elasticity of the smuggling supply curve. Hence, this type of liberalization will not necessarily be opposed by the privileged importers who benefit from the quota rent, if they perceive the demand curve as highly elastic.

These contrasted results have an important (although not unexpected) policy implication. During the era of adjustment, since the early 1980s, the Bretton Woods institutions have tried their best to convince African governments to lift the quantitative restrictions imposed on imports of many goods. As a transitional measure, the governments were advised first to replace the quotas by an equivalent tariff. Our analysis at Figure 8.3 suggests that such a move has no welfare effect if the tariff-inclusive price is set at p^R. The main effect is to transfer the value of the quota rent from the importers to the government, who will now get it as tax revenues. Obviously, if the government fixes the tariff rate so that the new tariff-inclusive price is above p^R, then welfare goes down as smuggling expands, if the latter entails any resource cost. However, this can hardly qualify as a trade liberalization.

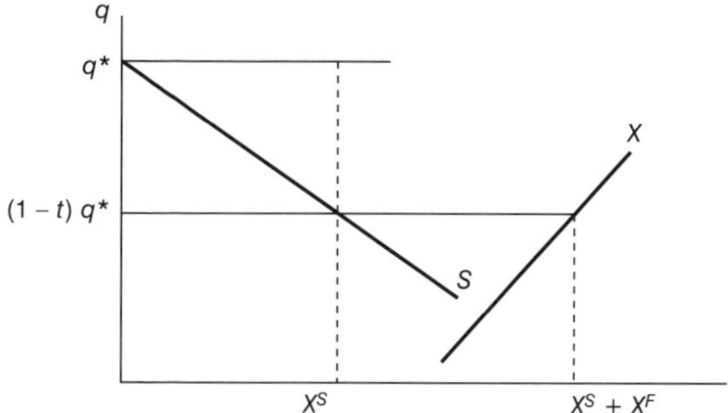

Figure 8.4

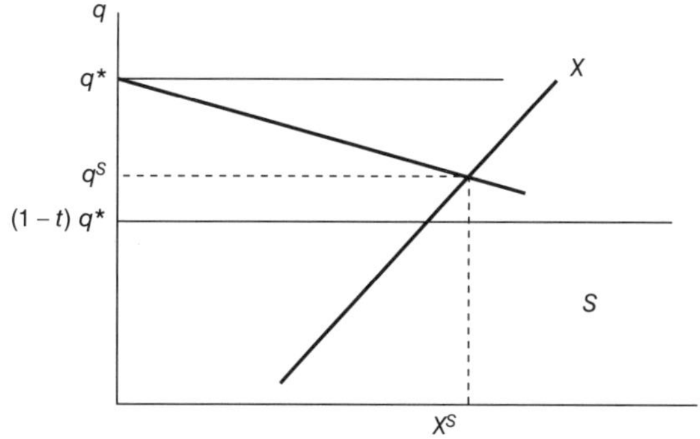

Figure 8.5

The Export Side

Let us now turn briefly to the analysis of unofficial exports. Figures 8.4 and 8.5 describe the case where the producer price is below the world price. In Africa, this mainly happens when a marketing board or a stabilization fund controls the official trade of an export crop. For the sake of simplicity, we deal with the case where no domestic demand for the good exists. This would be a widely unrealistic assumption for Ethiopian coffee, for example. However, it is straightforward to include a domestic demand in the analysis, so that our export supply function only needs to be interpreted as the net export function, or the excess of domestic supply over domestic demand.

The world price is denoted as q^*, and t denotes the (equivalent) tax rate. The supply curve is labelled X, while X^S and X^F denote the unofficial and the official quantities exported, respectively. The curve labelled S is the derived demand for unofficial exports, corresponding to equation (8.7) above. In Figure 8.4, both official trade and smuggling are non-zero, and we can see that smuggling has no welfare effect if it entails no real resource cost. If, on the contrary, all the smuggling cost is made of real resources, then the welfare loss entailed by smuggling is measured by the triangle above S, to the left-hand side of X^S, and between $(1 - t)q^*$ and q^*. If the cost of smuggling consists partly of transfers and partly of real resources, then only the fraction of this triangle that corresponds to the share of real resource cost should be counted as a welfare loss. If one regards smuggling as the automatic response of the economy to the export (explicit or implicit) tax, then in order to measure the total welfare loss entailed by the export tax, its resource cost must be added to the triangle above X, to the right-hand side of $X^S + X^F$, and between $(1 - t)q^*$ and q^*. The case for trade liberalization can then be discussed as above. Cutting t increases total exports and official exports, while it reduces smuggling. The area of the two triangles representing the welfare losses entailed by the export tax shrink, increasing the welfare of the producer, and may increase as well the welfare of the government if the relevant elasticities are right.

When the smugglers are able to drive out the official trade, as in Figure 8.5, then we get the same ambiguous result as above. The trade creation effect is dominant here, so that it is possible that it offsets the resource cost of smuggling and delivers an increase in welfare. If there is no real resource cost, then welfare is increased unambiguously.

Another typical case of exports involving smuggling in Africa is that re-export of subsidized goods. For example, assume that, as in Figure 8.6, an importable good can be bought in the world market at the price p^*, and sold in the domestic market at the price $(1 - s)p^*$. This is typically the case when there is a parallel market for foreign exchange. If the good under study can be imported at the official exchange rate, and re-exported at the parallel exchange rate, then the parallel market premium works like an import subsidy. Then, quantity Q^D will be consumed domestically, while an additional quantity Q^S will be imported by the country to be re-exported by smugglers at the non-subsidized price p^*. If smuggling

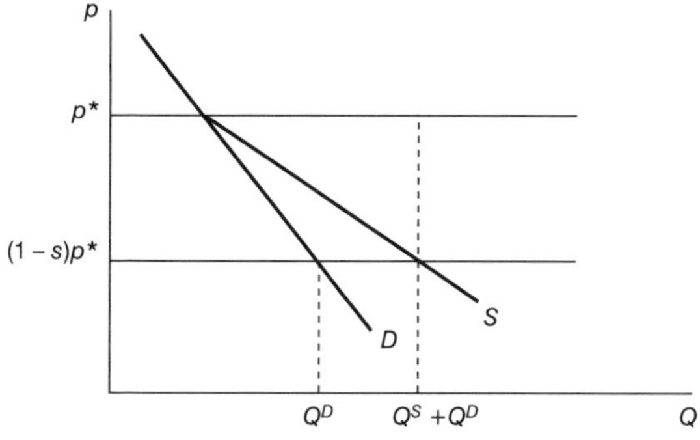

Figure 8.6

involves only real resource costs, the welfare loss is measured by the triangle above S, to the left-hand side of $Q^D + Q^S$, and between p^* and $(1 - s)p^*$. In West Africa, this type of re-export is well known, involving Nigerian fertilizers, or for example Algerian drugs.

The foregoing section has shown that, although the welfare impact of smuggling is generally ambiguous, unless one gets into detailed assumptions about the cause of the distortion and the nature of the smuggling cost, its existence usually strengthens the case for trade liberalization. This analysis was restricted to across-the-board trade liberalization. The next section shows that the same conclusion is found when only selective trade liberalization is analysed.

8.3 SMUGGLING AND THE CASE FOR REGIONAL INTEGRATION

The classical Vinerian analysis of regional integration can be easily extended to include smuggling. We restrict the analysis to the creation of a free-trade area, where two countries agree to have no tariff at all bearing on trade between them, while the importing country keeps a tariff against the rest of the world. Figure 8.7 represents the case where initially the country has a tariff bearing on all imports, and where official and unofficial trade exist side by side. Assume that initially the trade diversion effect of smuggling is dominant, as in Figure 8.1, with a negative welfare effect if there is any resource cost entailed by smuggling.

Assume now that the country under study creates a free-trade

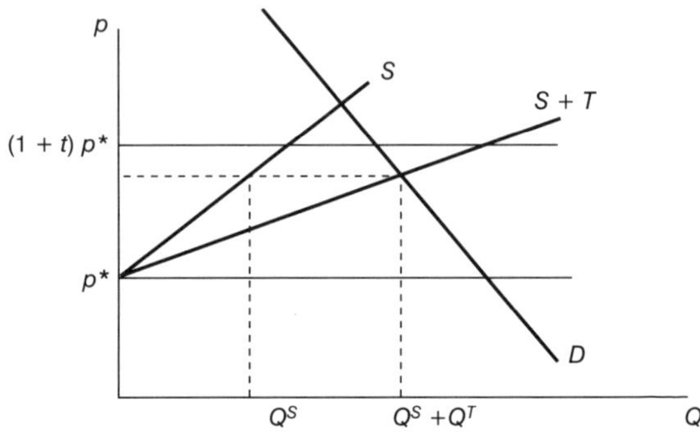

Figure 8.7

area with a neighbouring country. The two countries can trade among themselves with no tax or tariff being levied, while a tariff with the rest of the world is kept by the importing country. Define $T(p, p^*)$ as the net export function by the second member country of the free-trade area. In Figure 8.7 the curve labelled $S + T$ represents the import supply function comprising both smuggling and official imports from the free-trade area member country. We have represented the case where the selective liberalization provided by the creation of the free-trade area is enough for improving welfare. The curve labelled $S + T$ intersects the demand curve at a point below $(1 + t)p^*$, so that the trade-creation effect is dominant. In this case, all the imports are supplied by the smugglers and the union member country, and no more direct official trade with the world market, at the tariff-inclusive price, takes place. Hence, the government does not raise any funds through the tariff. Notice as well that the creation of the free-trade area in this case entails some trade diversion from the parallel to the official market, with positive welfare impact insofar as smuggling implies any real resource cost.

This example shows that smuggling strengthens the case for regional integration, understood here as the creation of a free-trade area, in the following sense. Assume that the neighbouring country is not large enough to offer an export function such that the trade-creation effect dominates the trade-diversion effect at the prevailing tariff-inclusive price, in which case regional integration is detrimental. Smugglers can complement the exports from the member country in such a way that any other trade flow with the rest of the world is driven out. Then, the trade diversion effect can be dominated by the trade creation effect, even if the opposite outcome would prevail in the absence of smuggling. Nevertheless, the other case is also possible – where the opening of trade to the imports from the neighbouring country is not enough to drive out any other direct official trade with the rest of the world, despite a positive level of smuggling. This suggests that the free-trade area should be created by involving large enough countries for driving out the rest of the world from the import market, with the help of the smugglers. Otherwise, the welfare effect would be negative.

However, the creation of a free-trade area is not only relevant to regional integration in Africa. It has even been shown by Foroutan (1993) that it has not been a very successful endeavour. On the contrary, monetary integration has been more successful, with the experience of the CFA franc zone and of the rand zone. We now analyse how smuggling bears on the desirability of monetary integration.

8.4 SMUGGLING AND THE CASE FOR MONETARY INTEGRATION

Monetary integration is generally understood as the fixing of the exchange rate among a group of countries, or the adoption of a common currency (De Grauwe, 1992). The issue of the optimum currency area is an active research topic, which lies to a large extent outside the scope of this chapter. Nevertheless, we can discuss some aspect of it, in the context of cross-border trading.

The classic discussion of the optimum currency area is based on the factors that reduce the effectiveness of the exchange rates as a tool for affecting relative prices between two countries. The exchange rate plays two different roles in any economy, labelled the 'nominal anchor approach' or the 'real target approach'. This refers respectively to the possibility of stabilizing the price level by fixing the exchange rate, and to the possibility of affecting the real exchange rate by changing the nominal exchange rate. There is usually a trade-off between these two functions of the nominal exchange rate, as in the case of the African CFA zone member countries. Fixing the exchange rate provides credibility to the government for fighting inflation but does not allow for accommodating external shocks, while the possibility of devaluing in response to an external negative shock creates a credibility problem, with an inflationary impact. Hence, the more effective the nominal exchange rate affecting the real exchange rate, the more costly it is to fix it as a means for controlling the price level. On the contrary, if the nominal exchange rate is not a very powerful tool for affecting the real exchange rate, then the opportunity cost of using it as a nominal anchor is reduced.

We can show now that the existence of smuggling flows, by increasing the tradeability of some goods, makes the real exchange rate less sensitive to the nominal exchange rate. In order to do that we use again the first model analysed above, where there is no cover effect, with simple changes made in order to make explicit the role of the exchange rate. Let us first assume that the world price of all goods is fixed and equal to 1. Then, denote as e the nominal exchange rate, so that $p^* = e$. We assume that there is no smuggling regarding some goods, called the tradeable goods, while some other goods are not tradeable at the margin, because of quantitative restrictions. Let p denote again their domestic price. We assume that these imperfectly tradeable goods are concerned by smuggling, which increases their tradeability at the margin. This is typical of African economies, where there are very few genuinely non-tradeable goods, while many goods are subject to quantitative restrictions and are involved in cross-border trade. Then, assuming that $c(Q^S) = p^* * (Q^S)$, the first order condition, equation (8.2) can be written as:

$$p = p^* (1 + \gamma^* (Q^S)) = e (1 + \gamma^* (Q^S)) \qquad (8.13)$$

Inverting equation (8.13) yields the following supply function:

$$Q^S = Q^S(e/p), \ Q^{S\prime} < 0 \qquad (8.14)$$

This equation simply states that a depreciation of the real exchange rate, by reducing the gap between the border price and the local price of the imperfectly tradeable good, reduces the incentive to smuggle.

We define the price index as the following function, assumed to be increasing in its two arguments, differentiable and homogenous of degree one:

$$v = v(e, p) \qquad (8.15)$$

Then the equilibrium in the market for theses imperfectly tradeable goods requires:

$$D(e/p, M/v) = Q^S(e/p)$$
$$(+) \ (-) \qquad\qquad (-)$$

$$(8.16)$$

where $D(-)$ is the domestic excess demand function for this good and M is the quantity of money. This equation simply states in equilibrium the excess of domestic demand for this good over the domestic supply is put up by smuggling. Differentiating Equation 16, holding m constant, yields:

$$\frac{d\log p}{d\log e} = \frac{D_e - S' - D_M v_e p^M/v^2}{D_e - S' + D_M v_p p^2 M/ev^2} < 1 \qquad (8.17)$$

The lower this elasticity, the more effective is a devaluation: that is, the more an increase in e can affect e/p. A look at equation (8.17) reveals that the more active is the smuggling sector, captured here by a higher S', the closer to 1 this elasticity becomes. In other words, if cross-border trade is not very active, so that a change in relative prices does not trigger any strong reaction by the smugglers, then a change in the nominal exchange rate is only partially passed on to the price of imperfectly tradeable goods. Thus the devaluation is quite effective. On the contrary, if cross-border trade is very active and responsive to relative price changes, then any change in e is passed on to p to a large extent, so that the nominal devaluation entails a weak real devaluation. In the limit, as S' becomes infinite, the degree of effectiveness falls to zero, as any change in e is entirely passed on to p.

Therefore, as smugglers increase the degree of tradeability of imperfectly tradeable goods, the nominal exchange rate loses its efficacy as a way to affect the real exchange rate e/p. Hence, in this case, it becomes more interesting to use the nominal anchor, irrespective or its impact on the real exchange rate, which is very weak. On the contrary, by reducing the scope for internal shocks to affect relative prices, the enhanced tradeability of the goods brought about by smuggling increases the power of the exchange rate as a tool for controlling inflation. However, the use of the exchange rate as a nominal anchor is not an easy task, as credibility problems can arise. Joining a monetary union is one of the best responses to the credibility constraint (de Grauwe, 1993). In other words, cross-border trade should be taken into account in the design of a currency area.

8.5 CONCLUSION

In this chapter, we have first shown that the welfare effect of smuggling depends on what type of distortion triggers it, and on the nature of the cost difference with official trade. If these costs are only some sort of transfers, like expected bribes of fines, then smuggling does not reduce welfare, and may well have a positive contribution if the trade-creation effect dominates the trade-diversion effect. If there is any real resource cost involved, then the welfare effect is more uncertain. A necessary condition for a positive welfare effect when smuggling is triggered by a tariff, in the case where official trade does not provide any cover effect, is that official trade is driven out. But this is not a sufficient condition, if the real resource cost involved offsets the benefit from trade creation. When smuggling is triggered by quantitative restrictions, smuggling necessarily increases welfare. Therefore, when due account is taken of smuggling, quotas turn out to be less damaging than suggested by the usual analysis that neglects it, while tariffs are more damaging, because of the diversion of trade from the official market to the parallel market that they entail. However, this result does not hold if the resource cost difference between official and unofficial trade is negligible, as argued by Deardoff and Stolper (1990). Then, smuggling is never harmful.

In this framework, trade liberalization never reduces welfare, and improves it in most cases. This is because a cut in tariff or a relaxation of a quota leads to some trade diversion from the parallel market to the official market, which is supposed to entail a lower resource cost. Similarly, a partial trade liberalization, like the creation of a free-trade area with some neighbouring country, is most likely to have a positive welfare effect, provided the trade creation effect is dominant. This occurs when trade within the free-trade area, added to the smuggling flow, adds up to a large enough level of trade to drive out any official direct trade with the rest of the world.

Lastly, we have shown that the existence of smuggling strengthens the case for monetary integration. The reason for this finding is that a lot of non-tradeable goods in Africa are not intrinsically non-tradeable, but are made non-tradeable at the margin by quantitative restrictions. Insofar as smuggling increases the tradeability of these goods, it makes the nominal exchange rate less powerful as a tool for affecting the real exchange rate, and a more powerful instrument for controlling inflation. Fixing the exchange rate within a monetary union might then be the right choice to make in small open economies where parallel markets are pervasive as in most African countries.

Note

1. I owe this interpretation to Nick Stern, at a seminar at the London School of Economics.

References

Azam, J.-P. (1990) 'Informal Integration through Parallel Markets for Goods and Foreign Exchange', in World Bank, *The Long-Term Perspective Study of Sub Saharan Africa*, vol. 4: *Proceedings of a Workshop on Regional Integration and Cooperation*, pp. 48–51 (Washington, DC: World Bank).

Azam, J.-P. (1991a) 'Cross-Border Trade between Niger and Nigeria, 1980–1987: The Parallel Market for the Naira', in M. Roemer and C. Jones (eds), *Markets in Developing countries. Parallel, Fragmented, and Black*, pp. 47–61 (San Francisco: ICS).

Azam, J.-P. (1991b) 'Niger and the Naira: Some Monetary Consequences of Cross-Border Trade with Nigeria', in A. Chhibber and S. Fischer (eds), *Economic Reform in Sub Saharan Africa*, pp. 66–75 (Washington, DC: World Bank).

Azam, J.-P. and T. Besley (1989a) 'General Equilibrium with Parallel Markets for Goods and Foreign Exchange: Theory and Application to Ghana', *World Development*, **17**: 1921–30.

Azam, J.-P. and T. Besley (1989b) 'The Case of Ghana', in J.-P. Azam, T. Besley, L. Maton, D. Bevan, P. Collier and P. Horsnell, *The Supply of Manufactured Goods and Agricultural Development*, Development Centre Studies (Paris: OECD).

Azam, J.-P. and C. Morrisson (1994) *The Political Feasibility of Adjustment in Cote d'Ivoire and Morocco*, Development Centre Studies (Paris: OECD).

Bhagwati, J. and B. Hansen (1973): 'A Theoretical Analysis of Smuggling', *Quarterly Journal of Economics*, **87**: 172–87.

Daubrée, C. (1994) 'Analyse microéconomique des marchés parallèles et de la fraude documentaire, avec références aux économies africaines', *Revue économique*, **45**: 165–92.

Daubrée, C. (1995): *Marchés parallèles et équilibrés économiques. Experiences africaines* (Paris: L'Harmattan).

De Grauwe, P. (1992) *The Economics of Monetary Integration* (Oxford University Press).

Deardoff, A. V. and W. F. Stolper (1990) 'Effects of Smuggling under African Conditions: A Factual, Institutional and Analytic Discussion', *Weltwirtschaftslisches Archiv*, **126**: 116–41.

Devarajan, S., C. Jones and M. Roemer (1989) 'Market under Price Controls in Partial and General Equilibrium', *World Development*, **17**: 1881–1993.

Johnson , O. E. G. (1987) 'Trade Tax and Exchange Rate Coordination in the Context of Border Trading', *IMF Staff Papers*, **34**: 548–64.

Foroutan, F. (1993) 'Regional Integration in Sub-Saharan Africa: Past Experience and Future Prospects', in J. de Melo and A. Panagariya (eds), *New Dimensions in Regional Integration* (Cambridge University Press).

Kamin, S. B. (1993) 'Devaluation, Exchange Controls, and Black Markets for Foreign Exchange in Developing Countries', *Journal of Development Economics*, **40**: 151–69.

Kidane, A. (1994) 'Indices of Effective Exchange Rates: A Comparative Study of Ethiopia Kenya and the Sudan.' AERC Research Paper no. 29: Nairobi: AERC.

Krueger, A. O. (1974) 'The Economies of the Rent-Seeking Society', *American Economic Review*.

May, E. (1985) *Exchange Controls and Parallel Market Economies in Sub-Saharan Africa*, Staff Working Paper no. 711 (Washington, DC: World Bank).

McKinnon, R. l. (1979) 'Foreign Trade Regimes and Economic Development. A Review Article', *Journal of International Economics*, **9**: 429–52.

O'Connell, S. (1992) 'Uniform Commercial Policy, Illegal Trade, and the Real Exchange Rate: A Theoretical Analysis', *World Bank Economic Review*, **6**, 459–79.

Odubogun, K. (1994) 'The Nigerian Foreign Exchange Market: Possibilities for Convergence in Exchange Rates', Interim Report (Nairobi: AERC).

Pitt, M. (1981) 'Smuggling and Price Disparity', *Journal of International Economics*, **11**: 447–58.

Pitt, M. (1984) 'Smuggling and the Black Market for Forcign Exchange', *Journal of International Economics*, **16**: 243–57.

Robson, P. (1987) *The Economics of International Integration*, 3rd edn (London: Unwin Hyman).

Roemer, M. (1987) 'The Simple Analysis of Segmented Markets: What Case for Liberalization?', *World Development*, **14**: 429–39.

Tanzi, V. (1987) 'Quantitative Characteristics of the Tax System of Developing Countries', in D. Newbery and N. Stern (eds), *The Theory of Taxation for Developing Countries* (Washington, DC: World Bank).

Tanzi, V. (1992) 'Structural Factors and Tax Revenue in Developing Countries: A Decade of Evidence', in I. Goldin and L. A. Winters (eds), *Open Economies: Structural Adjustment and Agriculture* (Cambridge: CEPR and OECD, Cambridge University Press).

Contents of Volumes 1, 2 and 4

Volume 4   Synthesis and Review

Index